# Atlantis Ambient and Pervasive Intelligence

## Volume 7

*Series Editor*

Ismail Khalil, Johannes Kepler University, Linz, Austria

For further volumes:
www.atlantis-press.com

## Aims and Scope of the Series

The book series 'Atlantis Ambient and Pervasive Intelligence' publishes high quality titles in the fields of Pervasive Computing, Mixed Reality, Wearable Computing, Location-Aware Computing, Ambient Interfaces, Tangible Interfaces, Smart Environments, Intelligent Interfaces, Software Agents and other related fields. We welcome submission of book proposals from researchers worldwide who aim at sharing their results in this important research area.

For more information on this series and our other book series, please visit our website at:

www.atlantis-press.com/publications/books
Atlantis Press
29, avenue Laumière
75019 Paris, France

Abderazek Ben Abdallah

# Multicore Systems On-Chip: Practical Software/Hardware Design

Second Edition

Abderazek Ben Abdallah
Adaptive Systems Laboratory
University of Aizu
Aizuwakamatsu
Japan

ISSN  1875-7669
ISBN  978-94-6239-050-8          ISBN 978-94-91216-92-3 (eBook)
DOI 10.2991/978-94-91216-92-3

Printed on acid-free paper

*To The University of Aizu in*
*commemoration of its 20th anniversary*

# Preface

Systems On-Chip designs have evolved over time from fairly simple unicore single memory designs to complex homogeneous/heterogeneous multicore SoC architectures consisting of a large number of IP (Intellectual Property) blocks on the same silicon. To meet the challenges arising from high computational demands posed by latest consumer electronic devices, most current systems are based on such paradigm, which represents a real revolution in many aspects of computing.

The attraction of multicore processing for power reduction is compelling. By splitting a set of tasks among multiple processor cores, the operating frequency necessary for each core can be reduced, thereby facilitating a reduction in the voltage on each core. Because dynamic power is proportional to the frequency and to the square of the voltage, we are able to obtain a sizable gain, even though we may have more (multiple?) cores running.

As more and more cores are integrated into these designs to share the ever increasing processing load, the primary challenges are geared toward efficient memory hierarchy, scalable system interconnect, new programming models, and efficient integration methodology for connecting such heterogeneous cores into a single system capable of leveraging their individual flexibility.

Current design methods are inclined toward mixed hardware/software (SW/HW) codesigns, targeting multicore SoCs for application specific domains. To decide on the lowest cost mix of cores, designers must iteratively map the devices functionality to a particular HW/SW partition and target architectures. In addition, to connect the heterogeneous cores, the architecture requires high performance-based complex communication architectures and efficient communication protocols, such as hierarchical bus, point-to-point connection, or the recent new interconnection paradigm—Network-on-Chip. Software development also becomes far more complex due to the difficulties in breaking a single processing task into multiple parts that could be processed separately and then reassembled later. This reflects the fact that certain processor jobs could not possibly be easily parallelized to run concurrently on multiple processing cores and that load balancing between processing cores especially heterogeneous cores is extremely difficult.

This second edition of this book stands independent and we have made every attempt to make each chapter self-contained as well. It is organized in 11 chapters. The first chapter introduces Multicore Systems On-Chip (MCSoCs) architectures and explores SoCs technology and the challenges it presents to organizations and developers building next generation multicore SoCs based systems.

Understanding the technological landscape and design methods in some level of details is very important. This is because so many design decisions in multicore architecture today are guided by the impact of the technology. Chapter 2 presents design challenges and conventional design methods of MCSoCs. It also describes a so called scalable core-based method for systematic design environment of application specific heterogeneous multicore SoC architectures. The architecture design used in conventional methods of multicore SoCs and custom multiprocessor architectures are not flexible enough to meet the requirements of different application domains and not scalable enough to meet different computation needs and different complexities of various applications. Therefore, designers should be aware of existing design methods and also be ready to innovate or adapt appropriate design methods for individual target platform.

Understanding the software and hardware building blocks and the computation power of individual components in these complex MCSoCs is necessary for designing power, performance, and cost-efficient systems. Chapter 3 describes in details the architectures and functions of the main building blocks that are used to build such complex multicore SoCs. Students with relevant background in multicore SoC building blocks could effectively skip some of the materials mentioned in this chapter. The knowledge of these aspects is not an absolute requirement for understanding the rest of the book, but it does help novice students or beginners to get a glimpse of the big picture of a heterogeneous or homogeneous MCSoC organization.

Whether homogeneous, heterogeneous, or hybrid multicore SoCs, IP cores must be connected in a high-performance, scalable, and flexible manner. The emerging technology that targets such connections is called an on-chip interconnection network, also known as a network on chip (NoC), and the philosophy behind the emergence of such innovation has been summarized by William Dally at Stanford University as *route packets, not wires*. Chapters 4–6 investigate 2D-NoC, 3D-NoC, and 2D/3D NoC Network Interface (NI) designs. These chapters focus on the architecture and design of Network-on-Chip (NoC) and the NI. Efficient, lightweight NI interfaces are critical for overall latency reduction. For an effective concurrent multicore SoCs, a programmer needs a fast on-chip network transport, fast and easy-to-use network interfaces, and predictable network performance. These three chapters are all very important part of the book since they allow the reader to understand what needed microarchitecture for on-chip routers and network interfaces are essential toward meeting latency, area, and power constraints. Reader will also understand practical issues about what system architecture (topology, routing, flow control, NI) is most suited for these on-chip networks.

With the rise of multicore and many-core systems, concurrency becomes a major issue in the daily life of a programmer. Thus, compiler and software development tools will be critical toward helping programmers create high performance software. Programmers should make sure that their parallelized program codes would not cause race condition, memory access deadlocks, or other faults that may crash their entire systems. Chapter 7 describes a novel parallelizing compiler design for high performance computing.

Power dissipation continues to be a primary design constraint and concern in single and multicore systems. Increasing power consumption not only results in increasing energy costs, but also results in high die temperatures that affect chip reliability, performance, and packaging cost. Chapter 8 provides a detailed investigation of power reduction techniques for multicore SoC at components and network levels. Energy conservation has been largely considered in the hardware design, in general and also in embedded multicore system components, such as CPUs, disks, displays, memories, and so on. Significant additional power savings could be also achieved by incorporating low power methods into the design of network protocols used for data communication (audio, video, etc.).

Soft-core processors are becoming increasingly common in modern multicore SoCs. A soft-core processor is a programmable processor that can be synthesized to a circuit, typically integrated into a larger multicore SoC. Chapter 9 describes architecture and design results of a low power Soft-core 32-bit QueueCore architecture. This core is an efficient architecture which can be easily programmed and integrated in a multicore SoC platform.

Chapter 10 introduces practical hardware design issues of a multi-mode processor architecture targeted for embedded applications. In an embodiment of this processor, a single instruction stream consists of two different programming models. This is effectively achieved dynamically with an execution-mode-switching and sources-results computing mechanisms.

Current and future generations of embedded biomedical applications require more flexible and cost-effective computing platforms to meet its rapidly growing market. The programmable embedded multicore SoC systems appear to be an attractive solution in terms of ease of programming, design cost, power, portability, and time-to-market. The first step toward such complex systems is to characterize biomedical applications on the target architecture. Such studies can help us understand the design issues and the trade-offs in specializing hardware and software systems. Chapter 11 ties together previous chapters and presents a real embedded multicore SoC system design targeted for biomedical applications (i.e., ECG processing). For this book, we used our experience to illustrate the complete design flow for a multicore SoC running an electrocardiogram (ECG) application in parallel. More specifically, discussions on how to design the algorithms, architecture, and register transfer level implementation for ECG processing; discussions of the FPGA prototype, and validation are described.

# Acknowledgments

The second edition of this book took nearly 3 years to write. It evolved and is derived from our teaching experiences in embedded system designs and architecture to both undergraduate and graduate students. Multicore paradigm created stupendous opportunities to increase overall system performance, but also created many design challenges that designers must now overcome. Thus, we must continue innovating new algorithms and techniques to solve these challenges. We must also continue with our efforts to better educate computer science and computer engineering students in both embedded multicore architectures and programming.

Abderazek Ben Abdallah

## Author Biography

**Abderazek Ben Abdallah** is currently a Senior Associate Professor in the School of Computer Science and Engineering, the University of Aizu, Japan where he is engaged in advanced computer system research and education. Previously, he was a Research Associate, then an Assistant Professor at the University of Electro-Communications at Tokyo (2002–2007). He has been a regular visiting Professor at Huazhong University of Science and Technology (HUST), and Hong Kong University of Science and Technology (KUST) since 2010. His research interests lie primarily in systems, including embedded real-time systems, energy-efficient system design, on-chip interconnection networks, parallel systems, and innovative architectures. He participated in new architecture development and led several middle-scale VLSI development efforts on several projects. He received the 2010 national prize for outstanding research in the field of computer systems and information technology. He has published more than 100 peer-reviewed journal and conference papers, edited one book, wrote one book, and several book chapters in these areas. He is a member of IEEE, ACM, and IEICE.

# Contents

# Figures

# Tables

# Chapter 1
# Introduction to Multicore Systems On-Chip

Systems On-Chip (SoCs) designs have evolved from fairly simple unicore, single memory designs to complex heterogeneous multicore SoC architectures consisting of large number of IP blocks on the same silicon. To meet high computational demands posed by latest consumer electronic devices, most current systems are based on such paradigm, which represents a real revolution in many aspects in computing.

This chapter presents a general introduction to the multicore System On-Chip (MCSoCs). We start this chapter by describing the needs for multicore systems by today's general and embedded application domains. Design challenges and basics multicore SoCs hardware and software design are also described.

## 1.1 The Multicore Revolution

Semiconductor companies and processor architects have historically invested time and money in micro-architectural and performance enhancements. Many of these efforts such as deep pipelining, increased large cache size, and sophisticated dynamic Instruction Level Parallelism (ILP) extraction exhibit diminishing returns due to increased area and power consumption. When considering the limitations associated with voltage supply scaling, threshold scaling, and clock frequency scaling, along with the above design complexity, architects were already looking for an alternative to the single core approach. Multicore was therefore the natural next revolution in staying on the ever increasing performance driven curve. But, was it really the good timing to switch from uni-processor approach to the more complex parallel structure of multiprocessor/multicore platforms? The direct answer from major hardware companies was very clear: yes; it is time for revolution and not for evolution! This decision was fueled by the shift that started from around 2004 when market leaders in the production of general purpose computer systems and embedded devices started offering an increasing number of multicore chips, contributing to an unprecedented paradigm that has led to what is know today as multicore revolution.

A. Ben Abdallah, *Multicore Systems On-Chip: Practical Software/Hardware Design*, Atlantis Ambient and Pervasive Intelligence 7, DOI: 10.2991/978-94-91216-92-3_1, © Atlantis Press and the author 2013

The main reason behind this shift can be simply explained by the limits of process technologies. As the computing needs of each processor type grew year by year, the traditional response by the semiconductor industries was to increase the clock frequency of the processor core. But as processor frequencies increase, other issues such as power consumption, thermal power, the inability to find sufficient parallelism in programs and lagging memory bandwidth become real obstacles to further advancements.

A promising solution seems to be the use of multiple cores operating at lower frequencies in a single chip. For embedded applications, multicore SoCs are becoming the preferable solution for several applications and design problems.

In a typical MCSoC architecture, a single physical chip integrates various components together. This single chip may contains digital, analog, mixed-signal, and often radio-frequency functions. Further, each individual core can run at a lower speed, which reduces overall power consumption as well as heat generation. This integration approach offers significant price, performance, and flexibility over higher speed single-core processor design.

## 1.1.1 Moore's Law

One of the guiding principles of computer architecture is known as Moore's Law. In April 1965, Gordon Moore wrote an article for Electronics magazine titled [Cramming more components onto integrated circuits] (Moore 1965). He predicted that the number of transistors on a chip would double every 12 months into the near future. Although this exponential trend has gradually lessen to doubling transistors every 18 months, it remains the driving force behind the integrated circuits industry. This law over the years has provided a road-map for product designers as they plan efficient and better usage of the transistors at their disposal. Figure 1.1 shows the scaling of transistor count and operating frequency in ICs.

## 1.1.2 On-Chip Interconnection Schemes

Shared bus was the dominant interconnect structure for the above somehow simple SoC systems. Most buses are bidirectional and devices can send or receive information. The good point in bus is that it allows to add new devices easily and facilitates portabilities of peripheral devices between different systems. However, if too many devices or processor cores are connected to the same bus, the bandwidth of the bus, clock skew and delay can become the bottlenecks.

A new interconnection scheme, known as on-chip network, or NoC, based on *packet switching* approach was proposed (Dally 2001; Ben-Abdallah 2006; Habibi 2011). NoCs are becoming an attractive option for solving shared bus problems. NoC is a scalable architectural platform with huge potential to handle growing

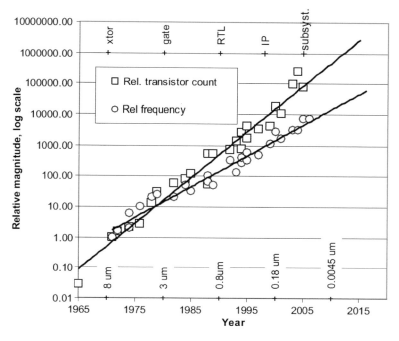

**Fig. 1.1** Scaling of transistor count and operating frequency in ICs. The feature size and design abstraction are also show in the graph

complexity (dozens of cores) and can provide easy reconfigurability, and scalability. The basic idea of NoC is that cores are connected via a *packet switching* communication on a single chip—similar to the way computers are connected to Internet.

The *packet switching* scheme supports asynchronous transfer of information. Yet, it provides extremely high bandwidth by distributing the propagation delay across multiple switches; thus pipelining the signal transmission. In addition, NoC offers several promising features. First, it transmits packets instead of words. Thus, dedicated address line like in bus systems are not necessary since the destination address of a packet is part of the packet itself. Second, transmission can be conducted in parallel if the network provides more than one transmission channel between a sender and a receiver. Thus, unlike bus-based system, NoC presents theoretical infinite scalability, facilitate IP core reusing, and higher parallelism.

During the last few years, several research groups adopted various concepts from conventional parallel and distributed (Internet) computing world and investigated various design issues related to NoCs. We will describe practical architecture and design of such promising interconnect in Chaps. 4 and 5.

## *1.1.3 Parallelism and Performance*

The prevalence of multicore and many-core technologies has brought ubiquitous parallelism and a huge theoretical potential for intensive tasks. Parallelism issue is now affecting all kinds of software development processes. Further, as software, hardware, and applications have evolved, there is a real need to run multiple such tasks simultaneously to benefit from the available hardware capability in multicore and many-core based systems. Thus, a good multicore programming model should be developed and should exploit all types of available parallelism (ILP, TLP, etc.) to maximize performance. For example, multimedia applications today often consist of multiple threads or processes. Recall that a thread can be defined as a basic unit of CPU utilization. It consists of a program counter register (PC), CPU state information for the current thread, and other resources such as a Stack (last-in-first-out data structure). However, finding and scheduling parallel instructions or threads is not an easy task since most applications and algorithms are not yet ready to utilize available multicore capabilities.

Embedded compute- and data-intensive applications can only benefit from the full multicore SoC hardware potential if all features on all system levels are taken into account. In addition, programmer should exploit different level of parallelisms which are found at several levels in the system. Existing approaches require the programmer/compiler to identify the parallelism in the program and statically create a parallel program using a programming model such as POSIX Threads (Pthreads) (IEEE 1995), Message Passing Interface (MPI), or task programming, expressed in an a high level language such as C. There are different types of parallelism that a programmer can exploit:

- *Bit-Level Parallelism (BLP)*: Bit-Level Parallelism extends the hardware architecture to operate simultaneously on larger data. However, by extending the word length from, for example 8–16, the operation can now be executed by a single operation. This is of course good for performance. Thus, word length has doubled from 4-bit processors through 8, 16, and even 64-bit in advanced processor cores.
- *Instruction-Level Parallelism (ILP)*: ILP is a well known and is (was) an efficient technique for identifying independent instructions and executing them in parallel. Generally, the compiler takes care about finding independent instructions and schedule them for execution by the hardware. Other known techniques are speculative and out-of-order (OoO) execution which are implemented in hardware. Because programs are written in sequential manner, finding independent instructions is not always possible. Some applications, such as for signal processing, can function efficiently and several existing DSP cores can execute 8 or even more instructions per cycle and per core (inst/cycle/core).
- *Thread-Level Parallelism (TLP)*: TLP is a software capability that enables a program, often a high-end program to work with multiple threads at the same time instead of having to wait on other threads. TLP can be exploited in single core or also in multicore systems. If used in multicore system, it allows closely

coupled cores that share the same memory to run in parallel on shared data structures.

- *Task-Level Parallelism (TaLP)*: TaLP (also known as function parallelism and control parallelism) focuses on distributing execution processes (or threads) across different parallel cores on the same or different data. Most real programs fall somewhere on a continuum between Task parallelism and Data parallelism. The difficulty with task parallelism is not on how to efficiently distribute the threads, rather is with how to divide the application program into multiple tasks. TaLP approach allows more independent processes to run in parallel, occasionally exchanging messages.
- *Data-Level Parallelism (DLP)*: DLP (also known as loop-level parallelism) allows multiple units to process data concurrently. One such technique implemented in hardware is single instruction multiple data (SIMD). In multiprocessor/multicore system, data parallelism is achieved when each core performs the same task on different pieces of distributed data. Data parallelism is where multicore plays an important role. Performance improvement depends on how many cores are able to work on the data at the same time. For example, consider adding two matrices using two cores (core0 and core1). In a data parallel implementation, core0 could add all elements from the top half of the matrices, while core1 could add all elements from the bottom half of the matrices. Since the two cores work in parallel, the job of performing matrix addition would take one half the time of performing the same operation in serial using one single core.

Since multicore based systems mainly exploit TLP approach (of course ILP can be also exploited within a single core in a given multicore based system), we will only focus on this parallelization technique. In order to support TLP, there are several software and hardware approaches that can be used. One approach involves using a preemptive multitasking operating system (OS). This approach involves the use of an interrupt mechanism which suspends the currently executing process and invokes the OS scheduler to determine which process should be executed next. As a result, all processes will get some amount of CPU time at any given time. The OS kernel can also initiate a context switch to satisfy the scheduling policy's priority constraint, thus preempting the active task. The other known approach to address TLP is called Time-slice multi-threading. This approach allows software developers to hide the latency associated with I/Os by interleaving the execution of multiple threads. But the main problem of this approach is that it does not allow for parallel execution because only one instruction stream can run on a processor at a time.

A more efficient approach for TLP is called simultaneous multi-threading (SMT), or Hyper-threading (HT) as called by Intel (Koufaty 2003). The goal of this approach is to efficiently utilize system's resources. SMP makes a single processor appears, from the programmer's view, as multiple logical processor cores. This means, instructions from more than one thread can be executing in any given pipeline stage at a time. This is done without great changes to the main basic building blocks of a processor.

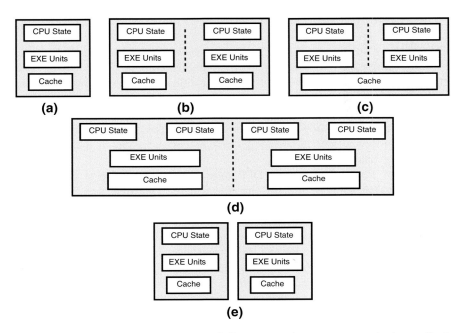

**Fig. 1.2** Different ways for exploiting parallelism over various system organization: **a** Single core, **b** Multicore with separate caches, **c** Multicore with shared cache, **d** Multicore with simultaneous threading, **e** Multiprocessor

The modern approach for SMP programming is to increase the number of physical processor cores in a computer system or the number of cores in a single die (multicore). As we earlier said, this shift becomes now possible due to the advance of semiconductor technology, which allows the integration of several cores in a single chip. Integrated cores have their own set of execution and architectural resources and may or may not share a large on-chip cache for better program locality exploitation. For application with large number of threads, individual cores may be implemented with SMP support (see Fig. 1.2d).

## 1.1.4 Parallel Hardware Architectures

Parallel hardware is becoming an important component in computer processing technology. Recently, there are many dual or quad-core CPUs and graphics processing units (GPUs) on the desktop computer market, and many MCSoC solutions are also in the embedded computing markets. Before we start discussing about multicore SoC architectures, let us first review the different types of parallel hardware architectures, including multiprocessor, dual-core, multicore, SoCs and FPGAs.

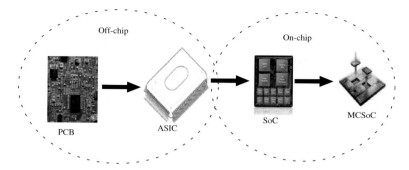

**Fig. 1.3**  From PCB to MCSoC

*Multiprocessors*: Multiprocessor systems contain multiple CPU cores that are not on the same chip. These systems were made common in the 1990s for the purpose of IT servers. Today, multiprocessors are commonly found on the same physical board and connected through a high-speed communication interface.

*Dual-Core and Multicore Processors*: Dual-core processors are two CPUs on a single chip (see Fig. 1.2b). Multicore processors are a family of processors that contain any number of multiple CPUs on a single chip, such as 2, 4, and 8. The challenge with multicore processors is in the area of porting existing sequential software (or writing new parallel model) so that it can benefit from the large number of available cores.

*FPGAs*: A Field Programmable Gate Arrays (FPGAs) is a device that contains a matrix of reconfigurable gate array logic circuitry. When a FPGA is configured, the internal circuitry is connected in a way that creates a hardware implementation of the software application. Unlike ASIC processors, FPGAs use dedicated hardware for processing logic and generally do not have an operating system.

*SoC*: A system-on-chip (SoC) is an integrated circuit (IC) that integrates all components of a system (generally embedded system) into a single chip. SoC consists of several building blocks including analog, digital, mixed-signal, and radio-frequency functions. These blocks are connected by either a custom or an industry-standard bus such as AMBA (2007).

A SoC is quite different from the so called microcontroller. Microcontrollers (i.e., 8051) typically have small RAM memory and are based on low performance processors, whereas an SoC is typically used with more powerful cores, and reconfigurable modules such as a FPGA device. Early SoCs used an interconnect paradigm inspired by the rack-based microprocessor systems of earlier days. Current SoCs use more advanced and scalable interconnects, such as network-on-chip approach (discussed later in Chaps. 4 and 5). Figure 1.3 illustrates the evolution of electronic circuits from simple PCB circuit of earlier days to a state of of the arts complex multicore SoC system.

## 1.1.5 The Need for Multicore Computing

As the computing needs of each processor type grew rapidly, the first response of
the computer architects and semiconductor companies was to increase the speed of
the CPU. Higher performance was mainly achieved by refining manufacturing
processes to improve the operating speed. However, this method requires finding
solutions for increased leakage power and other problems, making it unable to
keep pace with the current rate of evolution or revolution.

After several decades of singlecore processor devices production, major CPU
makers, such as Intel and AMD, decided to switch to multicore processor chips
because it was found that several smaller cores running at a lower frequency can
perform the same amount of work without consuming as much energy and power.
More precisely, this shift started when Intel's hardware engineers lunched the
Pentium 4; at that time, they expected single processor chip to scale up to 10 GHz
or even more using advanced process technologies below 90 nm. However, they
did not achieve their expectation since the fastest processor never exceeded
4 GHz. As a result, the trends followed by all major hardware makers is to use a
higher number of slower cores, building parallel devices made with denser chips
that work at low clock speed.

Of course, this revolution could not be achieved without an enormous progress
in the semiconductor technologies. That is, the exponential increase in the number
of transistors on a die is made possible by the progressive reduction in the characteristic dimensions of the integrating process, from the micrometer resolutions
of past decades (with tens of thousands transistors/chip in the 80's, until the recent
achievement below hundred manometers (with more than a hundred millions
transistor/chip).

Nowadays, semiconductor and hardware companies are fabricating devices
realized with technologies down to 45 nm and even less. The merit of reducing
dimensions of a chip lies not only in the higher number of gates that can fit on the
chip, but also in the higher working frequency at which these devices can be
operated. If the distance among every gate becomes small, propagation signals
have a lower path to cover, and the transitory time for a state transition decreases,
allowing a higher clock speed.

## 1.1.6 Multicore SoCs Potential Applications

To make it a simple discussion, we summarized nearly all potential multicore
SoCs applications in Fig. 1.4.

The above applications are mainly attractive for embedded systems market. Some
of them are also attractive for desktop applications. To meet the requirements of low
cost, high performance, and small size, multicore approach plays an important
role for system architecture and development. For embedded systems segment,
virtually most semiconductor houses are developing systems based on multicore SoC

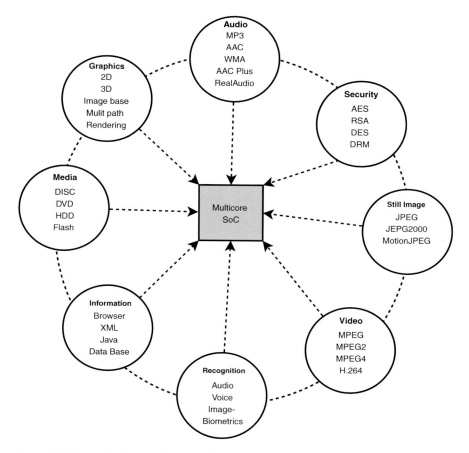

**Fig. 1.4** Multicore SoC potential applications

approach. Such multicore SoCs are growing day-after-day and are starting to find acceptance in various applications including, real-time mission critical, industrial automation, medical equipment, consumer electronic devices (PDAs, cellphones, laptops, cameras, etc) and high-performance computing as shown in Fig. 1.4.

High-end smart-phones already contain a plethora of micro-processors (MPUs) and digital signal processors (DSPs) to provide advanced modem and application processing, as well as WiFi, GPS and Bluetooth functionality.

Another important application is the multimedia domain. Multimedia applications with high-definition audio and video are being provided by embedded systems such as car navigation, cellular phones, and digital televisions. Multimedia schemes in general can be partitioned in stream oriented, block oriented, and DSP oriented functions, which can all run in parallel on different cores. Each core can be used to run a specific class algorithms, and individual tasks can be mapped efficiently to the appropriate core.

## 1.2 Multicore SoC Basics

Multicore SoCs are generally constructed with homogeneous or heterogeneous cores. Homogeneous cores are all exactly the same: equivalent frequencies, cache sizes, functions, etc. However, each core in a heterogeneous system may have a different function, frequency, memory model, etc. Homogeneous cores are easier to produce since the same instruction set is used across all cores and each core contains the same hardware. Each core in a heterogeneous multicore SoC, such as the case of CELL processor (Flachs 2005), could have a specific function and run its own specialized instruction set. This model could also have a large centralized core built for generic processing and running a Real-time Operating System (RTOS), a core for graphics, a communications core, an audio core, a cryptography core, etc.

A heterogeneous multicore SoC system is generally more complex to design, but may have better performance, and thermal power benefits that outweigh its complexity. A key difference with classic processor architecture is that the SoC model distinguishes two kinds of processor cores: (1) those used to run the end application, and (2) those dedicated to execute specific functions that could have been designed in hardware. The instruction set architectures (ISAs), programming, and interfacing of these two kinds of processor cores are quite different. Figure 1.5 shows typical multicore SoC architectural view.

## 1.2.1 Programmability Support

General applications usually consist of several tasks that can be executed on different cores in parallel or concurrently. For example, a multimedia application includes two concurrent tasks: an audio decoder task and a video decoder task. The task itself may consist of two types of parallelism: (1) functional parallelism and (2) loop-level parallelism. Therefore a multicore platform is needed for such application, and the main design challenge is how to exploit parallelism.

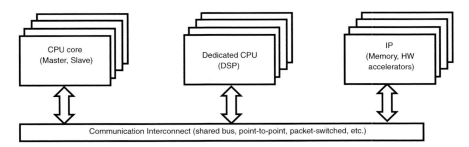

**Fig. 1.5** Typical multicore SoC architectural view

Programmability is also needed for supporting multiple standards and algorithms. For example, some digital video applications require support for multiple video standards, resolutions, and quality. It is easier to implement these on a programmable system. A programmable system can provide the designer the ability to customize a specific algorithm as necessary. This flexibility provides the application's developer with more control of the application.

A multicore SoC may have special instructions to speed up some applications. For example special instructions are implemented on a DSP core to accelerate operations such as: 32-bit multiply instructions (for extended precision computation), expanded arithmetic functions (to support FFT and DCT algorithms), double dot product instructions (for improving throughput of FIR loops), parallel packing instructions, and Enhanced Galois Field Multiply (EGFM).

### 1.2.1.1 Hardware Accelerators

Hardware accelerator is used on multicore SoCs as a way to efficiently execute some classes of algorithms. There are many applications that have algorithmic functions that do not map very well to a given architecture. Hardware accelerators can be used to solve this problem. Also, a conventional storage model may not be appropriate to execute these algorithms effectively. A specialized hardware accelerator can be built and performs bit manipulation efficiently which sits next to the CPU for bit manipulation operations.

Fast I/O operations are another area where a dedicated accelerator with an attached I/O peripheral will perform better. Finally, applications that are required to process streams of data do not map well to the traditional CPU architecture, especially those that implement caching systems. A specialized hardware accelerator with special fetch logic can be implemented to provide dedicated support to these data streams.

**Fig. 1.6** Software layers on top of the hardware

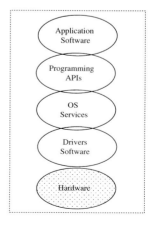

## 1.2.2 Software Organization

Each kind of multicore SoC employs different software organization. The application software generally consists of several layers on top of the hardware as shown in Fig. 1.6. For software designers, multicore SoC approach presents the interesting challenge of enabling applications to obtain all the processing power available from these multicore environments. How can developers make sure their applications scale linearly with the available cores, as well as fully utilize the other SoC hardware building blocks? The scalability question is still a real science issue for many applications.

## 1.2.3 Programming Multicore Systems

Given the various available multicore platforms, choosing the classical programming approach (i.e., OpenMP, MPI) is not always a good decision. The biggest hurdle is the non-deterministic nature of concurrent threads. Thus, to effectively exploit the full power of embedded multicore systems, a more efficient programming model is needed. The standard sequential programming approach cannot be used as it is and should be optimized or extended for such concurrent systems.

Software development for multicore SoCs involves partitioning a given application among the available PEs based on the most efficient computational model. The programmer also has to implement efficient static or dynamic techniques to synchronize between processes. The trend towards multicore systems is motivated by the performance gain compared to singlecore systems when a budget on power or temperature or both is given. The performance is expected to further increase with the increasing number of cores if TLP can be fully exploited. The typical goal of threading is to improve the application performance by either increasing the number of work items processed per unit of time (also called throughput) or reducing turnaround time (also called latency).

In order to effectively use *thread* to parallelize a given application, programmer needs a good plan for the overall partitioning of the system and the mapping of the algorithms to the respective processing elements. This may require a lot of trial and error to establish the proper partitioning. There are two main known categories used to do this partitioning: (1) Functional Decomposition—division based on the function of the work, and (2) Data decomposition. In Fig. 1.7, we show two simple examples with functional and data decomposition methods.

**Fig. 1.7** Sample OpenMP
code using *section* and
*parallel* directives:
**a** Functional decomposition,
**b** Data decomposition

```
#pragma omp parallel sections

{
#pragma omp section
    check_scan_attacks();


# pragma omp
    check_denial_service_attacks();


#pragma omp  section
    check_penetration_attacks
}
```

**(a)**

```
#pragma omp parallel for

{
for (j=0; j<1000 ; j++) {
    process_image(j);
}
```

**(b)**

## 1.2.4 Multicore Implementations

There are several manufacturers of multicore SoCs. Bellow, we will describe two
well known multicore systems as an example. Since the target applications of these
multicore SoC systems are different, the number of cores, interconnection types,
and memory configurations vary widely.

### 1.2.4.1 CELL Processor

A Sony-Toshiba-IBM partnership built the so called CELL processor for use in
Sony's PlayStation 3 (Flachs 2005). The CELL system is highly customized for
gaming/graphics rendering which means superior processing power for gaming
applications. The CELL architecture is a heterogeneous multicore processor that
combines a dual-threaded, dual-issue, 64-bit Power-Architecture compliant Power
processor element (PPE) with eight newly architected synergistic processor elements (SPEs) an on-chip memory controller, and a controller for a configurable
I/O interface (Flachs 2005). These units are interconnected with a coherent on-chip
element interconnect bus (EIB). Extensive support for pervasive functions such as

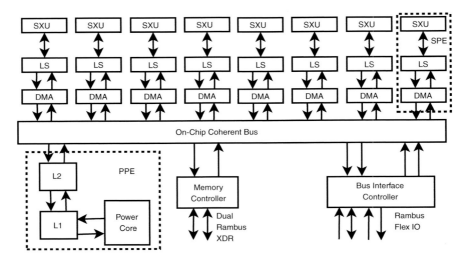

**Fig. 1.8** Heterogeneous multicore CELL organization

power-on, test, on-chip hardware debug, and performance-monitoring functions
are also included. With CELL's real-time broadband architecture, 128 concurrent
transactions to memory per processor are possible.

In CELL architecture (see Fig. 1.8), Direct Memory Access (DMA) is used to
transfer data between local storage and main memory which allows for the high
number of concurrent memory transactions. Other interesting features of this
architecture are the Power Management Unit (PMU) and Thermal Management
Unit (TMU). The PMU allows for power reduction in the form of slowing,
pausing, or completely stopping a unit. The TMU consists of one linear sensor and
ten digital thermal sensors used to monitor temperature throughout the chip and
provide an early warning if temperatures are rising in a certain area of the chip
(Flachs 2005).

### 1.2.4.2  Tilera TILE64

Tilera has developed a multicore chip with 64 homogeneous cores set up in a grid
(Bell 2008; Tilera 2011). The family of multicore processors delivers high
computing performance and targeted for embedded applications. The processor
features 64 identical processor cores (tiles) interconnected with a so called iMESH
on-chip network. Each tile works as a full-featured processor, including integrated
L1 and L2 caches and a non-blocking switch that connects the tile into the mesh. Each
tile can independently run a full OS, or a group of multiple tiles can run a multiprocessing OS such as SMP Linux. An application that is written to take advantage of
these additional cores will run far faster than if it were run on a single core.

The TILE64 also includes on-chip memory and I/O controllers. Like the CELL processor, unused tiles (cores) can be put into a sleep mode to further decrease power consumption. The TILE64 uses a 3-way VLIW pipeline to deliver 12 times the instructions as a single-issue, single-core processor. When VLIW is combined with the MIMD processors, multiple operating systems can be run simultaneously and advanced multimedia applications such as video conferencing and video-on-demand can be run efficiently (Tilera 2008).

## 1.3 Multicore SoCs Design Challenges

The introduction of multicore processors signals a major shift in the structure and design ways of all computing platforms. Before this shift, almost all embedded software could be written with the assumption that there is only a single processor core and where multiple processors were involved, they were either relatively loosely-coupled or were used in easily parallelized applications.

While multicore systems will change this model somewhat, there is a real expectation that the number of cores will grow rapidly, roughly doubling with each processor generation (Moore's Law still valid). This growth will create unique challenges for run-time systems and compilers. If multiple cores on a processor share a cache, contention for the shared cache memory and cache coherence are major issues.

Power and temperature management are also two concerns that can increase exponentially with the addition of multiple cores. The other issue is the problem of using a multicore processor to its full potential. Applications should be written in a good manner so that different parts of the program runs concurrently. Finally the necessity to move beyond parallel computing paradigm and towards heterogeneous embedded multicore distributed systems will likely drive changes in how embedded software will be created.

### 1.3.1 Cache Coherence

Allowing multiple processors to share memory complicates the design of the memory hierarchy in a multicore system. Cache coherency, or cache consistency, is a big concern in this multicore environment. Since each core has its own cache, the copy of the data in that cache may not always be the most up-to-date version. For example, imagine a processor with two cores where each core brought a block of memory into its private cache. One core writes a value to a specific location. When the second core attempts to read that value from its cache it will not have the updated copy unless its cache entry is invalidated and a cache miss occurs. This cache miss forces the second core's cache entry to be updated. This is a real trouble for the correctness of the application being executed.

A system is said to be coherent if all copies of the main memory location in multiple caches remain consistent when the contents of that memory location are modified. A cache coherency protocol (discussed later in Chap. 3) is the mechanism by which the coherency of the caches is maintained. Maintaining coherency means taking special actions when one core writes to a block of data that exists is other caches.

## 1.3.2 Power and Temperature

While multicore systems may limit power consumption in some areas, they present real challenges to energy management paradigms optimized for single chip systems. In particular, multicore limits the scope and capability of dynamic voltage and frequency scaling (DVFS) because most SoC subsystems share power supplies and clocks. As a result, scaling the operating voltage of one of several SoC subsystems may limit its ability to use local buses to communicate with other subsystems, and to access shared memory. Clock frequency scaling of a single SoC subsystem also presents a big challenges especially for synchronous buses.

To lessen the heat generated by multiple cores on a single chip, the chip is architected so that the number of hot spots does not grow too large and the heat is spread out across the chip. For example, the majority of the heat in the CELL processor is dissipated in the Power Processing Element and the rest is spread across the Synergistic Processing Elements. We will discuss in Chap. 8 in more details power optimization techniques.

## 1.3.3 Multi-Threading and Memory Management

The other important challenge is in using multi-threading or other parallel processing techniques to get the most performance out of the multicore system. Except Java, there are no widely used commercial development languages with multi-threaded extensions (Creeger 2005). To use multi-threading technique in a given multicore system, programmers have to write applications with subroutines able to be run in different cores, meaning that data dependencies will have to be resolved and applications should be balanced. If one core is being used much more than another, the programmer is not taking full advantage of the multicore system. Microsoft and Apple's newest operating systems can run on up to 4 cores, for example (Creeger 2005; Geer 2007).

On multicore SoC system, actual computing is not a problem since there are many processing elements. But, memory bandwidth remains the bottleneck because typical systems use a common bus which is shared by all processor cores. Therefore, efficient memory management is very critical for a scalable application on multicore SoCs.

## *1.3.4 Interconnection Networks*

Extra memory will be useless if the amount of time required for memory requests does not improve as well. Currently, on-chip interconnection networks are mostly implemented using buses, where several masters and slaves can be connected to a shared bus. However, an arbiter is needed with a bus to manage multiple requests. A bus arbiter periodically examines accumulated requests from the multiple master interfaces and grants access to a master using arbitration mechanisms specified by the bus protocol. Bus has simple topology, low area, low cost, and easy to build. The disadvantages of shared bus architecture are larger load per data bus line, longer delay for data transfer, large power consumption, and lower bandwidth. To this end, redesigning the interconnection network between cores is a major focus of chip manufacturers (Merritt 2007; Wentzlaff 2007).

## 1.4  Conclusion

Multicore SoCs are architected to adhere to reasonable power consumption, heat dissipation, and cache coherence protocols. In order to use a multicore system at full capacity, the applications must be multi-threaded. However, the difficult task is how to write parallel programs to exploit multicore systems. In addition, the memory systems and interconnection networks also should be carefully designed. This chapters introduced multicore SoC systems and their deign challenges.

# Chapter 2
# Multicore SoCs Design Methods

The strong demand for complex and high performance multicore systems-on-chip (MCSoCs) requires quick turn around design methodology. Thus, there is a clear need for efficient methodology for the design of these systems on platforms implementing both hardware and software modules.

This chapter describes conventional multiore SoC design methods in details. It also describes a so called scalable core-based methodology for systematic design environment of application specific heterogeneous multicore SoC architectures. Although the methodology presented here is general and not limited to special architecture, we will consider a real synthesizable core as a case study to make the discussion easy.

## 2.1 Introduction

Systems-on-chip designs have evolved from fairly simple uni-core, single memory designs to complex multicore SoCs consisting of tens or hundreds of cores in a single chip. As more and more cores are integrated into these chips to share the ever increasing processing load, the main challenges lie in how to efficiently and quickly integrate these cores together into a single system capable of leveraging their individual flexibility. Moreover, for better inter-core communication, the multicore system requires high performance communication architectures and efficient communication protocols, such as hierarchical bus (Diefendorff 1997; Liu 2005), point-to-point connection (Loghi 2004), Time Division Multiplexed Access (TDMA) based bus (Kulkarani 2002), or packet-switching networks (Ben-Abdallah 2006).

Recently, SoC design methods tend toward mixed hardware/software co-designs targeting multicore SoCs for specific applications (Ernst 1993; Jerraya 2005; Lennard 2000). To decide on the lowest cost mix of cores, designers must iteratively map the device's functionality to a particular hardware/software partition and target architecture (platform). When a designer wants to explore different system architectures, the interfaces must be redesigned. This method may lead to a narrow application domain. In addition, managing all these details is time

A. Ben Abdallah, *Multicore Systems On-Chip: Practical Software/Hardware Design*,
Atlantis Ambient and Pervasive Intelligence 7, DOI: 10.2991/978-94-91216-92-3_2,
© Atlantis Press and the author 2013

consuming that designers typically cannot afford to evaluate several different implementations.

Automating the interface generation is an alternative solution and a critical part of the development of embedded system' synthesis tools. Most existing automation algorithms implement the system based on a standard bus protocol (input/output interface) or based on a standard component (processing) protocol. Recent works have used a more generalize model consisting of heterogeneous multicore with arbitrary communication links. The SOS algorithm (Prakash 1992) uses an integer linear programming approach. The co-synthesis algorithm, developed in (Dave 1997), can handle multiple objectives such as cost, performance, power, and fault tolerance. Such design methods allow only limited automation and designers resort to manual architecture design which is time consuming and error-prone.

There are two fundamental steps needed for MCSoC design: (1) selection and construction of a target multicore platform, known as design space exploration phase, and (2) development of the parallel software for exploiting the application parallelism on the selected platform, known as parallel software development phase. We will describe these hardware and software design phases in the following two sections.

## 2.2 Design Space Exploration

There are various design axes that define the design space of multicore platforms, which include processor architectures and numbers, memory configuration, communication architectures, hardware accelerators, and so on. To determine the target platform, we need a technique that quickly evaluates the expected performance of each candidate and explores the wide design space without actual hardware implementation. Further, the gate densities achieved in current ASIC and FPGA devices give designers enough logic elements to implement all functionalities on the same chip by mixing self-design modules with third party ones (Kulkarani 2002; Sheliga 1996; Jerraya 2005). This possibility opens new horizons especially for embedded systems where space constraints are as important as performance. The most fundamental characteristic of a SoC is complexity. The SoC is generally tailored to the application rather than general-purpose chip, and may contain memory, one or several specialized cores, buses, and several other digital functions. Therefore, embedded applications cannot use general-purpose computers (GPPs) either because a GPP machine is not cost effective or because it cannot provide the necessary requirements and performance. In addition, a GPP machine can't provide reliable real-time performance.

In Fig. 2.1, a typical multicore SoC architecture block diagram is shown. This typical model is made of a set of cores communicating through an AMBA communication architecture (Diefendorff 1997). The communication architecture constitutes the hardware links that support the communication between cores. It also provides the system with the required support for the general data transfer

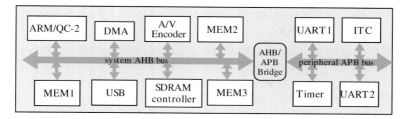

**Fig. 2.1** SoC typical architecture

with external devices common to most applications. Inter-component link is often in the critical path of such a system and is a very common source of performance bottlenecks (Pasricha 2006). Thus, it becomes imperative for system designers to focus on exploring the communication design space.

Conventional SoC architectures are generally classified into tow types: single-core based and multicore based systems. Single-core architecture consists of a single CPU core and one or several ASICs. A master-slave synchronization pattern is adopted in this type. The single-core SoC type can only offer a restricted performance capability in many applications because of the lack of true parallelism.

A multicore SoC architecture is a system that contains multiple CPU cores and also one or several ASICs. In term of performance, multicore SoCs perform better for several embedded applications. However, these systems generally introduce new challenges: first, the inter-processor communication may require more sophisticated networks than a simple shared bus, and second, the architecture may include more than one master processor. In both types, high processing performance is required because most of the applications for which SoCs are used have precise performance requirements deadlines; this is different from conventional general purpose computing.

In general, the architectures used in conventional methods of multicore SoC design and custom multicore architectures are not flexible enough to meet the requirements of different application domains (e.g. only point-to-point or shared bus communication is supported) and not scalable enough to meet different computation needs and different complexity of various applications. A promising approach was proposed in Dave (1997). This method is a core-based solution, which enables integration of heterogeneous processors and communications protocols by using abstract interconnections. Behavior and communication must be separated in the system specification. Hence, system communication can be described at a higher-level and refined independently of the behavior of the system. There are two known component-based design approaches: (1) usage of a standard bus (i.e., IBM Core-Connect) protocol, and (2) usage of a standard component protocol (Ernst 1993; Jerraya 2005; Lennard 2000). For the first approach, a wrapper is designed to adapt the protocol of each component to CoreConnect protocol. For the second case, the designer can choose a bus protocol and then design wrappers to interconnect components using the above protocol.

## 2.3 Parallel Software Development Phase

Embedded parallel software development for multicore platforms involves parallel programming for homogeneous and heterogeneous multicore SoC architectures under several design constraints such as power, area, cost, and timeliness.

The sequential Von Neumann programming model is not a good option for the multicore based systems because it simply cannot exploit the huge parallelism which is available in different forms in multicore platforms. Thus, it is clear that we now need new programming models and corresponding software development tools that are capable of exploiting all forms of available parallelism. Recently, big efforts have been made to develop methods and tools that solve the design problems of multicore SoCs targeted for various applications and under several design constraints. Bellow, we will describe these methods in details.

### 2.3.1 Compiler-Based Schemes

In compiler-based schemes, the sequential Von Neumann program is used as input, where all specifications are defined (Phase 1). Then, a parallelizing compiler automatically parallelizes (Phase 2) the source code (or binary) as illustrated in Fig. 2.2. Using several parallelizing techniques, this phase (Phase 2) analyses the input code and finds parallel regions. More specifically, Phase 2 parallelizes the serial code. A well known technique is to identify all loops and examine their dependencies by analyzing indexes. The mapper, then, transforms each parallel region into a set of concurrent tasks and maps them onto multiple cores (Phase 3).

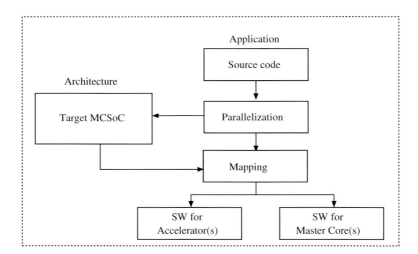

**Fig. 2.2** Compiler based scheme

## 2.3.2  Language Extensions Schemes

The *Language extension schemes* require that application programmer provides all parallelism information as well as where and how to parallelize the code with language extension that has annotations and/or additional application programming interfaces (APIs). As a result, compilers in *language-extension schemes* can focus on exploiting the specified parallelism according to the the target platform.

### 2.3.2.1  Language Extension with Annotations

The main merit of the language extension with annotations approach is simplicity. That is, it simplifies the compiler's job by relieving the burden of extracting parallelism while it gives only a little overhead of annotations to the software developer.

The Open Multiprocessing Standard [OpenMP] is an example of language extension with annotations. OpenMP is a widely used API for parallel programming and is attractive because programmers can continue using their familiar programming model while re-using their existing codes.

As an example, suppose a programmer is writing a ray tracing program, which goes through each pixel of the screen, and using lighting, texture, and geometry information, the color of that pixel is determined. The program goes on to the next pixel and repeats (loops) the process. The calculation for each pixel is completely separate from the calculation of any other pixel, therefore making this program highly suitable for OpenMP. The code for the above example is shown in Fig. 2.3. This piece of code simply goes through each pixel of the screen, and calls a function, RenderPixel, to determine the final color of that pixel. Note that the results are simply stored in an array. Because each pixel is independent of all other pixels, and because RenderPixel is expected to take a noticeable amount of time, this small snippet of code is a prime candidate for parallelization and can be simple annotated with OpenMP directive: *#pragma omp parallel for*.

We have to note here that OpenMP standard was originally developed for symmetric multiprocessor (SMP) computers with shared memory. Recently, it was ported to heterogeneous multicore platforms, such as in IBM Cell processor (Obrien 2008). GNU GCC also adopted the GOMP OpenMP implementation. Thus, many GCC-enabled multicore processors now support OpenMP [GOMP] The Cell processor is a heterogeneous multicore processor with one Power Processing Engine (PPE) core and eight Synergistic Processing Engine (SPE) cores. Each SPE has a directly accessible small local memory (256K), and it can access the system memory through DMA operations. Programming Cell system is difficult since an SPE core has a small local memory and accesses the system memory only through DMA operations. The other difficulty comes from the availability of several layers of parallelism in the architecture, including heterogeneous cores, multiple SPE cores, multi-threading. Cell compiler is built upon an IBM XL compiler therefore

**Fig. 2.3** Parallel for loop
with OpenMP

```
for(int x=0; x < width; x++)
{
  for(int y=0; y < height; y++)
  {
    finalImage[x][y] = RenderPixel(x,y, &sceneData);
  }
}
```
                    **(a)** Before parallelization

```
#pragma omp parallel for
for(int x=0; x < width; x++)
{
  for(int y=0; y < height; y++)
  {
    finalImage[x][y] = RenderPixel(x,y, &sceneData);
  }
}
```
                    **(b)** After parallelization

translates the parallel region into a set of concurrent tasks that run on the SPE cores
with a control task that schedules the SPE tasks (Obrien 2008).

## 2.3.3 Language Extensions with APIs

In this scheme, a software developer writes a parallel program with specifically
defined APIs for parallel execution. Compared with the annotation scheme, the
APIs based approach allows more low-level control of parallelism by the software
developer. Although this scheme has better performance, it requires that the
programmer manually discovers the parallel regions, distributes the code and data
to the processors, and restructures the code using the APIs.

Message passing interface (MPI) is an example of the language extension with
APIs since it started to find its use in embedded heterogeneous multicore SoCs.

## 2.3.4 Model-Based Schemes

Model-based schemes are advocated for multicore and MCSoC design since they
simplify the application behavior and reveals the top-level structure of the
behavior; this eliminates the complex low-level implementation details. In this
scheme, the software developer determines which model of computation is used to
capture application algorithms. For example, the actor based models are used to
specify the computation-oriented applications and the FSM (finite state machine)
model for control-oriented applications.

## 2.4 Generic Architecture Template for Real Multicore SoC Design

In this section we will describe a design design method based on a so called generic-architecture-template (GAT), where both processing and input/output interface may be customized to fit the specific needs of the application. GAT design method enables a designer to make a basic architecture design without detailed knowledge of the architecture.

A high performance synthesizable soft-core architecture, called QueueCore, is also presented here and is used as a task-distributor-core (TDC) in the a multicore SoC system design. The system may consist, then, of multiple processing cores of various types (i.e., QueueCore(s), general purpose processor(s), domain specific DSPs, and custom hardware), and communication links. The ultimate goal of the above systematic design automation and architecture generation is the to improve performance and the design efficiency of large scale heterogeneous multicore SoC.

### 2.4.1 Target Multicore SoC Platform

The target model of the architecture consists of CPUs (i.e., QueueCore (QC-2), GPPs), hardware blocks, memories, and communication interfaces. The addition of new core will not change the main principle of the proposed methodology. The core are connected to the shared communication architecture via communication network, which maybe of whatever complexity from a single bus to a network with complex protocols. However, to ensure modularity, standard and specific interfaces to link cores to the communication architecture should be used. This gives the possibility to design separately each part of the application. Reader can refer to Ben-Abdallah (2005) for more details about a modular design methodology. One important feature of the above method is that the generic assembling scheme largely increases the architecture modularity. Figure 2.4 shows a typical instance of the platform made of 4 cores (2*QC-2 cores and 2*SH cores). The QC-2 core is a special purpose synthesizable core (described in details in Sect. 2.4.3).

The designer can configure: the number of CPUs, I/O ports for each processor and interconnections between cores, the communication protocol and the external peripherals. The communication interface depends on the core attributes and on the application-specific parameters. The communication interface connects a given core to the communication architecture and consists of two parts: the first part specific to the core's bus and the second part is generic and depends on communication protocols and on the number of communication channels used. This structure allows the *isolation* of the cores from the communication network.

Each interface module acts as a co-processor for the corresponding core. The application dependent part may include several communication channels. The arbitration is done by the CPU-dependent part and the overhead induced by

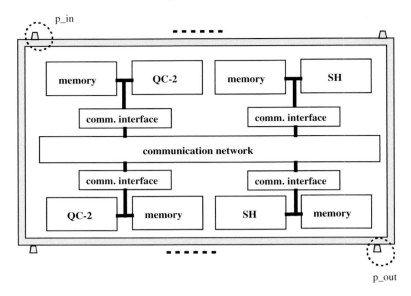

**Fig. 2.4** Multicore SoC system platform. This is a typical instance of the architecture, where the addition of a new core will not change the principle of the methodology

this communication co-processor depends on the design of the basic components and may be very low. The use of this architecture for interfaces provides huge flexibility and allows for modularity and scalability.

## 2.4.2 Design Method

In this methodology, the application-specific parameters should be used to configure the architecture platform and an application-specific architecture is produced. These parameters are determined from an analysis of the application to be designed. The design-flow-graph (DFG) is divided into 14 *linked-tasks* as shown in Fig. 2.5a, b and summarized in Table 2.1. The first task (node T1) defines the architecture platform using all fixed architectural parameters: (1) Network type, (2) Memory architecture, (3) CPU types, and (4) other HW modules.Using the application system level description (second task) and the architectural fixed parameters, the selection of the actual design parameters (number of CPUs, the memory sizes for each core, I/O ports for each core and interconnections, between cores, the communication protocols and the external peripherals) is performed in task 3 (node T3). The outputs of task 3 are: an abstract architecture description (node T7) and a mapping table (node T6). Node T7 is the internal structure of the

**Fig. 2.5** Linked-task design
flow graph (DFG).
**a** Hardware related tasks,
**b** Application related tasks

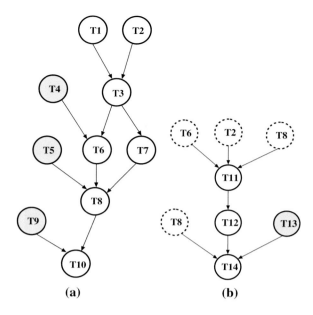

**(a)**                    **(b)**

target system architecture. It contains all the application specific parameters. The
mapping table (T7) contains the addresses allocation and memory map for each
core. The complete architecture design task (T8) is linked to the abstract architecture and the mapping table nodes (tasks). Finally, binary programs that will run
on the target processors are produced in task 11 (node T11). For validation, cycle
accurate simulation for CPUs and HDL (Verilog or VHDL) modeling for other
cores/modules can be used for the whole architecture.

**Table 2.1** Linked-task
description

| Task | Description |
|------|-------------|
| T1 | Define architecture platform |
| T2 | Describe application system level |
| T3 | Select design parameters |
| T4 | Instantiate Pr. att. |
| T5 | Instantiate communication |
| T6 | Mapping table |
| T7 | Describe abstract architecture |
| T8 | Design architecture |
| T9 | Inst. IP cores (Pr. and Mem) |
| T10 | H-SoC synthesis |
| T11 | Software adaptation |
| T12 | Binary code |
| T13 | Pr. and Memory emulators |
| T14 | H-SoC validation |

## 2.4.3 QueueCore Architecture

The key idea of the produced order queue computation model is the operands and results manipulation schemes (Ben-Abdallah 2004). The Queue computing scheme stores intermediate results into a circular queue-register (QREG).

A given instruction implicitly reads its first operand from the head of the QREG, its second operand from a location explicitly addressed with an offset from the first operand location. The computed result is finally written into the QREG at a position pointed by a queue-tail pointer (QT). An important feature of this scheme is that write-after-read false data dependency does not occur (Ben-Abdallah 2005). Furthermore, since there is no explicit referencing to the QREG, it is easy to add extra storage locations to the QREG when needed. The other feature of this computing model is its important affect on the instruction issue hardware.

The QC-1 core (Ben-Abdallah 2004) exploits ILP without considerable effort for heavy run time data dependence analysis, resulting in a simple hardware organization when compared with conventional Super-scalar processors. This also allows the inclusion of a large number of functional units into a single chip, increasing parallelism exploitation. Since the operands and result addresses of a given static-instruction (compiler generated) are implicitly *computed* during run-time, an efficient and fast hardware mechanism is needed for parallel execution of instructions. The queue processor implements a so named queue computation mechanism that calculates operands and result addresses for each instruction (discussed later). The QC-2 core implements all hardware features found in QC-1 core and also supports single precision floating point accelerator.

### 2.4.3.1 Hardware Pipeline Structure

The QC-2 supports a subset of the produced order queue processor instruction set architecture (Ben-Abdallah 2004). All instructions are 16-bit wide, allowing simple instructions fetch and decode stages and facilitate instructions pipelining. The pipeline's regular structure allows instructions fetching, data memory references, and instruction execution to proceed in parallel. Data dependencies between instructions are automatically handled by hardware interlocks. Bellow we describe the salient characteristics of the QueueCore architecture.

(1) *Fetch (FU)*: The instruction pipeline begins with the fetch stage, which delivers four instructions to the decode unit each cycle. This is the same bandwidth as the maximum execution rate of the functional units. At the beginning of each cycle, assuming no pipeline stalls or memory wait states occur, the address pointer hardware of the fetched instructions issues a new address to the Data/Instruction memory system. This address is either the previous address plus 8 bytes or the target address of the currently executing flow-control instruction.

(2) *Decode (DU)*: The QC-2 decodes four instructions in parallel during the second phase and writes them into the decode buffer. This stage also

calculates the number of consumed (CNBR) and produced (PNBR) data for each instruction. The CNBR and PNBR are used by the next pipeline stage to calculate source and destination locations for each instruction. Decoding stops if a queue becomes full.

(3) *Queue computation (QCU)*: The QCU calculates the first operand (*source*1) and destination addresses for each instruction. The QCU unit keeps track on the current value of the QH and QT pointers. Four instructions arrive to the QCU unit each cycle. To execute instructions in parallel, the QC-2 core must calculate the operands addresses (*source*1, *source*2 and *destination*) for each instruction. Figure 2.6 illustrates QC-2's next QH and QT pointers calculation mechanism. To calculate the *source*1 address, the consumed operands (CNBR) field (port field) is added to the current QH value (QH0). The second operand address in calculated as shown in Fig. 2.7. Similar mechanism is used for the other three instructions. Because the next QH and QT values are dependent on the current QH and QT values, the calculation is performed sequentially. Each QREG entry is written exactly once and it is busy until it is written. If a subsequent instruction needs its value, that instructions must wait until it is written. After QREG entry is written, it is ready.

(4) *Barrier*: The major goal of this unit/stage is to insert barrier flags for all barrier type instructions.

**Fig. 2.6** Next QH and QT pointers calculation mechanism

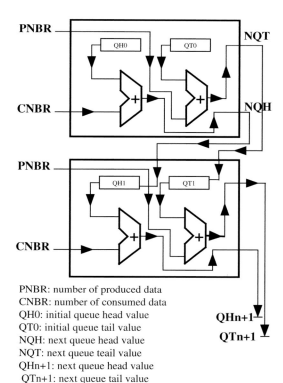

PNBR: number of produced data
CNBR: number of consumed data
QH0: initial queue head value
QT0: initial queue tail value
NQH: next queue head value
NQT: next queue teail value
QHn+1: next queue head value
 QTn+1: next queue tail value

**Fig. 2.7** QC-2's source 2
address calculation

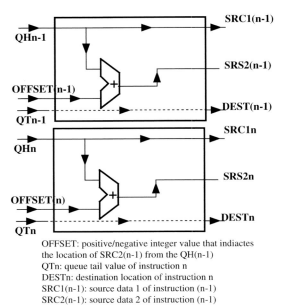

OFFSET: positive/negative integer value that indiactes
the location of SRC2(n-1) from the QH(n-1)
QTn: queue tail value of instruction n
DESTn: destination location of instruction n
SRC1(n-1): source data 1 of instruction (n-1)
SRC2(n-1): source data 2 of instruction (n-1)

(5) *Issue*: Four instructions are issued for execution each cycle. In this stage, the
second operand (*source*2) of a given instruction is first calculated by adding
the address *source*1 to the displacement that comes with the instruction. The
second operand's address calculation could be earlier calculated in the QCU
stage. However, for a balanced pipeline consideration, the *source*2 is calculated in this stage.

An instruction is ready to be issued if its data operands and its corresponding
functional unit are available. The processor reads the operands from the
QREG in the second half of stage 5 and execution begins in stage 6.

(6) *Execution (EXE)*: The macro-data flow execution core consists of 1 integer
ALU unit, 1 floating-point accelerator unit, 1 branch unit, 1 multiply unit, 4
set-units, and 2 load/store units.

The load and store units share a 16-entry address window (AW), while the
integer unit and the branch unit share a 16-entry integer window (IW). The FPA
has its own 16-entries floating point window (FW). The load/store units have
their own address generation logic. Stores are executed to memory in-order.

### 2.4.3.2 Floating Point Organization

The QC-2 floating-point accelerator (FPA) is a pipelined structure and implements
a subset of the IEEE-754 single precision floating-point standard (IEEE 1981,
1985). The FPA consists of a floating-point ALU (FALU), floating-point multiplier
(FMUL), and floating point divider (FDIV). The FALU, FMUL, FDIV and the

floating-point queue-register (FQREG) employ 32-wide data paths. Most FPA operations are completed within three execution cycles. The FPA's execution pipelines are simple in design for high speeds that the QC-2 core requires. All frequently used operations are directly implemented in the hardware. The FPA unit supports the four rounding modes specified in the IEEE 754 floating point standard: round toward-to-nearest-even, round toward positive infinity, round toward negative infinity, and round toward zero.

*Floating point ALU implementation*: The FALU does floating-point addition, subtraction, compare and conversion operations. Its first stage subtracts the operands exponents (for comparison), selects the larger operand, and aligns the smaller mantissa. The second stage adds or subtracts the mantissas depending on the operation and the signs of the operands. The result of this operation may overflow by a maximum of 1-bit position. Logic embedded in the mantissa adder is used to detect this case, allowing 1-bit normalization of the result on the fly. The exponent data path computes $(E + 1)$. If the 1-bit overflow occurred, $(E + 1)$ is chosen as the exponent of stage 3; otherwise, $E$ is chosen. The third stage performs either rounding or normalization because these operations are not required at the same time. This may also result in a 1-bit overflow. Mantissa and exponent corrections, if needed, are implemented exactly in this stage, using instantiations of the mantissa adder and exponent blocks.

The area efficient FADD hardware is shown in Fig. 2.8. The exponents of the two inputs (Exponent A and Exponent B) are fed into the exponent comparator,

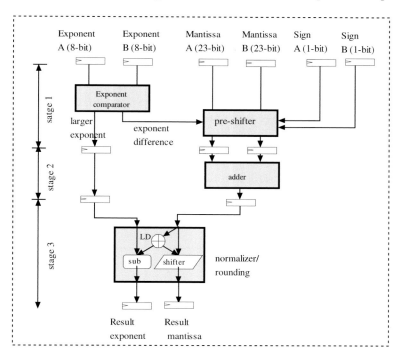

**Fig. 2.8** QC-2's FADD hardware

which is implemented with a subtracter and a multiplexer. In the pre-shifter, a new mantissa in created by right shifting the mantissa corresponding to the smaller exponent by the difference of the exponents so that the resulting two mantissas are aligned and can be added. The size of the pre-shifter is about $m * log(m) LUTs$, where $m$ is the bit-width of the mantissa. If the mantissa adder generates a carry output, the resulting mantissa is shifted one bit to the right and the exponent is increased by one. The normalizer transforms the mantissa and exponent into normalized format. It first uses a leading-one detector (LD) circuit to locate the position of the most significant one in the mantissa. Based on the position of the LD, the resulting mantissa is left shifted by an amount subsequently deducted from the exponent. If there is an exponent overflow (during normalization), the result is saturated in the direction of overflow and the overflow flag is set. Underflows are handled by setting the result to zero and setting an underflow flag.

We have to notice that the LD anticipator can be also predicted directly from the input to the adder. This determination of the leading digit position is performed in parallel with the addition step so as to enable the normalization shift to start as soon as the addition completes. This scheme requires more area than a standard adder, but exhibits reduced latency. For hardware simplicity and logic limitation, our FPA hardware does not support earlier LD prediction.

*Floating point multiplier implementation*: The data path of the FMUL hardware is shown in Fig. 2.9. As with other conventional architectures, QC-2's FMUL operation is much like integer multiplication. Because floating point numbers are stored in sign-magnitude form, the multiplier needs only to deal with unsigned integer numbers and normalization. Similar to the FALU, the FMUL unit is a three stages pipeline that produces a result on every clock cycle. The bottleneck of this unit was the $24 \times 24$ integer multiplications.

The first stage of the floating-point multiplier is the same denormalization module used in addition to insert the implied 1 to the mantissa of the operands. In the second stage, the mantissas are multiplied and the exponents are added. The output of the module are registered. In the third stage, the result is normalized or rounded.

The multiplication hardware implements the radix-8 modified Booth (Booth 1951) algorithm. Recoding in a higher radix was necessary to speed up the standard Booth multiplications algorithm since greater numbers of bits are inspected and eliminated during each cycle, effectively reduces the total number of cycles necessary to obtain the product. In addition, the radix-8 version was implemented instead of the radix-4 version because it reduces the multiply array in stage 2.

## 2.4.4 Performance Analysis

In order to estimate the impact of the description style on the target FPGAs efficiency, logic synthesis for FPGAs are explored. The idea of this experiment was to optimize critical design parts for speed or resource optimizations.

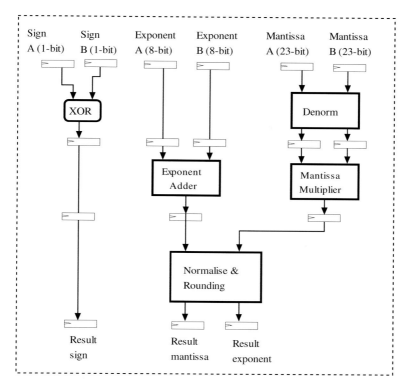

Sign A (1-bit)  Sign B (1-bit)  Exponent A (8-bit)  Exponent B (8-bit)  Mantissa A (23-bit)  Mantissa B (23-bit)

XOR

Denorm

Exponent Adder

Mantissa Multiplier

Normalise & Rounding

Result sign    Result mantissa    Result exponent

**Fig. 2.9** QC-2's FMUL hardware

Optimizing the HDL description to exploit the strengths of the target technology is of paramount importance to achieve an efficient implementation. This is particularly true for FPGAs targets, where a fixed amount of each resource is available and choosing the appropriate description style can have a high impact on the final resources efficiently (Micheli 2001; Gohringer 2008). For typical FPGAs features, choosing the right implementation style can cause a difference in resource utilization of more than an order of magnitude (Alsolaim 2000; Xilinx 2009). Synthesis efficiency is influenced significantly by the match of resource implied by the HDL and resources present in a particular FPGAs architecture. When an HDL description implies resources not found in a given FPGAs architecture, those elements have to be emulated using other resources at significant cost. Such emulation can be performed automatically by EDA tools in some cases, but may require changes in the HDL description in the worst case, counteracting aim of a common HDL source code base. In this work, our experiments and the results described are based on the Altera Stratix architecture. We selected Stratix FPGAs device because it has a good trade-offs between routability and logic capacity. In addition it has an internal embedded memory that eliminates the need for external memory module and offers up to 10 Mbits of embedded memory through the

**Table 2.2** QC-2 processor
design results: modules
complexity as LE (logic
elements) and TCF (total
combinational functions)
when synthesized for FPGA
(with Stratix device) and
Structured ASIC (HardCopy
II) families

| Descriptions | Modules | LE | TCF |
|---|---|---|---|
| Instruction fetch unit | IF | 633 | 414 |
| Instruction decode unit | ID | 2,573 | 1,564 |
| Queue compute unit | QCU | 1,949 | 1,304 |
| Barrier queue unit | BQU | 9,450 | 4,348 |
| Issue unit | IS | 15,476 | 7,065 |
| Execution unit | EXE | 7,868 | 3,241 |
| Queue-registers unit | QREG | 35,541 | 21,190 |
| Memory access | MEM | 4,158 | 3,436 |
| Control unit | CTR | 171 | 152 |
| Queue processor core | QC-2 | 77,819 | 42,714 |

TriMatrix TM memory feature. We also used Altera Quartus II professional
edition for simulation, placement and routing. Simulations were also performed
with Cadence Verilog-XL tool.

Figure 2.10 compares two different target implantations for $256 \times 33$ QREG
for various optimizations. Depending on the target implementations device, either
logic elements (LEs) or total combinational functions (TCF) are generated as
storage elements. Implementations based on HardCopy device, which generates
TCF functions give almost similar complexity for the three used optimizations—
area (ARA), speed (SPD) and balanced (BLD). For FPGA implementation, the
complexity for SPD optimization is about 17 and 18 % higher than that for ARA
and BLD optimizations respectively. Table 2.2 summarizes the synthesis results of
the QC-2 for the Stratix FPGA and HardCopy targets. The complexity of each core
module as well as the whole QC-2 core are given as the number of logic elements
(LEs) for the Stratix FPGA device and as the TCF cell count for the HardCopy
device (Structured ASIC). The design was optimized for BLD optimization guided
by a properly implemented constraint table. We also found that the processor
consumes about 80.4 % of the total logical elements of the target device.

The achievable throughput of the 32-bit QC-2 core on different execution
platforms is shown in Fig. 2.11. For the hardware platforms, we show the processor frequency. For comparison purposes, the Verilog HDL simulator performance has been converted to an artificial frequency rating by dividing the
simulator throughput by a cycle count of 1 CPI. This chart shows the benefits

**Fig. 2.10** Resource usage
and timing for $256 \times 33$ bit
QREG unit for different
coding and optimization
strategies

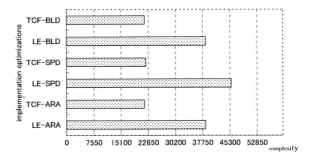

**Fig. 2.11** Achievable frequency is the instruction throughput for hardware implementations of the QC-2 processor. Simulation speeds have been converted to a nominal frequency rating to facilitate comparison

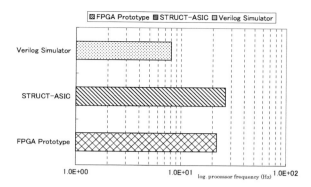

which can be derived from direct hardware execution using a prototype when compared to processor simulation. The data used for this simulation are based on event-driven functional Verilog HDL simulation.

## 2.5  Conclusion

SoC designs have evolved from fairly simple single-core designs to complex multicore SoCs consisting of hundreds of PEs in a single chip. As more and more cores are integrated into these chips, the main challenges lie in how to efficiently and quickly integrate these cores together into a single system capable of leveraging their individual flexibility.

There are two fundamental issues for MCSoC design: (1) design space exploration, and (2) parallel software development. This chapter focused on these two schemes. The chapter also presented a scalable core based methodology for generic architecture model and a synthesizable 32-bit soft core suitable for high performance multicore SoC architectures. The presented GAT method should permit a systematic generation of multicore architecture for embedded multicore SoCs.

# Chapter 3
# Multicore SoC Organization

Increasing processing power demand for new embedded consumer applications such asmobile multimedia devices, cell phones, and high definition televisions made convectionalsingle-core based designs no longer suitable to satisfy high performance and low powerconsumption demands. Moreover, continuous advancements in semiconductor technologyenable us to design more complex multicore systems-on-chip (MCSoCs) composed of tensor even hundreds of IP cores. General purpose CPUs, ASICs, DSPs, memory blocks, andI/O and networking devices on a single MCSoC chip are now possible and necessary forcurrent and future complex applications.

Understanding the software and hardware building blocks and the computation power ofindividual components in these complex MCSoCs is necessarily for designing power, performanceand cost efficient systems. This chapter describes in details the architectures andfunctions of the main building blocks that are used to build such complex MCSoCs.

## 3.1 Introduction

With increasing processing power demands of embedded applications and technology advances, MCSoCs become prevalent in embedded systems. A typical MCSoC includes several optimized components integrated together to execute a specific application. Applications range from digital cameras, cellular phones, set-top boxes, PDAs, to bio-medical and military instruments.

Different functions in these embedded MCSoCs are typically implemented with software running on a RISC, digital signal processors, or with dedicated hardware IP (Intellectual Property) blocks. These blocks are available from vendors as hard or soft cores. We will discuss later in this chapter how to select these IP cores to build power and performance efficient multicore systems. The availability of various IP cores with different performance and complexity from many existing providers makes the selection not easy. In addition, selecting suitable cores depends also on the available power, area, and cost budgets. Therefore, designer must be careful and aware about all these factors before even thinking about higher level organization of the target system.

A. Ben Abdallah, *Multicore Systems On-Chip: Practical Software/Hardware Design*, 37
Atlantis Ambient and Pervasive Intelligence 7, DOI: 10.2991/978-94-91216-92-3_3,
© Atlantis Press and the author 2013

Organization of a MCSoC architecture means the software and hardware relationships between different IP blocks (including on-chip/off-chip memory) and the interconnection network which links these IP cores together in an efficient manner, such that several design and performance constraints are satisfied. The hardware and software design team should be also aware about the real-time performance requirement of the system being designed. This is very important because generally a real-time system has more design constraints than a general multicore system. Consequently, the design of real-time MCSoCs is much more complex that the design of a general embedded systems.

Modern MCSoC organization guidelines include separation between computation and communication and between functions and architectures. The applications that need to run on these MCSoCs have become increasingly complex and have very tight power and performance requirements. Thus, achieving a satisfactory design quality under these circumstances is only possible when both communication and computation refinements are performed efficiently.

As we earlier stated, MCSoCs can be homogeneous or heterogeneous systems. The organization of each category is of course not similar. The main difference is in the type and computation power of integrated IP cores. Figure 3.1 shows a general view of a typical modern MCSoC organization and Fig. 3.2 shows an example of an embedded multicore system of a typical digital still camera device. The reader should be also aware that a number of programmable MCSoC platforms are now commercially available, such as Cell from IBM, Nomadik from STMicroelectronics, and many others.

To let the reader first get the "big picture" of such MCSoC system, we will explain in the next part of this section the two main MCSoC categories—homogeneous and heterogeneous. In this chapter, we only focus on the main building blocks of MCSoC system. The system which we assume here is generic and not restricted to a specific kind of embedded applications. The reason is that most building blocks, such as on-chip memory, microprocessor(s), peripheral interfaces, I/O logic control, data converters, and other components are found in most embedded applications. For example, the single chip phone, which has been introduced by several semiconductor vendors, is an example; it includes a modem, radio transceiver, a multimedia engine, security features and power management functionality all on the same chip.

## 3.1.1 Heterogeneous MCSoC

A heterogeneous MCSoC is a single chip which combines different cores having different instruction set architectures (ISAs) and computing power interconnected with a sophisticated network or simple shared medium to efficiently link all components together. Application designers or high-level compilers can choose the most efficient IP cores for the type of processing needed for a given application task.

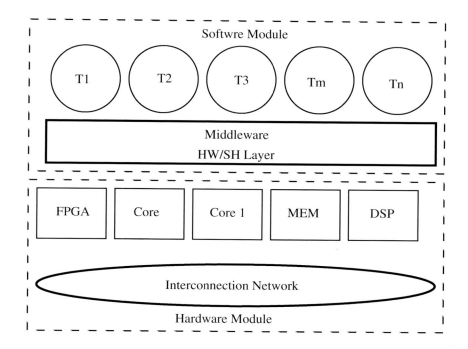

**Fig. 3.1** General organization view of a modern typical MCSoC

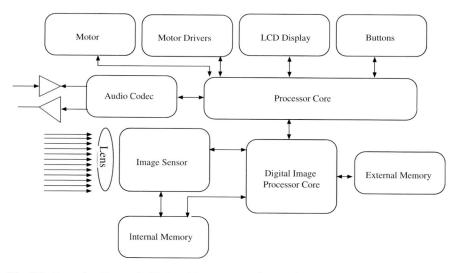

**Fig. 3.2** Example of an embedded multicore system for a typical digital still camera

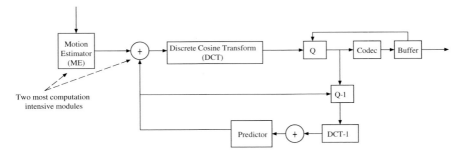

**Fig. 3.3** Example of MPEG-2 encoder for a heterogeneous MCSoC system

The main motivation of these systems is that many applications, such as MPEG-2 encoder (see Fig. 3.3), have more than one algorithm during their execution life. This means, a given application has different operations, different memory access patterns, and different communication bandwidth at different execution periods.

Another example is in the advanced safety automobile devices, where multiple applications, consisting of several tasks, are executed simultaneously. Each task, invoked by applications, such as image processing, recognition, control or measurement, is assigned to a single processor core. Heterogeneous MCSoCs provide the best performance/power efficiency trade-offs and are natural choice for embedded systems. The heterogeneous cores increase performance by dividing the work among well-matched cores. This requires many CPU cores for general-purpose processing as well as several SIMD processor cores to accelerate specific performance-critical processing. The heterogeneous SoC also can save energy almost at all levels (device, circuit, and logic) of abstraction. In addition, these systems generally use irregular memory and irregular interconnection networks that also save power by reducing the loads in the whole network.

Figure 3.4 shows and example of a heterogeneous MCSoC organization. The above system integrates several typical cores (RISC, accelerators, VLIW, SIMD, etc.) which are found in most modern heterogeneous MCSoC systems. The different cores are generally connected to a common pipelined bus (single or multi-layer) with a cache coherence mechanism (discussed later), such as the well known Modified, Exclusive, Shared or Invalid (MESI) protocol (Papamarco 1984).

The embedded L2 cache, internal I/O, synchronous dynamic random access memory (SDRAM) are all connected to the bus. The SIMD core is generally a highly specialized parallel processor and is used to process large amount of data, such as images. Additionally, a cache memory is shared by the CPU cores to reduce internal bus traffic and access to the main slow DRAM memory.

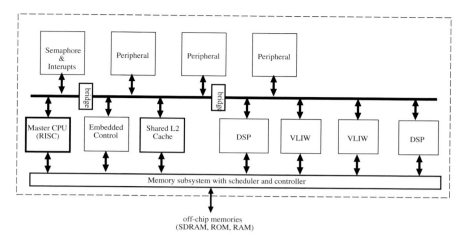

**Fig. 3.4** Heterogeneous MCSoC organization example

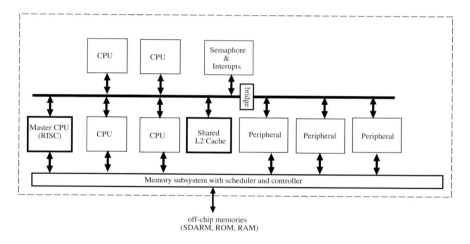

**Fig. 3.5** Homogeneous MCSoC organization example

## *3.1.2 Homogeneous MCSoC*

An alternative to the previously discussed system is called homogeneous MCSoC. This system is typically built with the same programmable building blocks instantiated several times. This alternative model is often referred in the literature to as parallel architecture model. Parallel architectures were particularly studied in computer science and engineering during the past 40 years. Nowadays, there is a growing interest for such approaches in embedded systems. Figure 3.5 illustrates an example of a typical homogeneous MCSoC organization example. The basic principle of an architecture that exhibit parallel processing capabilities relies on increasing the number of physical resource in order to divide the execution time of each resource.

## 3.1.3 Multicore SoC Applications

As with general architectures, MCSoCs are mainly driven by performance requirements of applications. Therefore, knowing the target application(s) of the system before starting the design is important not only for the selection of appropriate PEs, but also for reducing the overall cost of the applications.

*Wireless Applications::* In this class of applications, MCSoCs are mainly used as wireless base stations [i.e., Luceny Daytona (Knobloch 2000)] in which identical signal processing are performed on a number of data channels. Daytona is a homogeneous system with four SPARC V8 CPU cores attached to a high-speed split-transaction. Each CPU has an 8-KB 16-bank cache and each bank can be configured as instruction cache, data cache, or Scratchpad. The cores share a common address space (see Fig. 3.6).

*Network Applications:* In this second class, MCSoC can be used as a network processor for packet processing in off-chip networks. The C-5 processor is an example of network processor (C-5 2001). In this system, packets are handled by channel cores that are grouped into four clusters of four units each. The traffic of all cores is handled by three buses. In addition to the channel cores, there are also several specialized cores. The executive processor core is a RISC architecture.

*Multimedia Applications:* Multimedia applications implemented on consumer electronics devices span a vast range of functionality, from audio decoder such as MP3 via video decoder such as H.264 up to advanced picture quality processing such as frame rate up-conversion and Motion Accurate Picture Processing (MAPP). Hybrid TV solutions are a very good example because they are virtually capable of executing any of these multimedia applications.

*Mobile Applications:* The fourth class of MCSoCs application is in the mobile cell phone. Earlier cell phone processors performed base-band operations, including both communication and multimedia operations. As an example, the Texas Instruments' OMAP architecture has several implementations. The OMAP 5912 has two CPU cores: an ARM9 and a TMS320C55x digital signal processor (DSP). The ARM core acts as a master and the DSP core acts as a slave that performs signal processing operations. Another example was implemented by STMicro-electronics and is called Nomadik (ST 2005). It uses an ARM926EJ as its host processor. The ARM926EJ-S processor core runs at up to 350 MHz in 130 nm CMOS process and up to 500 MHz in 90 nm CMOS. The core includes on-board cache, Java acceleration in hardware, and strong real-time debug support Namdik systems are aimed at 2.5G and 3G mobile phones, personal digital assistants and other portable wireless products with multimedia capability.

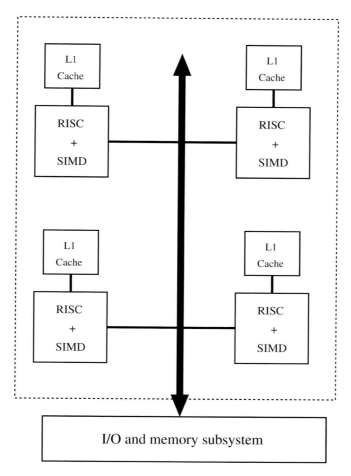

**Fig. 3.6** Example of MCSoC application in wireless communication: Lucent Daytona MCSoC

## 3.1.4 Applications Mapping

As discussed above, today's MCSoC architectures are composed of commercially of-the-shelf available IP blocks. Ultimately, we would like to design a generic heterogeneous MCSoC architecture that is flexible enough to run different applications. However, mapping an application to such heterogeneous SoC is more difficult compared to mapping to a homogeneous one. Today, general practice is to map applications to the architecture at design-time or run-time. Run-time mapping offers a number of advantages over design-time mapping. It mainly offers the following possibilities:

- To avoid defective parts of a SoC. Larger chip area means lower yield. The yield can be improved when the mapper is able to avoid faulty parts of the chip. Also aging can lead to faulty parts that are unforeseeable at design-time.
- To adapt to the available resources. Only at run-time the available resources are known to the mapping algorithm. In addition, the available resources may vary over time for example due to applications running simultaneously or adaptation of algorithms to the environment.
- To enable upgrades of the system.

The objective of the run-time mapping is to determine at run-time a near-optimal mapping of the application to the architecture using the library of process implementations and the current status of the system.

The mapping of the functional subsystems onto SoC hardware resources maybe based on a number of considerations:

- *Support:* support of industry standards. This is very important for processor cores that are programmed by the designers. Generally, industry standard CPU cores have extensive tool chain and library support that eases the application design and debug.
- *Performance:* computationally intensive algorithms such as HD H.264 decoder cannot be implemented effectively on a general purpose processor because of the computational complexity. Instead a function specific HW core is needed.
- *Flexibility:* evolving standards require flexibility in implementations so that new codecs can be added without the need for a new SoC. This reduce cost and time.
- *Re-usability* implementation, integration and verification are time consuming tasks and sometimes it is appropriate not to implement a function on the most optimum SoC HW resource in order to make it reusable in future SoCs0.

## 3.2 MCSoC Building Blocks

As we mentioned in Chap. 1, a typical MCSoC is composed of several components: memories, processing elements, input/output subsystem, and communication subsystem. In most of these MCSoC systems, the cores have separate L1 caches, but share a L2 cache, memory subsystem, interrupt subsystem, and peripherals. Figure 3.7 illustrates a simplified block diagram of a typical MCSoC architecture having different building blocks.

Figure 3.8 shows a general view of a state of the art MCSoC system based on NoC interconnection. In NoC interconnection, PEs communicate with each other using packets and not messages as with shared bus. We will explain this important interconnection paradigm later with more details in Chaps. 4 and 5.

Although systems which are built with NoC approach are scalable and power efficient, the design of such systems is not easy when compared with the design of systems based on shared buses. The reason for such complexity is that the designer

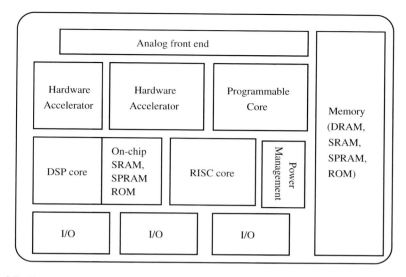

**Fig. 3.7**  Simplified view of a typical MCSoC architecture with different core and memory types

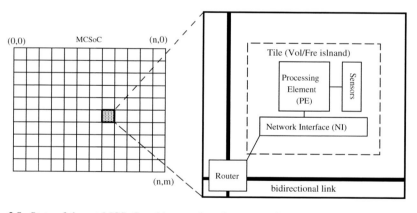

**Fig. 3.8**  State of the art MCSoC architecture based on network-on-chip paradigm

must care not only about the computational (PEs) part, but also he must care about the communication part (how to route packets). In other words, he must carefully select appropriate topology, routing scheme, control flow, and network interface (NI). Among these blocks, the NI is complex and very important component which must be carefully designed. That is why we dedicated a special chapter for it. We will explain the organization and design of the NI component later in Chap. 6.

The PEs type and computation power depends on the application context and requirements. As we explained in Sect. 3.1, we distinguish two types of architectures: (1) heterogeneous MCSoCs, and (2) homogeneous MCSoCs.

Heterogeneous systems are composed of different IPs, such as processors, memories, accelerators, and peripherals.

Homogeneous system is a system where the same tile is instantiated several times. Beyond its hardware architecture, MCSoC is generally running a set of software applications divided into tasks and an operating system devoted to manage both hardware and software through a middle-ware layer. Figure 3.1 shows a general view of a MCSoC and the interfacing between the software and hardware modules.

## 3.2.1 Processor Core

The type and the computation power of the processor core which is embedded in a given MCSoC depends on the target application and whether the core is used for control purpose (master) or computation purpose (slave). Figure 3.9 shows the pipeline stages of a typical RISC processor core. The stages are: fetch, decode, execute, memory access, and write-back stages.

## 3.2.2 Memory

In a MCSoC, several masters communicate with a single or at most few DRAM (dynamic RAM) memory slaves. The DRAM memory subsystem consists of a memory scheduler, a memory controller, and the DRAM memory. The scheduler arbitrates between multiple requests whereas controller takes care of bit-level protocol of the DRAM device and activates refreshes etc. In some design, a sophisticated scheduler reorder the requests such that the DRAM's efficiency is maximized by means of high page hit rate, and low Read-Write direction

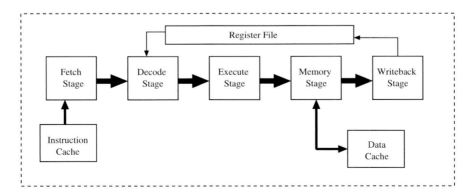

**Fig. 3.9** Typical 5 pipeline stages of a RISC processor core

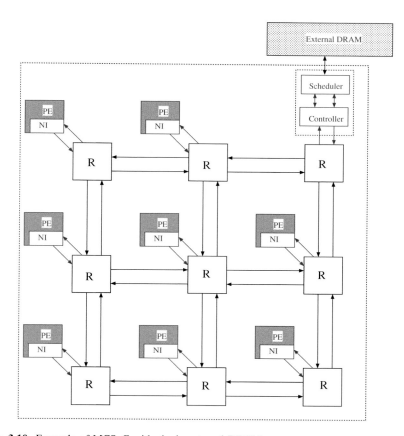

**Fig. 3.10** Example of MCSoC with single external DRAM memory

turnaround. Figure 3.10 shows an example of a MCSoC based on network-on-chip interconnection network with a single external DRAM memory. In this example the additional latency added by the router may become a real problem if the memory is highly utilized. That is, there is a high traffic between the external DRAM and one or more PEs within the system. Such traffic scenario is called traffic hot-spot, which affects large portion of the network because blocked traffic reserves many routers and links.

In addition, the requirement to refresh the DRAM at some regular periods reduces the total achievable bandwidth. Moreover, the efficiency is dependent upon the type of transactions, and the address patterns that are presented to the DRAM.

## 3.2.3 Cache

Most multicore systems today have one or two levels of dedicated private caches, backed up with a shared last level cache (LLC). The performance and power consumption of a MCSoC is strongly dependent of the performance of the LLC because the LLC can help reduce off-chip memory traffic and contention for memory bandwidth. Figure 3.11 shows three level of caches in a single node of a typical MCSoC. Cache is efficient because of a program property called *Locality*. The locality says that if a program accesses a particular memory address, it is likely that the next few accesses will be to nearby addresses (spatial locality), and also that the same address is likely to be accessed again within a short time (temporal locality). This is true for instruction fetches, and also for data reads and writes.

System designer can take advantage of the locality of references, to create a hierarchical memory with multiple levels of memory of different speed and size. At the top of this hierarchy, we have a fast, but small memory, which is directly connected to the processor core. The memory sizes increase as we move to lower levels of the hierarchy further away from the processor core. In contrary, the speed drops as we move to lower levels of the hierarchy further away from the processor core.

The minimum amount of data transfered between two adjacent memory levels is called a block or line. Although this could be as small as one word, the spatial locality principle suggests that designer should design caches with larger blocks. If the data requested by a given core is found at a memory level, we say that we have a *hit* at that level. If not, we have a *miss* and the request is send to the next level down and the block containing the requested data is copied at this level when the data is found. The reason for copying the missed block containing the requested data to the cache is that we want to ensure that next time this (or nearby) data is accessed there will be a hit at this level. The memory system in a MCSoC architecture generally consists of a four-level hierarchy: Registers, Scratchpad, cache, and main memory.

## 3.2.4 Communication Protocols

For a given number of cores, the most appropriate interconnection network depends on a combination of factors, including area/power budget, technology, performance objectives, and bandwidth requirements.

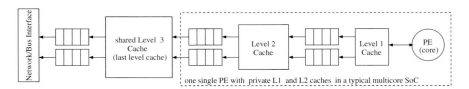

**Fig. 3.11** Cache organization in a single node of a typical MCSoC

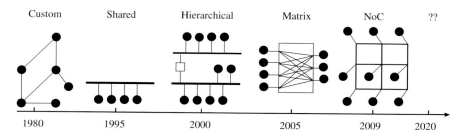

**Fig. 3.12** Evolution of On-Chip communication interconnect

We have to note here that unlike conventional multiprocessors, performance is not necessary maximized by the highest bandwidth interconnect available.

The traditional form of functional interconnect between different cores in a simple SoC is the on-chip bus which is an array of wires with multiple writers under a mutual-exclusion control scheme. Buses are very simple to design and permits the implementation of efficient hardware mechanisms to enforce cache consistency. In addition, bus-based systems have fair throughput as long as the system is small and there are few masters that initiate data transfers. This is the case with single-core SoC devices, where typically only the core and some advanced peripherals can function as bus masters. Typically, IPs are connected to the bus via standardized protocols, such as Advanced extensible Interface (AXI), Device Transaction Level (DTL), and Open Core Protocol (OCP).

By using large caches, it is possible to reduce the bus traffic produced by each core, thus allowing systems with greater numbers of cores to be built. Unfortunately, capacitive loading on the bus increases as the number of cores is increased. This effect increases the minimum time required for a bus operation; thus reducing the maximum bus bandwidth.

Multi-bus solutions have provided a temporary solution for small scale systems. However, for large scale systems a better solution is still needed. NoC is the promising interconnection paradigm (discussed in Chaps. 4 and 5) for these complex multi and many-core SoCs. Figure 3.12 shows the evolution chart of on-chip communication interconnects for single and MCSoCs.

### 3.2.4.1 Packet-Switched Interconnect

The PEs integrated within modern and future MCSoC are (will be) mostly inter-connected by a packet-switched network also called network-on-chip (NoC) (Ben-Abdallah 2006). NoC consists of a network of shared communication links and routers, which connect to the various cores through network interfaces (NIs). These NIs convert between the internal NoC protocol on one side and the core's protocol on the other side. For reasons of compatibility and reuse, the latter is typically one of the standardized bus protocols, such as AXI, DTL, and OCP.

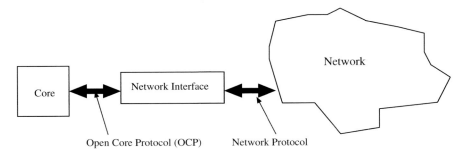

**Fig. 3.13** Open core protocol (OCP) and network protocol (NP) interfacing

The NI module decouples computation from communication functions. Routers are in charge or routing and are arbitrating the date between the source and destinations PEs through links (Fig. 3.13).

Several network topologies have been studied. The NoCs facilitate the design of Globally Asynchronous Locally Synchronous (GALS) property by implementing asynchronous-synchronous interfaces in the NIs. Figure 3.14 shows an example of NoC operation.

### 3.2.5 Intellectual Property Cores

An IP core is a block of logic or a software library that we use to design a SoC based on single or multicore. These software and hardware IPs are designed and highly optimized in advance (time to market consideration) by specialized companies and area ready to be integrated with our new design. For example, we may buy a software library to perform some complex graphic operations and integrate that library with our existing code. We may also obtain the above code freely from an open-source site on-line. Universal Asynchronous Receiver/Transmitter (UARTs), central processing units (CPUs), Ethernet controllers, and PCI interfaces are all examples of hardware IP cores.

As essential elements of design reuse, IP cores are part of the growing electronic design automation (EDA) industry trend towards repeated use of previously designed components. Ideally, an IP core should be entirely portable. This means the core must be able to easily be integrated (plug-and-play style) into any vendor technology or design methodology. Of course there are some IPs that are not standard and may need some kind of interface (called wrapper) before integrating it into our design. IP cores fall into one of two main categories: soft cores, and hard cores:

(1) Soft IP Core: Soft IP cores refer to circuits which are available at a higher level of abstraction, such as register-transfer level (RTL). These type of cores can be customized by the user for specific applications.

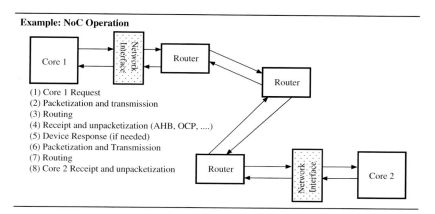

**Example: NoC Operation**

(1) Core 1 Request
(2) Packetization and transmission
(3) Routing
(4) Receipt and unpacketization (AHB, OCP, ....)
(5) Device Response (if needed)
(6) Packetization and Transmission
(7) Routing
(8) Core 2 Receipt and unpacketization

**Fig. 3.14** NoC operation

(2) Hard IP Core: A hard IP core is one where the circuit is available at a lower level of abstraction such as the layout-level. For this type of core, it is impossible to customize it to suit the requirements of the embedded system. As a result, there are limited opportunities in optimizing the cost functions by modifying the hard IP.

A good IP core should be configurable so that it can meet the needs of many different designs. It also should have a standard interface so that it can be integrated easily. Finally, a good IP core should come in forms of complete set of deliverables: synthesizable RTL, complete test benches, synthesis scripts, and documentation. The example shown in Fig. 3.15 is for a hardware IP core from Altera FPGA provider (Altera 2012).

## 3.2.6 IP Cores with Multiple Clock Domains

The IP cores integrated within a given MCSoC may work at different clock rates. For example, some SoC may have more than three clock domains. In addition, many embedded cores operate internally using multiple frequencies. Figure 3.16 shows a simple design that comprises three cores with three different physical clocks. In this example, Core 2 consists of three modules operating at different frequencies (f1, f2, and f3). A physical clock is a chip-level clock; for example it can come from an oscillator, or a phase locked loop (PILL). All the internal clocks generated from the same physical clock are considered to be a part of the same physical clock domain.

In a MCSoC system, the multi-frequency blocks communicate one with each other through synchronization logic and/or FIFO memory blocks. Such design has the advantage of low power and low silicon area. However, the main design

---

**Example:  Altera Intellectual Property**

The Altera IP core site ( http://www.altera.com/products/ip/ip-index.jsp)
Altera IP site provides access to a wide variety of IP blocks of different
size and complexity:

- basic arithmetic blocks to transceivers,
- memory controllers,
- microprocessors,
- signal processing, and
- protocol interfaces

---

**Fig. 3.15**  Intellectual property example

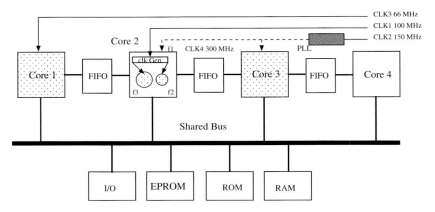

**Fig. 3.16**  Three clock domains MCSoC

difficulties with multi-frequency embedded cores are the clock skew, and synchronization problems.

## 3.2.7  Selection of IP Cores

This section investigates the classification and selection of processor cores and
considers the MCSoC infrastructure that allows an efficient mix of different types
of cores and function-specific hardware cores to access shared resources in the
SoC. Selection of appropriate IP cores depends on the application mapping output.
Depending of the target application, mapping of the functional subsystems to a
MCSoC hardware resources generally involves the following cores:

- *Host CPU:* The host CPU is generally an industry standard core such as, MIPS,
  and ARM CPUs. Typically, these cores have a large application code and thus
  need to access code and data in an external SDRAM memory.

- *VLIW processor:* Generally, this core provides scalability and processing power. This processor core exploits fine-grained data parallelism. Code and data segments are typically large, so the VLIW processor core also needs access to SDRAM.
- *Embedded control CPU:* Small to medium sized code base. For architectural and commercial reasons often use processor core from the same processor provider as the host CPU. For architectural consistency, such core is connected to the same bus structures as the host CPU or VLIW processor cores.
- *Fixed point DSP:* generally deeply embedded into the MCSoC architecture. Often, DSP cores are connected into the SoC infrastructure via HW semaphore mechanisms.
- *Function-specific HW core:* massively parallel computation core that make use of fine-grained parallelism as well as coarser parallelism and typically processes large data sets. Some cores are connected to external real-time interfaces, and therefore need real-time performance.

As an example of mapping a given application to different cores within a MCSoC system, consider an example of an MPEG-2 decoder application which consists of a baseline unit, a motion compensation (MC) unit, a recovery unit, and the associated buffers. The baseline unit consists of a variable length decoder (VLD), an inverse quantization/inverse zigzag (IQ/ IZZ) module, inverse discrete cosine transform (IDCT) modules, and the buffer. Figure 3.17 shows this application running on a multicore system with two or three cores.

## 3.3 MCSoC Memory Hierarchy

The memory architecture of an embedded MCSoCs strongly influences area, power and performance of the entire system. In these systems, more on-chip silicon is devoted to memory than to anything else on the chip. This requires special attention that must be dedicated for the on-chip memory organization.

The memory organization of embedded MCSoC systems varies widely from one to another, depending on the application and market segment for which the SoC is targeted. Broadly speaking, program memories for MCSoCs are classified into: (1) primary memory, and (2) secondary memory.

The primary memory is the memory that is addressed by core(s) and holds current data set that is being processed as well as the program (text) code. This memory may consist of main memory typically implemented in DRAM technology, and a hierarchy of smaller and faster caches (SRAMs) or Scratchpad memories (SPRAMs), that hold the copies of some of the data from the main memory.

The secondary memory maybe be also used for long-term storage. Embedded MCSoC systems often include flash memory as the secondary storage, e.g., for storing pictures in a digital camera.

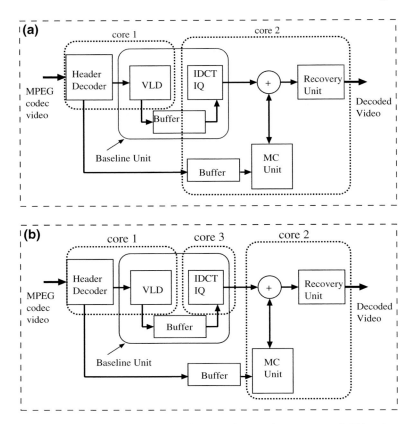

**Fig. 3.17** Example of mapping of an MPEG-2 decoder. **a** Using two cores, **b** Using three cores

In the remaining part of this section, we will discuss in a fair amount of details the many alternatives for on-chip and off-chip memory usage that SoC designers must understand.

### 3.3.1 Types on On-Chip Memory

There are three broad categories of on-chip memories that system designer can use. The first type is called Static Random Access Memory (SRAM). This is quite known memory architecture and is found in almost all type of computers and not only embedded multicore systems. SRAM is very common in SoC designs because it is fast and is built from the same transistors used to build all of the logic on the SoC, so no process changes are required. Further, due to its good characteristics (mainly speed), SRAMs are generally used for caches to solve the processor-memory speed mismatches.

Most SRAM bit-cells require at least four transistors and some require as many as ten; so on-chip dynamic RAM or DRAM is becoming increasingly popular. DRAM stores bits as capacitive charge, so each DRAM bit cell requires only one transistor and a capacitor. DRAM's main advantage is density. But, DARM is slower than SRAM and has some particular requirements that affect system design such as the need for periodic refresh. Further, the capacitors in the DRAM bit-cells require specialized processing, which increases die cost. This is of course not a good situation for strictly cost constrained embedded MCSoC systems.

Every SoC needs memory that remembers code and data even when the power is off. Thus, the cheapest and the least flexible memory is ROM and so is our second type of memory in this discussion. ROMs are not flexible since their contents cannot be changed after the system is fabricated. Fortunately, EPROM and flash memory are good alternatives. Figure 3.18 illustrates a simplified view of a MCSoC architecture with different core and memory types.

A given memory bank can be organized as a single-access RAM or a dual-access RAM to provide single or dual access to the memory bank in a single cycle. Also the on-chip memory banks can be of different sizes.

The good thing for smaller banks is that they consume less power per access than the larger memories. Embedded multicore systems may also be interfaced to off-chip memory, which can include SRAM and DRAM. If the system is targeted

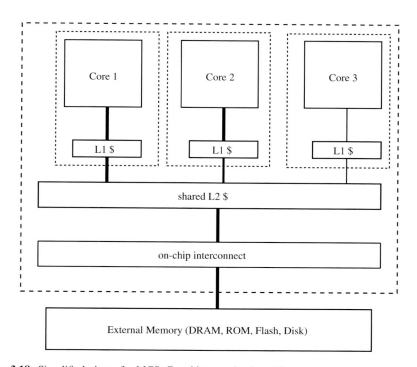

**Fig. 3.18** Simplified view of a MCSoC architecture having different memories

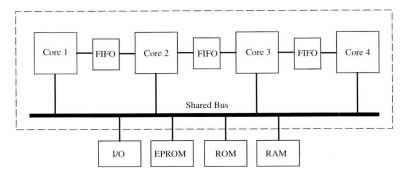

**Fig. 3.19** Example of four cores communicating via FIFOs

for low to medium complex embedded applications, purely SPRAM based on-chip organization is recommended. FIFO memories can be also used to inter-core communication inside the MCSoC chip as shown in Fig. 3.19.

### 3.3.2 Scratchpad Memory

Scratchpad memory (SPRAM) is a high-speed internal memory directly connected to the CPU core and used for temporary storage to hold very small items of data for rapid retrieval. Scratchpads are employed for simplification of caching logic, and to guarantee a unit can work without main memory contention in a system employing multiple cores, especially in embedded MCSoC systems. They are suited for storing temporary results.

While a cache memory uses a complex hardware controller to decide which data to keep in cache memories (L1 or L2) and which data to prefetch, the SPRAM approach does not require any hardware support in addition to the memory itself, but requires software to take control of all data transfers to and from Scratchpad memories. That is, it is the responsibility of the programmer to identify data section that should be placed in SPRAM or place code in the program to appropriately move data from on-chip memory to SPRAM. For this reason, SPRAMs are sometimes called "software controlled caches". Figure 3.20 illustrates the memory subsystem architecture with 2 SPARMs (level 1 and level 2).

### 3.3.3 Off-Chip Memory

When embedded system designers need a large amount of RAM storage, then off-chip DDR (double-data-rate) SDRAM is likely to be the good choice. Even if an embedded design only requires a small fraction of the capacity of a DDR memory

**Fig. 3.20** MCSoC memory subsystem with SPARM (only interconnection for one node is shown for simplicity)

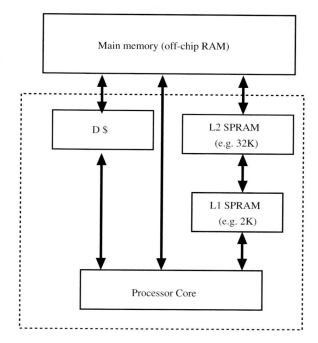

chip or module, it may still be more economical to pay for the excess capacity because the system price will still be lower.

Adding a DDR memory port to a MCSoC design creates the need for an on-chip DDR memory controller. In the same way, system design considerations may make it more desirable to have nonvolatile memory reside off-chip. Again, this option is adopted when a large nonvolatile memory is needed or when the manufacturing costs needed to add EEPROM to the MCSoC are expensive due to limited available budget. In this case, the hardware design team should add a Flash memory controller which of course will add some extra hardware and cost to the system.

### 3.3.4 Memory Power Reduction in SoC Designs

Due to recent increases in VLSI density, SoC designers have exploited the additional silicon available on chips to integrate embedded memories such as SPRAMs, FIFOs and caches to store data for the large number of cores.

Since these embedded memories are implemented inside the chip, the communication latency is low or even negligible. Thus, they allow for significantly better system performance and lower power compared to a solution where off-chip memories are used.

It was found by several researchers that the memory subsystem accounts for up to 50–70 % of the total power consumption of the system (ITRS 2005). This reflects the importance of limiting the energy consumption of memory subsystem. One possible architectural approach for memory energy reduction is the replacement of traditional cache-based memory subsystem by customized SPRAM based one.

The energy savings from this solution comes from the fact that SRPARM consumes less energy per access than a cache due to the absence of additional hardware (e.g., tag memory) present in a cache.

With more transistors becoming available on chip, the percentage of area taken by memory is increasing. In addition to the power projection, the ITRS 2003 report projects that in 2012 memory will occupy about 90 % of a chip. This means that only about 10 % will be left for the processor's computing blocks. Figure 3.21 shows the projection of memory/logic composition of a power-constrained SoC chips.

As we mentioned earlier, most memories embedded in MCSoCs use SRAM technology. The key sources of power consumption in such memories are:

- Static or leakage power dissipated by the logic in the periphery and memory array.
- Dynamic or switching power dissipated when read or write operations are performed.

The dynamic power consumed by a memory when a read or write operation occurs, can be divided into the power consumed by the following components:

- Toggling of the clock network
- Registers for data/address latching on memory I/Os
- Bit-lines in the memory array
- Peripheral logic to decode the address
- Core memory cells changing state.

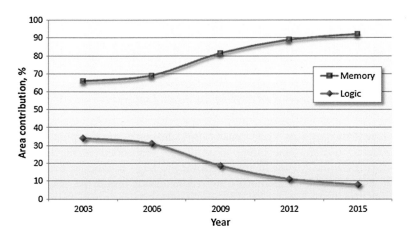

**Fig. 3.21** Projection of memory/logic composition of power-constrained SoC chips (ITRS 2003)

## 3.4 Memory Consistency in Multicore Systems

In the traditional Von Neumann machines, instructions appear to execute in the order specified by the programmer or compiler regardless if the implementation of the machine actually executes them in a different order. For example, a load instruction should return the last value written to the memory location. Likewise a store instruction to a memory location determines the value of the next load. All sequential programs assume this strict rule when they are executed on a uni-processor.

Multithreaded programs running on multicore systems complicate both the programming model and the implementation to enforce a given model. More precisely, the value returned by a given load is not clear because the most recent store instruction may have occurred on a different core. Thus, system designers generally define memory consistency models to specify how a processor core can observe memory accesses from other cores in the same system. Serial consistency is a model defined such that the result of any execution is the same as if the operations of all processor cores were executed in some serial order, and the operations of each individual core behave in this sequence in the order specified by its program. The addition of cache memories to these systems affects how such consistency is implemented.

A cache memory allows processor speed to increase at a greater rate than the main memory speed by exploiting what is known as "time" and "space" localities.

The process of connecting memory locations with cache lines is called "mapping". Since cache is smaller than the main memory, the same cache lines are shared for different memory locations. Each cache line has a record of the memory address called tag. This tag is used to track which area of memory is stored in a particular cache line.

The way these tags are mapped to cache lines can have a beneficial effect on the way a program runs. Caches can be organized in one of several ways: direct mapped, fully associative, and set associative. Figure 3.22 shows an example of direct-mapped cache organization. Cache operations are mainly done in hardware and their operation is all hardware-based and automatic from a programmer's point-of-view. In other words, details of the cache hierarchy does not affect the instruction set architecture of the processor. While caches do not present a real problem in a uni-processor system, they considerably complicate memory consistency for systems designed with multi and many-cores. This problem is known in the literature as *cache coherence* problem.

### 3.4.1 Cache Coherence Problem

In a single-core system, the coherence problem appears when an I/O peripheral bypasses the cache on the system bus and flows directly to and from the main memory (DRAM). This problem can be easily solved by software (compiler)

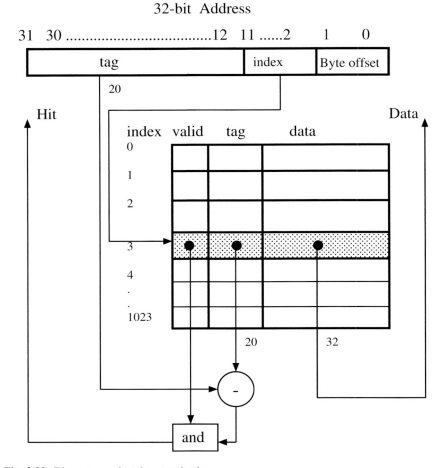

**Fig. 3.22** Direct-mapped cache organization

because the single-thread context imposes a well-defined thread order and the software is always informed on each trap and interrupt caused by a given I/O. The compiler, then, tags data as cacheable and non-cacheable. Only read-only data is considered cacheable and put in private cache. All other data are non-cacheable, and can be put in a global cache, if available.

In multicore based systems things are quite different and more serious because it is difficult to keep record about the order of instructions in different threads running in simultaneously and in different processor cores.

This "coherence" problem comes from the multiple copies of the same memory location, not only in the cache hierarchy, but also in more low-level hardware buffers for memory accesses inside the processor core. The coherence problem here is more difficult to solve than in singlecore system because the software is not

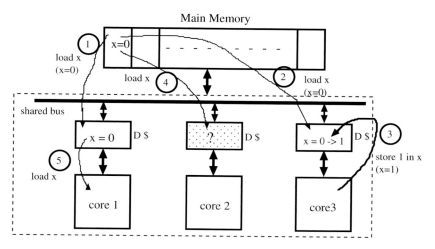

**Fig. 3.23** Cache coherence problem example without coherence protocol

always informed and on-chip communication patterns are not clearly seen by the system'software.

Figure 3.23, illustrates an example of cache coherence problem. As shown in the above figure, the value returned by a given load is not clear because the most recent store may have occurred on a different core. We have to note here that this problem is not very different from multiprocessor (multiple chips) cache coherence problem. Thus, system designers generally define memory consistency models to specify how a processor core can observe memory accesses from other processor cores in the system.

A multicore system is said to be *cache coherent* if the execution of a given program leads in a valid ordering of reads and writes to a memory location.

## 3.4.2 Cache Coherence Protocols

We have to note first that the solution for cache coherence problem is a general problem with multiprocessors and only limited to multicore systems or MCSoCs. There exist many coherence algorithms and protocols.

For a small-scale bus based system, snooping bus is generally used. There are two basic methods to utilize the inter-core bus to notify other cores when a core changes something in its cache. One method is referred to as *update*. In the update method, if core 1 modifies variable 'y' it sends the updated value of 'y' onto the inter-core bus. Each cache is always listening (snooping) to the inter-core bus so that if a cache sees a variable on the bus which it has a copy of, it will read the updated value. This ensures that all caches have the most up-to-date value of the variable.

**Table 3.1** Cache coherence states

| State | Permission | Definition |
|---|---|---|
| Modified (M) | Read, write | All other caches in I or NP |
| Exclusive (E) | Read, write | The addressed line is in this cache only |
| Owned (O) | Read | All other caches in S,I, or NP |
| Shared (S) | Read | All other caches in M or E |
| Invalid (I) | None | None |
| Not present (NP) | None | None |

Another method which utilizes the inter-core bus is called *invalidation*. This method sends an invalidation message onto the inter-core bus when a variable is changed. The other caches will read this invalidation signal and if its core tries to access that variable, it will result in a cache miss and the variable will be read from main memory.

The update method causes a significant amount of traffic on the inter-core bus because the update signal has to be sent onto the bus every time the variable is updated. However, the invalidation method only requires that an invalidation signal be sent the first time a variable is altered; this is why the invalidation method is the preferred method. Table 3.1 shows all cache coherence states.

*Modified, Shared, and Invalid (MSI) Protocol*: MSI is a basic but well known cache coherency protocol. These are the three states that a line of cache can be in. The *Modified* state means that a variable in the cache has been modified and therefore has a different value than that found in main memory. The cache is responsible for writing the variable back to main memory. The *Shared* state means that the variable exists in at least one cache and is not modified. The cache can evict the variable without writing it back to the main memory. The *Invalid* state means that the value of the variable has been modified by another cache and this value is invalid.

*Modified, Exclusive, Shared, and Invalid (MESI) Protocol:* Another well known cache coherency protocol is the MESI protocol. The Modified and Invalid states are the same for this protocol as they are for the MSI protocol. This protocol introduces a new state; the Exclusive state. The Exclusive state means that the variable is in only this cache and the value of it matches the value within the main memory. This now means that the Shared state indicates that the variable is contained in more than one cache.

*Modified, Owned, Shared, and Invalid (MOSI) Protocol):* The MOSI protocol is identical to the MSI protocol except that it adds an Owned state. The Owned state means that the processor "Owns" the variable and will provide the current value to other caches when requested (or at least it will decide if it will provide it when asked).

### 3.4.2.1  Directory-Based Cache Coherency

The snooping protocol works well with system based on shared bus (natural broadcast medium). However, large-scale MCSoC (and multiprocessors) may connect cores/processors with memories using switches or some other kind of complex interconnects. Thus, a new method is needed.

The alternative for the "snoopy-bus" scheme is a protocol known as "directory" protocol (Censier 1978; Chaikem 1990). The basic idea in this scheme is to keep track of what is being shared in one centralized place called directory. This method scales better than snoopy-bus. In this approach each cache can communicate the state of its variables with a single directory instead of broadcasting the state to all cores.

Cache coherence protocols guarantee that eventually all copies are updated. Depending on how and when these updates are performed, a read operation may sometimes return unexpected values. Consistency deals with what values can be returned to the user by a read operation (may return unexpected values if the update is not complete). Consistency model is a contract that defines what a programmer can expect from the system.

## 3.5  Conclusion

Increasing processing power demand for new embedded consumer applications made the convectional single-core based designs no longer suitable to satisfy high performance and low power consumption demands. In addition, continuous advancements in semiconductor technology enable us to design a complex multicore systems-on-chip (MCSoCs) composed of tens or even hundreds of IP cores.

Integrating multiple cores on a single chip has enabled embedded system hardware designers to provide more features and higher processing speeds using less power, thus solving many design problems. However, no thing is really free! The designer of these embedded MCSoCs is no longer dealing with the familiar homogeneous and symmetric multiprocessing (SMP) model of large computer systems. Rather, he may have dozens or hundreds of processor core to program and debug, a heterogeneous and unbalanced mix of DSP, RISC, IPs and complex on-chip network architectures, operating asymmetrically. This is not an easy task.

In this chapter we tried to explain the main components of a typical MCSoC system. The goal is to give a clear idea about the architecture and function of the main building blocks . In the next two chapters we will describe in details the network-on-chip interconnection which is a promising on-chip interconnection paradigm for future multi and many-core SoCs.

# Chapter 4
# 2D Network-on-Chip

Global interconnects are becoming the principal performance bottleneck for high performance MCSoCs. Since the main purpose for this system is to shrink the size of the chip as smaller as possible while seeking at the same time for more scalability, higher bandwidth and lower latency. Conventional bus-based-systems are no longer reliable architecture for SoC due to a lack of scalability and parallelism integration, high latency and power dissipation, and low throughput. During this last decade, Network-on-Chip (NoC) has been proposed as a promising solution for future systems on chip design. It offers more scalability than the shared-bus based interconnection, allows more processors to operate concurrently. This chapter presents architecture and design of a 2D NoC system suitable for medium scale multicore SoCs.

## 4.1 Introduction

Future high-performance embedded SoCs will be based on multi and manycore approaches with nano-scale technology consisting of hundreds of processing and storage elements. These new paradigms are emerging as a key design solution for today's nano-electronics design problems. The interconnection structure supporting such systems will be closer to a sophisticated network than to current bus-based solutions. Such network must provide high throughput and low latency while keeping area and power consumption low.

Network-On-Chips (NoCs) (Dally 2001; Morales 2004; Ben-Abdallah 2006; Samman 2008) provide a good way of realizing interconnections on silicon and largely alleviate the limitations of bus-based solutions. Deep sub-micron processing technologies have enabled the implementation of new application-specific architectures that integrate multiple software programmable cores and dedicated hardware components together onto a single chip. Recently, this kind of architecture has emerged as key design solutions for today's design challenges, which are being driven by emerging applications in the areas of: (1) wireless communication, (2) broadband/distributed networking, (3) distributed computing, and (4) multimedia computing.

A. Ben Abdallah, *Multicore Systems On-Chip: Practical Software/Hardware Design*,
Atlantis Ambient and Pervasive Intelligence 7, DOI: 10.2991/978-94-91216-92-3_4,
© Atlantis Press and the author 2013

NoC is a scalable interconnect with a huge potential to handle the increasing complexity of current and future multicore SoCs. In such paradigm, cores are connected via a packet-switching communication network on a single chip. This scheme is similar to the way that computers are connected to the Internet. The packet-switching network routes information between network clients (e.g. PEs, memories, and custom logic devices). Figure 4.1 illustrates a typical NoC paradigm and point-to-point network.

Packet switching approach supports asynchronous data transfer and provides extremely high bandwidth by distributing the propagation delay across multiple switches and effectively pipelining the packet transmission. In addition, it offers several other promising features. First, it transmits packets instead of words. As a result, dedicated address lines, like those used in bus based systems, are not necessary since the destination address of a given packet is included in the packet's header. Second, transmission can be conducted in parallel if the network provides more than one transmission channel between a sender and a receiver. Thus, unlike bus-based systems, NoC (packet switching network) presents theoretical infinite scalability, facilitates IP cores reusing, and has higher level of parallelism. A NoC architecture, named OASIS NoC (ONoC), was developed in Ben Ahmed et al. (2010). The above network is based on mesh topology (Kumar 2002) and uses wormhole like switching, a First-Come-First-Served (FCFS) scheduler, and re-transmission flow control similar to conventional ACK/NACK flow control.

Figure 4.2 illustrates typical NoC topologies. Each processing element (PE) is connected uniformly without consideration of the network load balance and spots where increasing traffic is concentrated and may cause packet drops or stall transactions; hence, performance degradation. Some researchers attempted to solve these problems by increasing buffer size and the wires width at the expense of extra area utilization and power consumption.

The other type of topology is called custom topology. In this type, routing algorithm is quite difficult to implement. All routers have identical components (numbers of port, physical wires, etc.). Figure 4.3 illustrates a typical custom topology. The significant increased design complexity of the NoC based system

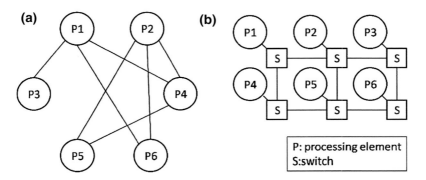

**Fig. 4.1** Typical paradigms: **a** circuit switching, **b** packet switching

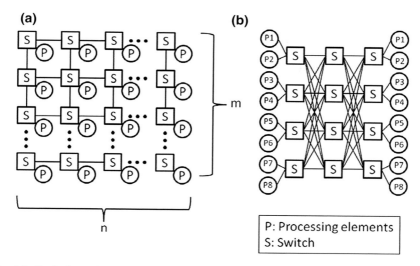

**Fig. 4.2** Typical standard topology: **a** N × M mesh topology, **b** 3 stage Clos topology

causes unacceptable simulation time with the traditional simulation methods (Genko 2005; Holsmark 2004).

NoC research issues include a lot of trade-offs such as: topology, routing, switching, scheduling, flow control, buffer size, packet size, and any optimization techniques. It is difficult to analyze these parameters using only high-level simulations. Therefore NoC prototype is an essential design phase for evaluating the performance of the NoC architectures under real applications (Pande 2005).

The remaining of this chapter presents architecture and design details of a 2D-mesh NoC architecture. The chapter also describes a so called short pass link (SPL) to optimize mesh topology by reducing (in some cases) the number of hopes between nodes experiencing heavy traffic.

**Fig. 4.3** Typical customized topology

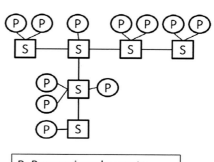

## 4.2 2D NoC Architecture

As we earlier stated, an NoC architecture is generally characterized by its topology, routing, switching, flow control, and arbiter techniques. There are various trade-offs when selecting these parameters. So, designers need to take care and deeply understand about all the design choices.

### 4.2.1 Topology and Routing

As we explained in previous section, topology is commonly selected from two types: standard or customized. The routing methods are selected depending on the topology (Mello 2004; Li 2006). Routing algorithm can be easily implemented in a standard topology (e.g. Mesh, Torus, Star) because each router sends the same routing path to its neighboring nodes. However, for customized topology, routing is generally more difficult and it is necessary to design specific routing mechanism. Thus, the design time may be longer than standard (Bononi 2006; Bolotin 2004). Figure 4.4 illustrates a 3 × 3 NoC based on mesh topology.

### 4.2.2 Switching

In packet switching, how packets move between the different nodes is known as switching scheme. The switching scheme influences the buffering in the routing nodes and how resources are used (Rasmussen 2006). Store and Forward (SF),

**Fig. 4.4** 3 × 3 NoC based on mesh topology. *S* switch, *PE* processing element, *NI* network interface

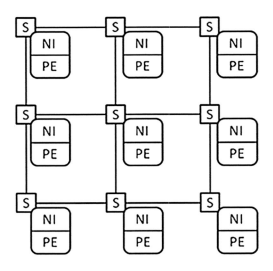

Wormhole (WH), and Virtual Cut Through (VCT) are all well known switching schemes for NoC systems. These switching methods transmit flits (flow control units), which are parts of individual packets.

### 4.2.3  Flow Control

Flits must be transmitted in a way such that there are no dropped flits, or with some kind of resend protocol. Low power consumption, and execution time are not dependent on situation of the network and are ideal for flow control. ON/OFF, Credit-based, Handshaking, and ACK/NACK are the commonly control flows used in NoC (Pullini 2005).

### 4.2.4  Arbiter

Round Robin arbiter is a known technique for many applications (Goossens 2005). In particular, it is a crucial building block for high-speed network routers. For instance, when inputs of a network router are competing for the usage of the router to send traffic to their respective outputs, Round Robin-based arbitration schemes, such as iSLIP or Ping-Pong Arbitration are used for fair sharing of switch band-width between inputs.

In traditional networks, the distance between routers is generally large and the arbitration task has multiple clock cycles to complete. However, for NoC the arbitration generally need to complete within one clock cycle to avoid large latencies between the cores on the chip (e.g., between a processing element and a memory block). To achieve this goal of one clock cycle arbitration, the overall delay introduced by the arbitration task should be low so that it will not impact the overall system clock frequency, which introduces new challenges for the design of the arbiters.

### 4.2.5  Network Interface

Network interfaces (NI) is the interface between cores and the network itself. NI design has received considerable attention in parallel computers and computer networks. These designs are generally optimized for high throughput and low latency and often consist of a dedicated processor, and large amount of buffering.

The NI must provide low area overhead because NoC designs are generally constrained by area and power. In addition, a good NI design must provide throughput and/or latency guarantees, which are essential for the design of NoC based complex multicore SoCs. We will describe in Chap. 6 real architecture and design of a network interface.

## 4.3 2D NoC Hardware Design Details

In this section, we explain the router architecture and design. We use Verilog-HDL codes to describe the main router building blocks, such as buffer, routing calculation, arbiter, flow control and crossbar.

### 4.3.1 Topology Design

Figure 4.6 illustrates the topology of a so called OASIS NoC (ONoC) and Fig. 4.5 illustrates the external connections to a router ($i = 0$ is Local port, $i = 1$ is "North" port, $i = 2$ is "East" port, $i = 3$ is "South" port and $i = 4$ is "West" port). The corresponding Verilog RTL code is shown in code 4.1.

As we mentioned earlier, ONoC is $n \times m$ mesh topology. Parameters $X - WIDTH$ and $Y - WIDTH$ means network size, when $i == 1$, each router's north input port receives data from south port of $currentx, currenty+1$ router. $(y - pos == Y - WIDTH - 1)$ indicates the router position is north edge, so there are no input data from north port. All ports connections can be written using the same method.

Code 4.1: Verilog RTL coding for a mesh topology.

```
//y loop
for (y_pos=0; y_pos<Y_WIDTH; y_pos=y_pos+1) begin:y_loop
  //x loop
 for (x_pos=0; x_pos<X_WIDTH; x_pos=x_pos+1) begin:x_loop

 router #(NOUT, FIFO_DEPTH, FIFO_LOG2D, FIFO_FULL_LVL)
     rtr(.clk(clk), .reset(reset),
 .data_in(net_data_in[x_pos][y_pos]),
 .data_out(net_data_out[x_pos][y_pos]),
 .stop_in(net_stop_in[x_pos][y_pos]),
 .stop_out(net_stop_out[x_pos][y_pos]),
 .xaddr(x_pos['L2NET_SIZE-1:0]), .yaddr(y_pos['L2NET_SIZE-1:0]));

for (i=0; i<NOUT; i=i+1) begin:i0
 //tile interface of router
 if(i==0) begin
   assign net_data_in[x_pos][y_pos]['WIDTH*(i+1)-1:'WIDTH*i] = data_in[('WIDTH*
       X_WIDTH*y_pos)+('WIDTH*(x_pos+1))-1:('WIDTH*X_WIDTH*y_pos)+('WIDTH*x_pos)
       ];
   assign data_out[('WIDTH*X_WIDTH*y_pos)+('WIDTH*(x_pos+1))-1:('WIDTH*X_WIDTH*
       y_pos)+('WIDTH*x_pos)] = net_data_out[x_pos][y_pos]['WIDTH*(i+1)-1:'WIDTH
       *i];
   assign net_stop_in[x_pos][y_pos][i] = stop_in[(X_WIDTH*y_pos)+x_pos];
   assign stop_out[(X_WIDTH*y_pos)+x_pos] = net_stop_out[x_pos][y_pos][i];
 end
 //north edge of router
 if(i==1) begin
  if(y_pos==Y_WIDTH-1) begin
   assign net_data_in [x_pos][y_pos]['WIDTH*(i+1)-1:'WIDTH*i] = 0;
   assign net_stop_in [x_pos][y_pos][i] = 1'b1;
  end else begin
     assign net_data_in [x_pos][y_pos]['WIDTH*(i+1)-1:'WIDTH*i] = net_data_out[
         x_pos][y_pos+1]['WIDTH*(3+1)-1:'WIDTH*3];
     assign net_stop_in [x_pos][y_pos][i] = net_stop_out[x_pos][y_pos+1][3];
  end
 end
 //east edge of router
 if(i==2) begin
 ...
```

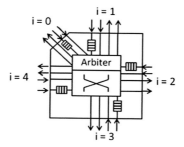

**Fig. 4.5** External connections to one router

## 4.3.2 Pipeline Design

ONoC architecture has three pipeline stages. The first stage includes the *Buffer module*. The second stage includes the *Routing module, buffer overflow module* and *scheduling module*. The last stage includes the *Crossbar module*.

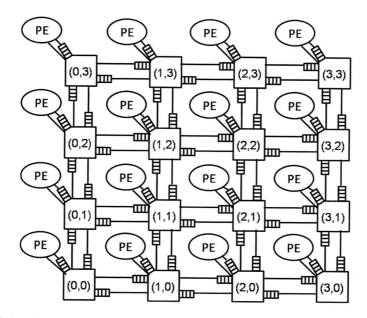

**Fig. 4.6**  4 × 4 mesh topology

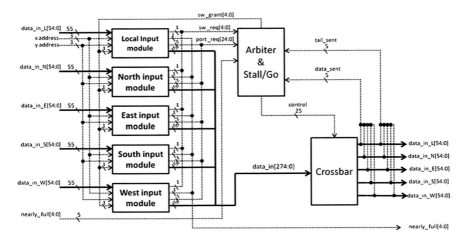

**Fig. 4.7** ONoC router block diagram

Figure 4.7 illustrates the router micro-architecture. The five modules in the left side of the figure are the input port modules with buffers and routing modules. The other important module is the switch allocation (sw-alloc) module which mainly implements the scheduler and flow control modules. Finally, the crossbar module implements the crossbar circuitry and has an array of data input and output paths.

### 4.3.2.1 Input Port Design

ONoC router has 5 independent input ports. The input port has two main functions: buffering, and routing calculation. The *buffering* task is described by the RTL Code 4.2. This module manages the FIFO pointers (head and tail) calculation (lines 2–9), and *stop_out* signal is also calculated (lines 11–22) for upstream router's flow control.

The RTL code for the *Routing calculation* task is shown in Code 4.3. As shown in the above code, the look-ahead XY routing is performed. The next port address which is used in routing calculation phase is computed (lines 2–8 in Code 4.3).

Code 4.2: Verilog RTL coding for manging FIFO.

```
always @(posedge clk) begin
 if (!reset) begin      //If out of reset
  if (enqueue) begin //Write a flit to the buffer
   fifo[tail_ptr] <= data_in;
   tail_ptr <= tail_ptr + 1;
  end
  if (dequeue) begin //Read a flit from the buffer
   head_ptr <= head_ptr + 1;
  end

  //nearly full signal = stop_out,
  if (((tail_ptr + FULL_LVL[LOG2D-1:0] + 1'b1)==head_ptr) && enqueue && !
       dequeue)begin
   stop_out <= 1'b1;
  end
  if (((tail_ptr + FULL_LVL[LOG2D-1:0])==(head_ptr+1'b1)) && !enqueue &&
       dequeue)begin
   stop_out <= 1'b1;
  end
  if ((tail_ptr + FULL_LVL[LOG2D-1:0])==head_ptr)begin
   if ((enqueue && !dequeue) || (!enqueue && dequeue))begin
    stop_out <= 1'b0;
   end
  end
 end
 else ...
end
```

Code 4.3: XY routing code.

```
//assign next addresses
if (nextport == 'EAST) next_xaddr = xaddr + 1'b1;
  else if (nextport == 'WEST) next_xaddr = xaddr - 1'b1;
    else next_xaddr = xaddr;

if (nextport == 'NORTH) next_yaddr = yaddr + 1'b1;
  else if (nextport == 'SOUTH) next_yaddr = yaddr - 1'b1;
    else next_yaddr = yaddr;

//evaluate next port
if (next_xaddr == xdest) begin
  if (next_yaddr == ydest) route = 'SELF;
    else if(next_yaddr < ydest) route = 'NORTH;
      else route = 'SOUTH;
end else begin
  if (next_xaddr < xdest) route = 'EAST;
    else route = 'WEST;
end
```

### 4.3.2.2 Switch Allocator Design

The *Switch Allocator* includes a *Scheduler*, *Matrix Arbiter*, and a *Stop Go* flow control modules. Code 4.4 shows part of the *Matrix Arbiter* module. Lines 1–15 generate grant $i$, and lines 17–23 calculate next state of all matrix elements. Finally, lines 25–30 update these states.

The block diagram of the arbiter is shown in Fig. 4.8. Each row of the matrix means competitive inputs and has priority level. After the highest priority input is served, the priority will be changed to lowest by inversing one's row and column. Figure 4.8a shows an example of how the matrix arbitration works.

**Fig. 4.8** Matrix arbitration
example

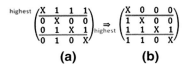

$$\begin{pmatrix} X & P_{12} & P_{13} & P_{14} \\ P_{21} & X & P_{23} & P_{24} \\ P_{31} & P_{32} & X & P_{34} \\ P_{41} & P_{42} & P_{43} & X \end{pmatrix}$$

When the priority i > j, P(i,j) becomes 1 and P(j, i) become 0

$$\underset{\text{highest}}{} \begin{pmatrix} X & 1 & 1 & 1 \\ 0 & X & 0 & 0 \\ 0 & 1 & X & 1 \\ 0 & 1 & 0 & X \end{pmatrix}_{\text{highest}} \Rightarrow \begin{pmatrix} X & 0 & 0 & 0 \\ 1 & X & 0 & 0 \\ 1 & 1 & X & 1 \\ 1 & 1 & 0 & X \end{pmatrix}$$

**(a)**                **(b)**

Code 4.4: Matrix Arbiter RTL code.

```
//Matrix Arbiter
generate
 for (i=0; i<SIZE; i=i+1) begin:ol1
  for (j=0; j<SIZE; j=j+1) begin:il1
   if (j==i)
    assign pri[i][j]=request[i];
   else
   if (j>i)
    assign pri[i][j]=!(request[j]&&state[j*SIZE+i]);
   else
   assign pri[i][j]=!(request[j]&&!state[i*SIZE+j]);
   end
       assign grant[i]=&pri[i];
 end
endgenerate

generate
for (i=0; i<SIZE; i=i+1) begin:ol2
 for (j=0; j<SIZE; j=j+1) begin:il2
  assign new_state[j*SIZE+i]=(success&&((state[j*SIZE+i]&&!grant[j])||(grant[i
      ])))||(!success&&state[j*SIZE+i]);
      end
 end
endgenerate

always@(posedge clk) begin
 if (reset) state<=-1;
 else begin
 if (|request) state<=new_state;
 end
end
```

## 4.3.3  Arbiter Design

For the flow control, ONoC employs *stop-go* scheme. This technique ovoids
buffers overflow. Data transfer is controlled by signals indicating the buffers
condition. In the absence of *stall-go* function, the receiver cores need to judge
whether there are dropped packets or not. If so, the transmitter must resend the
dropped packets using a receiving request signal from master cores. In addition,
*stall-go* scheme reduces blocking, but at the same time it may increase latency in
some situations. Figure 4.10a illustrates the state machine of this approach and
Fig. 4.10b shows the input FIFO state of *nearly-full* signal output.

Code 4.5 shows the RTL code of the state machine. State *Go* indicates that the
receiving FIFO can store more than two flits. State *Sent* means that it can store one
flit and state *Stop* means that it cannot store any more flits. Figure 4.9 shows the
*stop-go* control flow scheme.

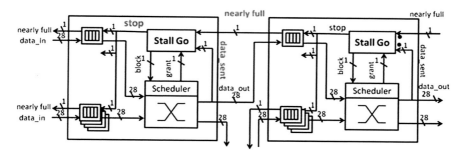

**Fig. 4.9** Stall-go block diagram

Code 4.5 is the RTL for stall-go state machine.

```
//Stall-go state machine.
   always @(posedge clk) begin

if (!reset) begin
 if ((state=='GO) && stop_in && data_sent)
 state <= 'SENT1;
 if (state=='SENT1) begin
  if (stop_in && !data_sent)
   state <= 'GO;
  if (!stop_in && data_sent)
   state <= 'STOP;
 end

if ((state=='STOP) && stop_in) // stop_in = nearly_full
 state <= 'GO;
    end else
 state <= 'GO;
end

   assign blocked = ( ((state=='STOP) && !stop_in) || ((state=='SENT1) && !
       stop_in && data_sent) );
```

## 4.3.4 Crossbar Design

The crossbar in ONoC architecture is a an important module that connects multiple inputs to multiple outputs. It is basically an assembly of single switches between multiple inputs and multiple outputs. Code 4.6 is the Verilog RTL code for the crossbar (Fig. 4.11).

**Fig. 4.11** Arbiter control signals

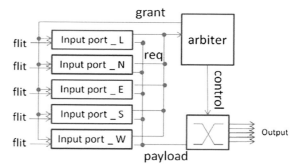

**Fig. 4.10  a** State machine
design. **b** Nearly full signal
output

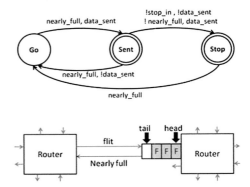

Code 4.6 RTL code for Crossbar.

```
// Crossbar
generate
 for (i=0;i<NOUT;i=i+1) begin:output_loop
 mux_out #(NIN, WIDTH) cbar_mux(.cntrl(cntrl_reg[NIN*(i+1)-1:NIN*i]),
.data_in(data_in), .data_out(data_out[WIDTH*(i+1)-1:WIDTH*i]));
 end
endgenerate

//mux_out
generate
 //loop over each bit of data
 for (i=0;i<WIDTH;i=i+1) begin:bit_loop
  assign data_out[i] = mux(cntrl, data_bits[i]);
  //loop over each input channel
  for (j=0;j<n_in;j=j+1) begin:input_loop
   assign data_bits[i][j] = data_in[WIDTH*j+i];
  end
 end
endgenerate

function mux;
 input [n_in-1:0] cntrl;
 input [n_in-1:0] data_in;
 integer i;

begin
 mux = 0;
 for (i=0; i<n_in; i=i+1) begin
  if(cntrl[i] == 1'b1) mux = data_in[i];
 end
end
endfunction // mux
```

## 4.3.5 Network Interface

The NI module is divided in two sub-modules: transmitter and receiver.
Figure 4.12 shows the transmitter NI block diagram and Fig. 4.13 shows the
receiver NI block diagram. This NI design is used for the Dimension Reversal,
Hotspot and JPEG Encoder benchmarks. Dimension reversal and Hotspot
benchmarks have the same NI structures. JPEG encoder transmitted data size is
assumed to be 9 bits, 25 bits and 39 bits as illustrated in Fig. 4.15.

For the ONoC system, we simplified the NI design and we set the *Payload* to its
largest size (39 bits) as shown in Fig. 4.14. The reader can easily notice that the

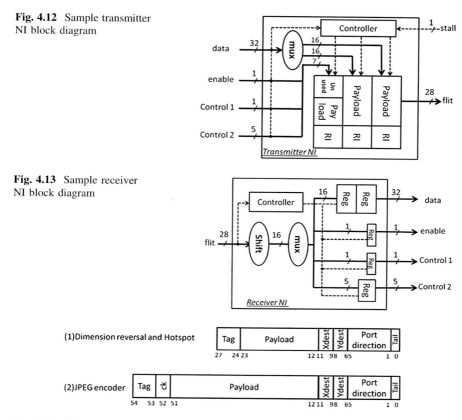

**Fig. 4.12** Sample transmitter NI block diagram

**Fig. 4.13** Sample receiver NI block diagram

**Fig. 4.14** Flit structure

above NI design can be also used with other target applications if the format of the flit (mainly the Payload item) is slightly modified. A more detailed design for a general NI will be given later in Chap. 6.

### 4.3.6 Limitations of Regular Mesh Topology

The ONoC communication architecture considered so far is based on regular mesh topology. This provides well-controlled electrical parameters and reduced power consumption across the links. However, because of the nonexistence of short (fast) paths between remotely situated nodes, such architectures may suffer from long packet latencies. To solve this problem, a so called *short-path-link (SPL)* is used to shorten the path; thus, decreasing the latency.

Figure 4.16 shows a simple example showing SPL insertion between two remote nodes. To support optimization with SPL insertion, a new port should be

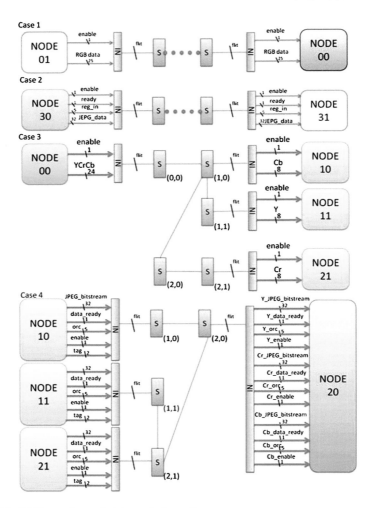

**Fig. 4.15** JPEG encoder packet transmission patterns

added to the 5 ports in each router. Consequently, each router will have 6 ports instead of only 5 ports in fully regular mesh topology.

### 4.3.7 SPL Insertion Algorithm

The SPL algorithm selects communication paths that need optimization. The available SPL resources should be decided first so that the power and area are not increased. Then, the communication costs for all communication patters are calculated using the communication frequencies and the distance between different

**Fig. 4.16** Short-Path-Link
(SPL) insertion example

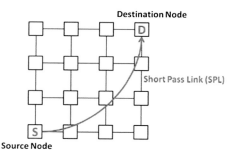

nodes. Depending on the output of this computation, the SPL is inserted to the highest communication cost. After adding an SPL, the algorithm loops until the available SPL budget is exhausted.

$$f_{ij} = \max \frac{V_{ij}}{\sum_p \sum_{p \neq q} V_{pq}} \qquad (4.1)$$

$$d_M(i,j) = |i_x - j_x| + |i_y - j_y| \qquad (4.2)$$

$$C_{ij} = f_{ij} \times d_M(i,j) \qquad (4.3)$$

Where, $S$ is the available resource, $i$ is the target sender router, $j$ is the target receiver router, $f_{ij}$ is the target communication frequency, and $C_{ij}$ is the target communication total cost.

Figure 4.17 shows the SPL insertion algorithm. Equation 4.1 is used to measure the communication frequency by calculating the whole communication with all neighbor nodes and the target communication for the whole neighbor nodes usability volume.

The whole communication volume is expressed by $\sum_p \sum_{p \neq q} V_{pq}$; where $p$ indicates the sender node, $q$ indicates the receiver node. Notice that $p$ and $q$ are always neighbors. Then, the target communication frequency is expressed by $V_{ij}$; where $i$ indicates the sender node, and $j$ indicates the receiver node.

To calculate the distance (number of hops) of communications, *Manhattan distance* is employed (Eq. 4.2). The address of $i$ node is expressed by $(i_x, i_y)$, and the address of $j$ node is expressed by $(j_x, j_y)$. Finally, the total cost calculation is computed using Eq. 4.3 with computed values from the previous two equations.

#### 4.3.7.1 SPL Complexity

Tables 4.1 and 4.2 show the area utilization of 5-port and 6-port routers respectively. From these results, we can see that the 6-port router's ALUTs utilization is increased by 33.2 % and the registers utilization is increased by 56.6 % when compared with 5-port router.

**Fig. 4.17** SPL insertion
algorithm

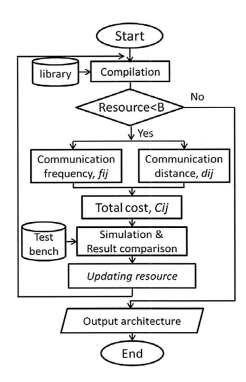

**Table 4.1** Area utilization for a 5-ports router

| Parameters | | Input port | Switch allocator | Crossbar | Total |
|---|---|---|---|---|---|
| ALUTs | 1-port | 71 (7.4%) | 300 (31%) | 310 (32.1%) | 965 |
| | 5-ports | 355 (36.8%) | | | |
| Registers | 1-port | 72 (15.2%) | 90 (18.9%) | 25 (5.3%) | 475 |
| | 5-ports | 360 (75.8%) | | | |

**Table 4.2** Area utilization for 6-port router

| Parameters | | Input port | Switch allocator | Crossbar | Total |
|---|---|---|---|---|---|
| ALUTs | 1-port | 75 (5.8%) | 469 (36.5%) | 366 (28.5%) | 1285 |
| | 6-ports | 450 (35%) | | | |
| Registers | 1-port | 99 (13.3%) | 144 (19.4%) | 36 (4.8%) | 744 |
| | 6-ports | 594 (79.8%) | | | |

## 4.3.7.2 Hardware Modification for SPL Support

Initially, each router has 5 in/out ports: Local, North, East, South, and West. In order
to optimize the system with SPL approach, it is essential to add another port.
Figure 4.18 shows the extra-port addition for both sender and receiver nodes. Flit
structure also needs to be modified to support SPL. Initially, ONoC has 5 bits

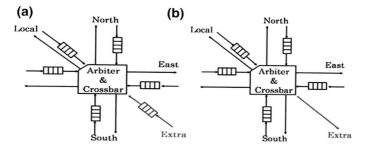

**Fig. 4.18** Extra-Port insertion. **a** Receiver. **b** Transmitter

dedicated used for the *next-port* field direction. To support SPL, it is also necessary to modify the network connection between routers and also extend the *next-port* field by 1 bit. That is, from 5 bits to 6 bits. Figures 4.19, 4.20 and 4.21 illustrate the application mapping with SPL links. We assume here that the resource budget is 5 % of the original area utilization. Code 4.7 shows the modified code for SPLs insertion.

We mainly modified the loop function for the mesh topology because it is necessary to simplify the connection of all routers (lines 1–4). After that, designers can easily insert one or more SPLs. For example, lines 15–17 show the address (0,3) north output connects to (1,0) south input port, and the address (1,0) south port has no connections. Thus, the south port can use SPL without adding an extra port.

As we mentioned, ONoC router employs *look-ahead* XY routing, so the routing stage calculates next router's output direction. The SPL is inserted from source node to destination node directly. Lines 6–13 in code 4.8 shows routing calculation for (0,3) to (1,0) communications.

Code 4.7 RTL code Modification for SPL.

```
// code Modification for SPL.
//y loop
for (y_pos=0; y_pos<Y_WIDTH; y_pos=y_pos+1) begin:y_loop2
 //x loop
 for (x_pos=0; x_pos<X_WIDTH; x_pos=x_pos+1) begin:x_loop2
  ...
  ///(1,0)
  if (x_pos == 1 )begin
   if (y_pos == 0)begin
    //tile interface of router, x_pos = 1, y_pos = 0, i = 0
    ....
    //north edge of router, x_pos = 1, y_pos = 0, i = 1
    ....
    //east edge of router, x_pos = 1, y_pos = 0, i = 2
    ....
    //south edge of router, x_pos = 1, y_pos = 0, i = 3
    assign net_data_in [x_pos][y_pos]['WIDTH*(3+1)-1:'WIDTH*3] = net_data_out
         [0][3]['WIDTH*(1+1)-1:'WIDTH*1];
    assign net_stop_in [x_pos][y_pos][3] = net_stop_out[0][3][1];

    //west edge of router, x_pos = 1, y_pos = 0, i = 4
    ...
   end
  ...
```

**Fig. 4.19** Dimension
reversal with 2 SPLs

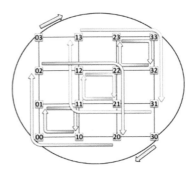

**Fig. 4.20** Hotspot with 2
SPL

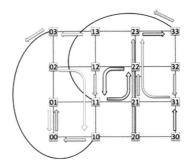

**Fig. 4.21** JPEG encoder with
3 SPL

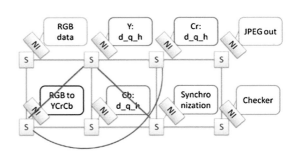

Code 4.8 Code Modification for *look-ahead* routing.

```
if(nextport == 'WEST) begin
 next_xaddr = xaddr - 1'b1;
end else if (nextport == 'EAST) next_xaddr = xaddr + 1'b1;
else next_xaddr = xaddr;

if(nextport == 'NORTH)begin
 if((xaddr==0&&yaddr==3)&&(xdest==1&&ydest==0))begin
  next_xaddr = 1;
  next_yaddr = 0;
 end
 else next_yaddr = yaddr + 1'b1;
end else if (nextport == 'SOUTH) next_yaddr = yaddr - 1'b1;
else next_yaddr = yaddr;
```

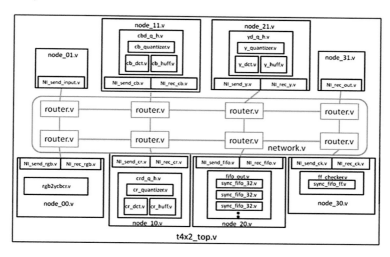

**Fig. 4.22** The top module of designed circuit with file names

## 4.3.8 Putting it all Together

Figure 4.22 illustrates the whole system architecture, and Fig. 4.23 shows the router architecture. Figure 4.24 shows ONoC block diagram with JPEG encoder.

## 4.4 Evaluation

This section explains the described ONoC architecture and evaluation results using three different benchmarks: Dimension Reversal, Hotspot, and JPEG encoder.

## 4.4.1 Environments and Parameters

The proposed architecture is designed in Verilog-HDL. Synthesized and simulated with industrial tools. The target device is Altera Stratix III EP3SL150F1152C2.

Table 4.3 shows the design and the simulation parameters for Dimension reversal benchmark. The input data is continuously injected and both transmitter and receiver nodes are assigned (6 nodes). Each transmitter node sends 1000 flits.

Table 4.4 shows design and the simulation parameters for Hotspot benchmark. Here, both transmitter and receiver nodes are mapped to 8 nodes and continuously inject flits. Each transmitter also sends 1000 flits. Table 4.5 shows JPEG encoder design and the simulation parameters. The algorithm (Fig. 4.17) starts from budget selection.

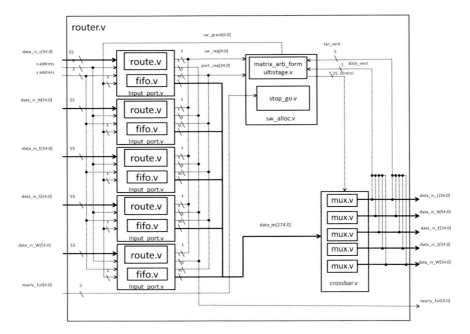

**Fig. 4.23** Router top module with file names

## 4.4.2 Dimension Reversal and Hotspot Simulation Results

The number of SPL depends on the available budget. Here we again assume 5 % area budget (Table 4.6). Hotspot's budget (Table 4.7) is also 5 %. Figure 4.25 shows the comparison results between the base architecture (OASIS-2) and the designed ONoC-SPLs. The execution time includes packetization and depacketization latencies. Figure 4.25 shows the execution time, and throughput for different NoC architectures (OASIS-2 (ONoC2), ONoC-SPL1, and ONoC-SPL2).

Form these results, we can conclude that the throughput was increased by 49.6 % and the execution time was reduced by 29.7 % with ONoC-SPL3 configuration. Figure 4.26 shows the Hotspot simulation result, where the throughput is increased by 24.8 %, and the execution time is reduced by 16.9 %.

## 4.4.3 JPEG Encoder Simulation Results

For JPEG benchmark evaluation, the SPL budget is again assumed to be 5 % (Table 4.8). Figure 4.27 shows the throughput, the execution time, and latency evaluation results. With this benchmark, it was also found that the throughput

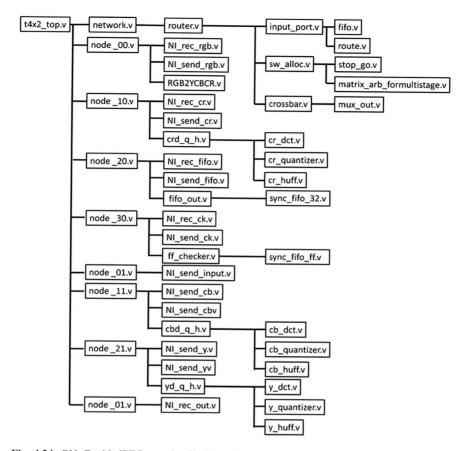

**Fig. 4.24** ONoC with JPEG encoder file hierarchy

**Table 4.3** Dimension reversal simulation environment

| Parameters | OASIS-2 | ONoC with SPL |
|---|---|---|
| Topology | Mesh | Mesh with SPL |
| Budget | 0 | 5 % |
| Flow control | ACK/NACK(at PE) | Stall go |
| Routing algorithm | XY-routing | XY-routing |
| Switching method | Wormhole | Wormhole |
| Flit size | 28 bit | 28 bit |
| Buffer depth | 4 | 4 |

increases by 22.6 %, the latency decreased by 41.7 % and the execution time decreases by 43.7 % with ONoC-SPL3 configuration. Tables 4.6, 4.7, and 4.8 show power consumption evaluations.

**Table 4.4** Hotspot simulation environment

| Parameters | OASIS-2 | ONoC with SPL |
|---|---|---|
| Topology | Mesh | Mesh with SPL |
| Budget | 0 | 5 % |
| Flow control | ACK/NACK(at PE) | Stall go |
| Routing algorithm | XY-routing | XY-routing |
| Switching method | Wormhole | Wormhole |
| Flit size | 28 bit | 28 bit |
| Buffer depth | 4 | 4 |

**Table 4.5** JPEG encoder simulation environment

| Parameters | OASIS-2 | ONoC with SPL |
|---|---|---|
| Topology | Mesh | Mesh with SPL |
| Budget | 0 | 5 % |
| Flow control | ACK/NACK(at PE) | Stall go |
| Routing algorithm | XY-routing | XY-routing |
| Switching method | Wormhole | Wormhole |
| Flit size | 28 bit | 28 bit |
| Buffer depth | 4 | 4 |

**Table 4.6** Hardware complexity: Dimension reversal

| Parameters | OASIS-2 | ONoC-SPL1 | ONoC-SPL2 | ONoC-SPL3 |
|---|---|---|---|---|
| Area (ALUTs) | 9,008 (8 %) | 9,119 (8 %) | 9,272 (8 %) | 9,605 (8 %) |
| Speed (MHz) | 182.78 | 169.58 | 171.53 | 167.28 |
| Power consumption (mW) | 660.61 | 663.12 | 662.54 | 661.46 |
| Additional hardware | 0 | 1.23 % | 2.93 % | 6.63 % |

**Table 4.7** Hardware complexity: Hotspot

| Parameters | OASIS-2 | ONoC-SPL1 | ONoC-SPL2 | ONoC-SPL3 |
|---|---|---|---|---|
| Area (ALUTs) | 10,041(9 %) | 10,130 (9 %) | 10,302 (9 %) | 10,911 (10 %) |
| Speed (MHz) | 187.62 | 180.41 | 178.83 | 169.78 |
| Power consumption (mW) | 666.01 | 667.29 | 667.33 | 669.20 |
| Additional hardware | 0 | 0.89 % | 2.60 % | 8.66 % |

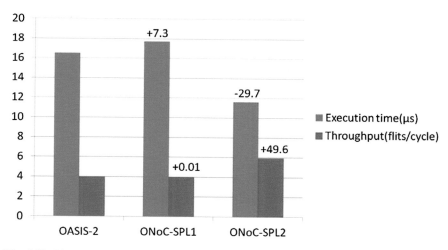

**Fig. 4.25**   Dimension reversal simulation result

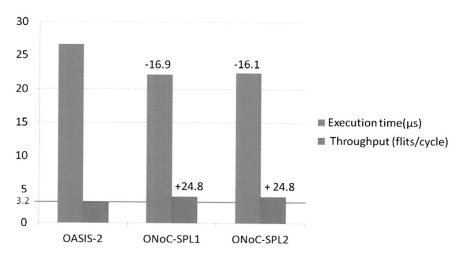

**Fig. 4.26**   Hotspot simulation result

**Table 4.8** Hardware complexity: JPEG encoder

| Parameters | OASIS-2 | ONoC-SPL1 | ONoC-SPL2 | ONoC-SPL3 |
|---|---|---|---|---|
| Area (ALUTs) | 28,401(25 %) | 28,733 (25 %) | 29,138 (26 %) | 29,616 (26 %) |
| Speed (MHz) | 193.8 | 173.13 | 176.03 | 171.79 |
| Power consumption (mW) | 815.90 | 815.84 | 823.32 | 823.92 |
| Additional hardware | 0 | 1.17 % | 2.59 % | 4.28 % |

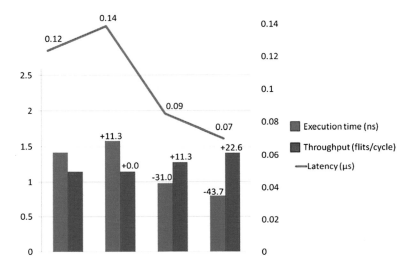

**Fig. 4.27**  JPEG encoder simulation result

## 4.5  Conclusion

The interconnection structure supporting future complex multi and manycore SoCs will be closer to a sophisticated network than to current bus-based solutions. Such network must provide high throughput and low latency while keeping area and power consumption low. NoCs provide a good way of realizing interconnections on silicon and largely alleviate the limitations of bus-based solutions. NoC is a scalable interconnect with a huge potential to handle the increasing complexity of current and future multicore SoCs. In such paradigm, cores are connected via a packet-switching communication network on a single chip.

This chapter presented in details architecture, design, and evaluation of a real Network-on-Chip architecture, which utilizes a Short-Path-Link (SPL) insertion customization to reduce the communication latency which directly affects the overall system performance. Evaluated of performance in terms of hardware complexity, execution time and throughput were also given.

# Chapter 5
# 3D Network-on-Chip

Two-dimensional Networks-on-Chip (2D-NoCs) are proposed to be used in medium-scale multicore SoCs because of scalability, better throughput and low power consumption. However, for large-scale many-core SoCs, just increasing the number of cores over a 2D-NoC is not efficient due to large number of hops—long interconnects. With the emergence of three-dimensional (3D) integration technologies, a new opportunity emerges for chip architects by porting the 2D-NoC to the third dimension. In 3D integration technologies, multiple layers of active devices are stacked above each other and vertically interconnected using through-silicon via (TSV). As compared to 2D-IC designs, 3D ICs allow for performance enhancements even in the absence of scaling because of the reduced interconnect lengths. Yet, package density is increased, power consumption is reduced, and the system is more immune to noise. This chapter describes a 3D-NoC architecture and design to overcome the limitations of 2D-NoC systems.

## 5.1 Introduction

As we mentioned in Chap. 1, the number of transistors kept increasing along the past few decades. That made shrinking the chip size while maintaining high performance possible. This technology scaling has allowed Systems-on-Chip (SoCs) to grow continuously in component count and complexity, which significantly led to some very challenging problems, such us power dissipation, and resource management (Habibi 2011; Leary 2010).

As moving to sub-20 nm CMOS technology poses real design and manufacturing problems, 3D integration becomes an attractive option for increasing transistor density for complex application to meet high performance demand. By stacking dies or wafers we can reduce wire-length. As a result, the performance is increased and the power consumption is reduced.

The on-chip interconnection network starts to play a more and more important role in determining the performance and also the power consumption of the entire chip (Kumar 2005). Conventional shared bus interconnect is no longer reliable

A. Ben Abdallah, *Multicore Systems On-Chip: Practical Software/Hardware Design*,
Atlantis Ambient and Pervasive Intelligence 7, DOI: 10.2991/978-94-91216-92-3_5,
© Atlantis Press and the author 2013

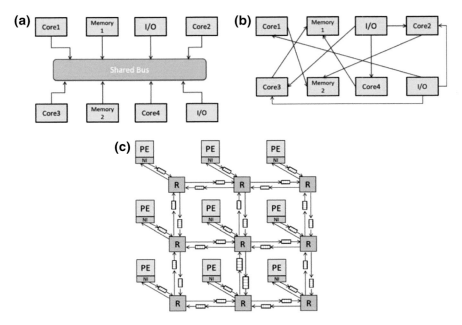

**Fig. 5.1** SoC interconnection types: **a** Shared bus, **b** Point-2-Point, **c** NoC

architectures for multicore SoCs, due to the lack of scalability and parallelism integration, high latency and power dissipation, and low throughput.

As was described in Chap. 4, 2D-NoC paradigm was introduced as a promising method that can respond to the bus-based design challenges. Based on a simple and scalable architecture platform, NoC connects processing cores, memories and other custom designs together using switching packets on a hop-by-hop basis. The ultimate goal is to provide a higher bandwidth and higher performance.

Figure 5.1a, b show some well-known architectures which are respectively Point-to-Point (*P2P*) and shared bus systems. As shown in Fig. 5.1c, NoC architectures are based upon connecting segments (or wires) and switching blocks to combine the benefits of the two previous architectures while reducing their disadvantages, such us the large numbers of long wires and the lack of scalability in shared-bus systems.

### 5.1.1  Why 3D-NoCs?

Future applications are getting more and more complex, demanding good architecture to ensure a sufficient bandwidth for any transaction between memories and cores as well as communication between different cores on the same chip. Because of these and other factors, 2D-NoC interconnect become not suitable candidate for future large scale many-core SoCs that are expected to accommodate hundreds of cores. More specifically, the limitation of the 2D-NoC paradigm comes from the high diameter that conventional 2D-NoC suffers from. The network's diameter is the number of hops that a flit traverses in the longest possible minimal path between a (source, destination) pair.

In 2D-NoC, if a given packet traverses a large number of hops to reach its destination, the communication time (latency) will be long and hence the throughput will be low. In other words, large network diameter has a negative impact on the worst case routing latency in the system.

The seek for optimizing 2D-NoC based architecture becomes more and more necessary, and many researches have been conducted to achieve this goal in various approaches, such as developing fast routers (Kim 2003, 2006; Kumar 2007; Mullins 2004) or designing new high-throughput, and low latency network topologies (Dally 1991; Kim 2007; Ogras 2006).

One of these proposed solutions was porting the 2D-NoC architecture to the third dimension (Philip 2008). In the past few years, 3D-ICs have attracted a lot of attention as a potential solution to resolve the interconnect bottlenecks. A 3D chip is a stack of multiple device layers with direct vertical interconnects tunneling through them (Das 2004; Morrow 2004).

So far, the achieved researches in this area have shown that 3D-ICs can achieve higher packing density due to the addition of a third dimension to the conventional two-dimensional layout; thanks to the reduced average interconnect length, 3D-ICs can achieve higher performance. Besides this important benefit, this reduction of total wiring, a lower interconnect power consumption can be obtained (Joyner 2001; Topol 2006), not to forget that circuitry is more immune to noise with 3D-ICs (Philip 2008). This may offer an opportunity to continue performance improvements using CMOS technology with smaller form factors, higher integration densities and supporting the realization of mixed-technology chips (Carloni 2009). As Topol (2006) stated, 3D-IC can improve the performance even in absence of scalability.

3D NoC architecture responds to the scaling demands for future multicore and many-core SoCs, exploiting the short vertical links between the adjacent layers that can clearly enhance the system performance. This combination is expected to provide a new horizon of NoC and IC designs in general.

One of the important design steps that should be taken into consideration while designing an 3D-NoC is to implement an efficient router since it is the backbone of any NoC architecture. The router's performance depends on many factors and techniques such as the traffic pattern, the router pipeline design and the network topology. As Feihui (2006) stated, among these three factors we have less control over the traffic patterns compared with the topology and the pipeline design. Following this logic and assuming the topology choice was already taken, one of the most important router enhancements that can be done is to improve the pipeline design. By reducing the pipeline delay via pipelining optimization, not only we decrease the per-hop delay, but also the whole network latency will be reduced.

On the other hand, the pipeline design is strongly associated with the adopted routing algorithm. Routing is the process of determining the path that a flit should take between one source and one destination nodes. Routing algorithm can be classified into minimal or non-minimal, depending on whether flits traveling from source to destination always use the minimal possible path or not.

Minimal routing schemes are shorter and require less complex hardware, but allowing non-minimal routes increases the path diversity and decreases the network congestion. Also the routing algorithms can be adaptive, where routing decisions are made based on the network congestion status and other information about network links or buffer occupancy of the neighboring nodes, or alternatively are deterministic.

There are a large number of sophisticated adaptive routing algorithms. However, they require more hardware and are difficult to implement. That's why deterministic routing schemes has been adopted for 3D-NoC designs. One of the well used routing schemes used in 3D-NoCs is the Dimension Order Routing (DOR) XYZ algorithm. XYZ is a simple scheme, easy to implement and free of deadlock and life-lock. But on the other hand, it suffers from a non-efficient pipeline stage usage. This can introduce an additional packet latency which has an important effect on the router delay and eventually on the system overall performance. Enhancing this algorithm while keeping its simplicity may improve the system performance by reducing the packet delay.

A 2D-NoC, named OASIS NoC, was presented in Ben-Abdallah (2006), Mori (2009, 2010). Although this architecture has its advantages over the shared-bus based systems, it has also several limitations such as high power consumption, high cost communication, and low throughput.

The presented 3D-OASIS-NoC (3D-ONoC) uses the earlier proposed efficient routing scheme—Look-ahead-XYZ (LA-XYZ). This algorithm improves the router pipeline design by parallelizing some stages while taking advantage at the same time of the simplicity of the conventional XYZ. As a result, this routing scheme aims to enhance the router performance thereby achieving a low-latency design.

## 5.1.2  3D-NoC Versus 2D-NoC

3D-NoC is a widely studied research topic, and many related works have been conducted in the past. Few of them focused on the benefits of the 3D-NoC architecture over the traditional 2D-NoC design. Feero (2007) showed that 3D-NoC has the ability to reduce latency and the energy per packet by decreasing the number of hopes by 40 % which is a basic and important factor to evaluate the system performance (Feero 2007). Pavlidis (2007) analyzed the zero-load latency and power consumption, and demonstrated that a decrease of 62 and 58 % in power consumption can be achieved with 3D-NoC when compared to a traditional 2D-NoC topology for a network size of $N = 128$ and $N = 256$ nodes, respectively, where N is the number of cores connected in the network. This power consumption reduction can simply be related to the reduction of number of hops, since a flit has less hops to traverse to go from one source to its destination, and that includes less buffer access, less switch arbitration, and less link and crossbar traversal. All of these factors will eventually lead to decrease the power consumption.

### 5.1.3 Router Architectures

Another part of previous works focused on the router architecture. For example, Li (2006) has modified the conventional $7 \times 7$ 3D router using a shared bus as a communication interface between the different layers of the router, to create a *3D NoC-Bus Hybrid* router. This kind of routers reduces in fact the number of ports in each router from 7 to 6, but on the other hand flits wishing to travel from one layer to another should compete the access to the shared bus, since it's the only inter-layer communication interface. This may lead to undesirable performance degradation especially under a heavy inter-layer traffic.

Yan (2008), also proposed another architecture for the 3D-router, by implementing all the vertical links into a single 3D-crossbar. In this case, the router has only 5 ports since we do not need any more additional ports for the vertical connections. This technique reduces the inter-layer distance, and makes the travel between the different layers in one single hop possible. But this router also engenders a high router cost besides the implementation complexity of such router, which cannot be acceptable for some simple application that actually does not need such a complex router.

For all these facts, we adopted the conventional $7 \times 7$ 3D-router, as it is the lowest cost among the other architectures and also the simplest to implement showing several properties like regularity, concurrent data transmission, and controlled electrical parameters (Glass 1992; Hu 2003). All the benefits are acquired while making sure that this low cost and simple implementation does not affect the performance of our system.

### 5.1.4 Routing Algorithms

Many routing algorithms have been proposed for MCSoC systems but most of them focus only on 2D-network topologies. Also, among all the studies conducted for 3D-NoC, few of them focused on routing algorithms. Among the few proposed ones, there are some custom routing schemes that aims to reduce the power consumption and thermal power which is a very challenge design for 3D-NoC systems. For instance, Ramanujam (2008) presented an oblivious routing algorithm called randomized partially minimal (RPM) that aims to load balance the traffic along the network improving then the worst case scenario. RPM sends packets to a random layer first, then route them along their X and Y dimensions using either XY or YX routing with equal probability. Finally packets are sent to their final destination along the Z dimension.

In a quiet similar technique, Chao (2010) addressed the thermal power problem in 3D-NoC, which is one of the most important issues in the 3D-NoC designs. Starting from the fact the upper layer in the network detains the highest thermal power in the design, they proposed a thermal aware downward routing scheme that sends first the traffic to a downer layer, routes along the X and Y dimension before sending the packets back up to their destination layer. This technique avoids communication in upper layers, where the thermal power is more important than the downer ones, and then may reduce the overall thermal power in the design. Thus, ensuring thermal safety while guaranteeing less performance impact from temperature regulation.

Both of these two routing algorithms have their advantages in term of load balancing and thermal power reduction. But the routing used is not minimal, which effect in a direct way the number of hops. By adopting a non-minimal routing, the packet delay may increase in the system, especially when we talk about a large number of connected nodes.

To ensure a minimal path for flits when traveling the network while making the routing as simple as possible, the majority of the remaining 3D-NoC systems have been using the conventional minimal Dimension Order Routing (DOR) XYZ routing scheme. Other introduced a routing scheme based upon XYZ such as the case of *Tyagi* in Tyagi (2009) who extended a previous routing algorithm (Montana 2009) called *BDOR* designated for 2D-NoC. *BDOR* forwards packets in one of two routes (XY- or YX-orders), depending on relative position of a source-destination pair, and that aims to improve the balance of paths along the network also when taking into account the destination.

XYZ routing scheme, and all the routing algorithms based upon it, is presented as a vertically balanced routing algorithm which has the best performance, since it's simple to implement, it is free of deadlock and life-lock, and also because packet ordering is not required (Chao 2010; Lahiri 2000; Dev 2002). On the other hand, it cannot always make the best use of each pipeline stage. For the simple reason that since the Switch Allocation stage (SA) is always dependent on the previous Routing Calculation (RC) one. This dependency can be explained by the fact that SA stage needs information about the desired output-port calculated from the RC stage, where the incoming flits should go through in order to pass to the next neighboring node. To solve this problem in 2D-NoC systems using the Dimension Order Routing (DOR) XY routing scheme, a smart pipeline design can be adopted with the help of some advanced techniques like look-ahead routing (Tyagi 2009). This kind of routing has been used to reduce the pipeline stages in the router, by parallelizing some of these stages then reducing the router delay and then enhancing the system performance. Look-ahead routing has indeed been used with 2D-NoC but it hasn't been adopted for 3D Network-on-Chip architectures before.

A second problem that can be seen with a lot of conventional router using XYZ-based routing schemes, is in case of no-load traffic and when the input buffer is empty, the flit entering the router should be first stored in the input buffer before advancing the next RC stage even there is no any flit under process in the next stages. This unnecessary stall will increase the packet latency in the router, and its associated power consumption, adding a performance overhead to the whole system even in a light traffic case where the system is supposed to have a close-to-optimal performance since there is no congestion that may increase the latency. In order to face this problem, a technique called no-load bypass is used (Xin 2010). This technique allows the flit to advance to the RC stage in case where the buffer is empty. Then overlapping the unnecessary buffer writing stage (BW) then decreasing the router delay.

Previously in Ben (2010), a part of this research has been including architecture of a 3D Network-on-Chip architecture (named 3D-OASIS-NoC) based on a previously designed 2D-OASIS-NoC. The design's performance was evaluated using a simple application that randomly generates flits and sends them along the network. But real application could not be evaluated due to the absence of some components in the design such us the network interface. For that reason, a network interface has been added to 3D-ONoC, the optimized version of 3D-OASIS-NoC, in order to make our system able to be evaluated with our real selected target applications (JPEG encoder and Matrix Multiplication).

In this chapter we present a complete architecture and design of 3D-OASIS-NoC. Also evaluation results are presented using real applications (JPEG encoder and Matrix Multiplication). We provide more details about the different components of 3D-OASIS-NoC including a new Look-ahead-XYZ routing scheme (LA-XYZ) and its ability to take advantage of the simplicity of the conventional XYZ algorithm, while improving the pipeline design of the 3D-NoC router then enhancing the overall performance. The lookahead routing scheme means that each flit additionally carries one hot encoded *Next-Port* identifier used by the downstream router. The no-load bypass technique is also associated with LA-XYZ in order to get more pipeline improvement.

## 5.2 Topology Design

3D-ONoC is a scalable Network-on-Chip based on *Mesh* topology. The packets are forwarded among the network using *Wormhole-like* switching policy and then routed according to *Look-Ahead-XYZ* routing algorithm (LA-XYZ). Many topologies exist for the implementation of NoCs, some are regular (*Torus, tree-based*) and other irregular topologies are customized for some special application. We choose the Mesh topology for this design thanks to its several properties like regularity, concurrent data transmission, and controlled electrical parameters (Glass 1992; Hu 2003).

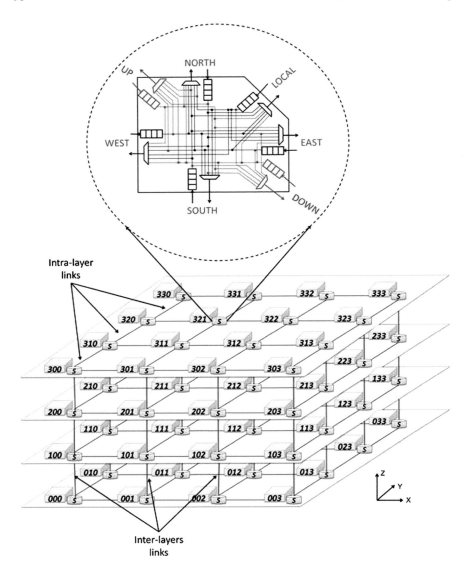

**Fig. 5.2** Configuration example of a 4×4×4 3D-ONoC based on mesh topology

Figure 5.2 shows a configuration example of 4×4×4 3D-ONoC design. We can see in this figure that different layers are linked between each other via inter-layer channels. On the other side, each layer is composed of different switches which are connected to each other using some intra-layer links, each one of them is connected to one single processing element.

Code 5.1 illustrates the RTL (in Verilog-HDL) code of the 3D-ONoC top module that defines the mesh topology. The z-loop, y-loop and x-loop are used to define the dimensions of 3D-NoC. While the internal i-loop (line 17) is used to define the different input and output ports for each direction. For example, $i = 0$ refers to the local port where, the outputs and inputs of this port will be allocated later to the attached PE.

Taking the example of the *Down port* (line 31–39) , the output and input of this port are allocated to the UP port of the router situated just below the current router, which means the one in the downer layer. As it will be explained later, the unused ports should eliminated in order to reduce the area and power consumption. Continuing with the same *Down port*, it should be disabled when the router is located at the bottom of the topology, which means when $z - pos = 0$. In this case, as it is illustrated in Code 5.1 (line 32–35), net-data-in and net-stop-in are assigned to 0.

Code 5.1: Verilog-HDL code for topology design.

```
generate
//z loop
for (z_pos=0; z_pos<Z_WIDTH; z_pos=z_pos+1) begin:z_loop

    //y loop
    for (y_pos=0; y_pos<Y_WIDTH; y_pos=y_pos+1) begin:y_loop

    //x loop
    for (x_pos=0; x_pos<X_WIDTH; x_pos=x_pos+1) begin:x_loop

    router #(NOUT, FIFO_DEPTH, FIFO_LOG2D, FIFO_FULL_LVL) rtr(.clk(clk), .reset(
        reset),
        .data_in(net_data_in[x_pos][y_pos][z_pos]), .data_out(net_data_out[x_pos][
            y_pos][z_pos]),
        .stop_in(net_stop_in[x_pos][y_pos][z_pos]), .stop_out(net_stop_out[x_pos][
            y_pos][z_pos]),
        .xaddr(x_pos['L2NET_SIZE-1:0]), .yaddr(y_pos['L2NET_SIZE-1:0]), .zaddr(
            z_pos['L2NET_SIZE-1:0]));

    //set up inter-router connections with correct boundary conditions
    for (i=0; i<NOUT; i=i+1) begin:i0

        //tile interface of router
        if(i==0) begin
    assign net_data_in[x_pos][y_pos][z_pos]['WIDTH*(i+1)-1:'WIDTH*i] = data_in
        [('WIDTH*X_WIDTH*z_pos*Y_WIDTH)+('WIDTH*X_WIDTH*y_pos)+ ('WIDTH*(x_pos
        +1))-1: ('WIDTH*X_WIDTH*z_pos*Y_WIDTH)+('WIDTH*X_WIDTH*y_pos)+('WIDTH*
        x_pos)];
    assign data_out[('WIDTH* X_WIDTH*z_pos*Y_WIDTH)+('WIDTH*X_WIDTH*y_pos)+('
        WIDTH*(x_pos+1))-1: ('WIDTH*X_WIDTH*z_pos*Y_WIDTH) +('WIDTH*X_WIDTH*
        y_pos)+ ('WIDTH*x_pos)] = net_data_out[x_pos][y_pos][z_pos]['WIDTH*(i+1)
        -1:'WIDTH*i];

    assign net_stop_in[x_pos][y_pos][z_pos][i] = stop_in[(X_WIDTH* z_pos *
        Y_WIDTH)+(X_WIDTH*y_pos)+x_pos];
    assign stop_out[(X_WIDTH* z_pos * Y_WIDTH)+(X_WIDTH*y_pos)+x_pos] =
        net_stop_out[x_pos][y_pos][z_pos][i];
        end
...
```

## 5.3 Switching Policy

Considered as a very important choice for any NoC design, switching establishes the type of connection between any upstream and downstream node. It is important to deploy an efficient switching policy to ensure less blocking communication while trying to minimize the system complexity. When it is related to packet switching, three main switching policies have been mostly used for NoC: *Store and Forward (SAF)*, *Virtual Cut Through (VCT)* and *Wormhole (WH)* (Rasmussen 2006).

Code 5.2: Verilog-HDL code for flit design.

```
// Flit structure
'define DATA          37:0
'define TAIL          0
'define NEXT_PORT     7:1
'define XDEST         10:8
'define YDEST         13:11
'define ZDEST         16:14
'define DATA          37:17
```

3D-ONoC adopts *Wormhole-like* switching and Virtual-Cut-Through forwarding method. The forwarding method which is chosen in a given instance depends on the level of packet fragmentation. For instance, each router in 3D-ONoC has input buffers which can store up to four flits by default. When a packet is divided into more than four flits, 3D-ONoC chooses Virtual-Cut-Through switching. When packets are divided into less than four flits, the system chooses Wormhole. In other words, when buffer size is greater than or equal to the number of flits, Virtual-Cut-Through is used, but when buffer size is less than or equal to the number of flits, Wormhole switching is employed. By combining the benefits of both switching techniques, packet forwarding can be executed in an efficient way while guaranteeing a small buffer size. As a result the system performance is enhanced while maintaining a reasonable area utilization and power consumption.

## 5.3.1 Flit Format Design

Figure 5.3 shows the 3D-ONoC flit format. The first bit indicates the *tail* bit informing the end of the packet. The next 7-bit are dedicated for the *Next-Port* that will be used by the *Look-Ahead-XYZ* routing algorithm to define the direction of the next downstream neighboring node where the flit will be sent to. Then, 3-bit are used to store destination information of each *xdest*, *ydest* and *zdest*. Having 3-bit for each destination field allows the network to have a maximum size of $8 \times 8 \times 8$ 3D-ONoC. But if the network size needs to be extended, the addresses fields may also be increased to accommodate a larger network size. Finally the

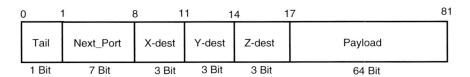

**Fig. 5.3** 3D-ONOC flit format

remaining 64 bits are dedicated to store the payload. Since 3D-ONoC is targeted for various applications, the payload size can be easily modified in order to respect the requirements of some specific applications. Code 5.2 shows the structure of the 3D-ONoC flit. In addition, as we previously stated, the architecture does not provide for a separate head flit and every flit therefore identifies its destination X, Y, and Z addresses and carries an additional single bit to indicate whether it is a tail flit or not.

## 5.4 3D-NoC Router Architecture Design

The router is considered as the back-bone element in the whole 3D-ONoC design. The 3D-ONoC router architecture is based upon the $5 \times 5$ 2D-ONoC router where, as shown in Fig. 5.2, each switch has a maximum number of 7-input by 7-output port, where 4 ports are dedicated to connect to the neighboring routers in north, east, south and west direction using the intra-layer links. One port is used to connect the router to the local computation tile where the packet can be injected into or ejected from the network. The remaining two ports are added to connect the switch to the upper and downer layers to ensure the inter-layer communication.

As we previously stated, the number of ports depends on the position of the switch in the design, since we have to eliminate any unused links that have no connections with other switches in order to reduce power consumption. For example, as it is depicted in Fig. 5.2, switch-000 have only four connected ports (north, east, up and local) and the remaining three ports (south, west and down) have been disabled since there are no connections to any neighboring routers along those directions.

Figure 5.4 represents 3D-ONoC router architecture and that the routing process at each router can be defined by three main pipeline stages: Buffer writing (BW), Routing Calculation and Switch Allocation (RC/SA), and the Crossbar Traversal stages (CT). Observing the Verilog HDL code for the *Router* module depicted in Code 5.3, 3D-ONoC contains seven *Input-port* modules for each direction represented in *input-port* module in line 4. This seven modules allocation are defined by the i-loop in line 2, where each value of i refers to the seven direction (Local, North, East, South, West, Up, Down), and *NOUT* parameter in line 2 refers to the number of ports. The outputted *sw-req* signal defining the input port asking the grant and the output port requested defined by the *port-req* signal are sent from the seven input port to be an input port for the Switch allocator as it shown at line 19 and 20 of Code 5.3.

In addition to the *Switch-Allocator*, the *Crossbar* module is also defined (line 22–25). The crossbar circuit takes as input the *sw-cntrl* from the switch allocator and *data-in* coming from the seven input ports.

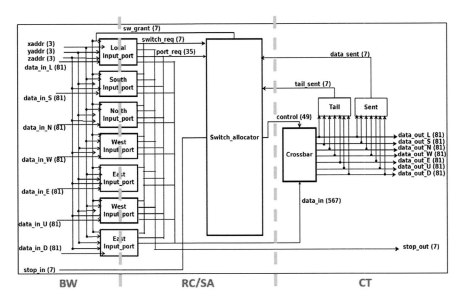

**Fig. 5.4** 3D-ONoC pipeline stages: Buffer writing (BW), Routing Calculation and Switch Allocation (RC/SA) and Crossbar Traversal stage (CT)

Code 5.3: Verilog-HDL code for Router.

```
//instantiate input ports
for (i=0; i<NOUT; i=i+1) begin:il

  input_port #(NOUT, FIFO_DEPTH, FIFO_LOG2D, FIFO_FULL_LVL) ip
    (.clk(clk), .reset(reset),
     .data_in(data_in['WIDTH*(i+1)-1:'WIDTH*i]),
     .data_out(cbar_data_in['WIDTH*(i+1)-1:'WIDTH*i]),
     .sw_req(sw_req[i]), .port_req(port_req[NOUT*(i+1)-1:NOUT*i]),
     .sw_grant(sw_grant[i]), .stop_out(stop_out[i]),
     .xaddr(xaddr), .yaddr(yaddr), .zaddr(zaddr));

  assign data_sent[i] = |data_out['WIDTH*i+'NEXT_PORT_END:'WIDTH*i+'
    NEXT_PORT_START];
  assign tail_sent[i] = data_out['WIDTH*i];

 end
endgenerate

  sw_alloc #(NOUT) sw_allc(.clk(clk), .reset(reset),
 .sw_req(sw_req), .stop_in(stop_in), .data_sent(data_sent), .tail_sent(
    tail_sent),
 .port_req(port_req), .grant_out(sw_grant), .sw_cntrl(sw_cntrl));

  crossbar #(NOUT, NOUT, 'WIDTH) cbar(.clk(clk), .reset(reset),
         .cntrl(sw_cntrl),
         .data_in(cbar_data_in),
         .data_out(data_out));
```

Now we analyze each component of the switch separately. Starting with the *Input-port*, the *Switch-Allocator* and finally *Crossbar* module.

### 5.4.1 Input-Port Module Design

Starting with the *Input-port* module represented in Fig. 5.5 (and where the Verilog code is represented in Code 5.4), each one of the seven modules is composed of two main elements: *Input buffer* and the *Route* module.

Code 5.4: Verilog-HDL code for Input-port.

```
//instantiate FIFO
  fifo #(NOUT, FIFO_DEPTH, FIFO_LOG2D, FIFO_FULL_LVL) ff
      (.data_in(data_in), .data_out(fifo_data_out),
       .second_item_nextport(second_fifo_nextport),
        .enqueue(enqueue), .dequeue(sw_grant),
        .stop_out(stop_out), .nearly_empty(fifo_nearly_empty),
       .empty(fifo_empty),
        .clk(clk), .reset(reset));

//instantiate lookahead routing module
  route #(NOUT) rr
      (.xdest(fifo_data_out['XDEST]), .ydest(fifo_data_out['YDEST]),.zdest(
          fifo_data_out['ZDEST]),
       .xaddr(xaddr), .yaddr(yaddr), .zaddr(zaddr),
       .nextport(fifo_data_out['NEXT_PORT]), .new_nextport(lookahead_route));
```

Incoming 81-bit flits *data-in* from different neighboring switches, or from the connected computation tile, are first stored in the *Input buffer* and waiting to be processed. This step is considered as the first pipeline stage of the flit's life-cycle (BW). As it is illustrated in Code 5.5, arbitration between different flits is managed using FIFO queue technique. Each input buffer has by default four as depth, which means that it can host up to four 81 bits flits. Buffers occupy a significant portion of router area but can imply also increase in overall performance.

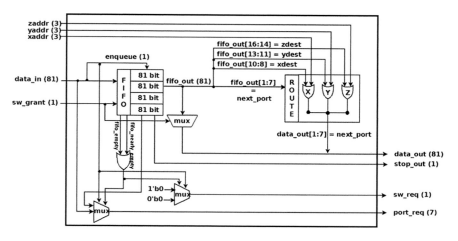

**Fig. 5.5** Input-port module architecture

Code 5.5 Verilog-HDL Code for Input-FIFO-buffer.

```
always @(posedge clk) begin
 if (!reset) begin       //If out of reset
  if (enqueue) begin //Write a flit to the buffer
  fifo[tail_ptr] <= data_in;
  tail_ptr <= tail_ptr + 1;
  end
  if (dequeue) begin //Read a flit from the buffer
  head_ptr <= head_ptr + 1;
  end
//nearly full signal = stop_out,
  if (((tail_ptr + FULL_LVL[LOG2D-1:0] + 1'b1)==head_ptr) && enqueue && !
      dequeue)begin
  stop_out <= 1'b1;
  end
  if (((tail_ptr + FULL_LVL[LOG2D-1:0])==(head_ptr+1'b1)) && !enqueue &&
      dequeue)begin
  stop_out <= 1'b1;
  end
  if ((tail_ptr + FULL_LVL[LOG2D-1:0])==head_ptr)begin
  if ((enqueue && !dequeue) || (!enqueue && dequeue))begin
   stop_out <= 1'b0;
  end
...
```

After being stored, the flit is fetched form the *FIFO* buffer and advanced to the next pipeline stage (RC/SA). The destination addresses (*xdest*, *ydest* and *zdest*) are then decoded in order to extract the information about the destination address in addition to the *Next-Port* pre-calculated in the previous upstream node. Those values are then sent to the *Route* circuit where La-XYZ routing scheme is executed to determine the *New-next-Port* direction for the next downstream node. At the same time the *Next-Port* identifier is also used to generate the request for the *Switch-Allocator* asking for grant to use the selected output port via *sw-req* and *port req* signals.

As we stated in previous section, 3D-ONoC uses lookahead routing scheme *LA-XYZ* for fast routing. This scheme is based upon the dimension order (DOR) X-Y-Z static routing algorithm, where the X,Y and Z coordinates are satisfied in order. X-Y-Z routing is presented as the vertically balanced routing algorithm which has the best performance, since it's simple to implement, it is free of deadlock and live-lock, and also because packet ordering is not required. In addition to that each flit additionally carries one hot encoded *Next-Port* identifier used by the downstream router. Since *LA-XYZ* is based upon *XYZ* routing, it is considered also as a minimal routing where each flit from any source and destination pair traverses the minimal number of hops.

## 5.4.2 Semi-Adaptive Look-Ahead Routing

To understand better how the *Next-Port* is decided, we designed the Verilog HDL code depicted in Code 5.6. As it is shown in this Code (line 1–12), the routing decision starts first by finding the next node's address. It is done by evaluating the actual *Next-Port* fetched from the flit, which gives a hint about which neighboring node the flit is going to be routed to and eventually knowing its exact address by incrementing *xaddr* or *yaddr* or *zaddr*. Depending on the resulted next address from the later step, the new *Next-Port* can be determined. As demonstrated between line 15 and 31 in Code 5.6, *LA-XYZ* compares the resulted next node's address (*next-xaddr*, *next-yaddr* and *next-zaddr*) and the destination addresses (*xdest*, *ydest* and *zdest*). At the end of the execution of this comparison, the new *Next-Port* (defined by *route* in Code 5.6) can be determined then embedded in the flit back again to be sent to the next node as Fig. 5.5 illustrates.

Code 5.6 Verilog HDL implementation of LA-XYZ routing algorithm.

```
//assign next addresses
 if (nextport == 'EAST) next_xaddr = xaddr + 1'b1;
  else if (nextport == 'WEST) next_xaddr = xaddr - 1'b1;
    else next_xaddr = xaddr;

 if (nextport == 'NORTH) next_yaddr = yaddr + 1'b1;
    else if (nextport == 'SOUTH) next_yaddr = yaddr - 1'b1;
      else next_yaddr = yaddr;

       if (nextport == 'UP) next_zaddr = zaddr + 1'b1;
    else if (nextport == 'DOWN) next_zaddr = zaddr - 1'b1;
      else next_zaddr = zaddr;

//evaluate next port
 if (next_xaddr == xdest)
 begin   if (next_yaddr == ydest)
 begin   if (next_zaddr == zdest) route = 'SELF;
  else begin if(next_zaddr < zdest) route = 'UP;
             else route = 'DOWN;
       end
  end
    else  begin
    if(next_yaddr < ydest) route = 'NORTH;
    else route = 'SOUTH;
    end
 end
 else  begin
    if (next_xaddr < xdest) route = 'EAST;
      else route = 'WEST;
 end
end
```

If we take a look at Fig. 5.2, and assume for example that a flit coming from switch-200 enters switch-201 (where the *xaddr*, *yaddr* and *zaddr* addresses are defined by 001, 000 and 001 respectively) trying to reach its destination node switch-313 (where the *xdest*, *ydest* and *zdest* addresses are defined by 011, 001 and 011 respectively). This flit caries "EAST" as a *nextport* identifier pre-calculated in the previous node (switch-200). According to the he first phase of the LA-XYZ algorithm, *next-xaddr= xaddr+1* which is the x-address of switch-202. In the second phase of the algorithm, *next-xaddr* is then compared with *xdest*. The comparison result will determine "EAST" as *route* (the new *Next-Port* for switch-202) which will be re-updated in the flit.

In order to enable the bypass technique, two signals are issued from the buffer to give information about the buffer occupancy status. These two signals are *fifo-empty* and *fifo-nearly-empty*. When the *fifo-empty* signal is issued, it means that the

input buffer is empty and when an incoming flit arrives to the input port, it doesn't
need to be stored in the buffer. Then overlapping the buffering stage and advancing
to the next stage (RC and SA).

## 5.4.3 Switch Allocator Design

The *sw-req* and *port req* signals issued from each *Input-port* module, and giving
information about the desired output-port, are transmitted to the *Switch-Allocator*
module to perform the arbitration between the different requests. When more than
two input flits from different input-ports are requesting the same output-port at the
same time, the *Switch-Allocator* manages to decide which output-port should be
granted to which input-port, and when this grant should be allocated. This process
is done in parallel with the routing computation done in *Input-port* to form the
second pipeline stage.

As indicated in Fig. 5.6, the switch allocator circuit has two output signals: one
is *sw-cntrl* and the second one is *grant-out*. *sw-cntrl* contains all the information
needed by the crossbar circuit about the scheduling result as it is explained later.

On the other hand, the *grant-out* is sent back to the *Input-port* module and gives
the grant to the appropriate input-port to send its data to the crossbar before
reaching its next neighboring node. Figure 5.6 shows that the switch allocator
module is composed of two main components: *Stall-Go flow control* and *Matrix-
Arbiter Scheduling*.

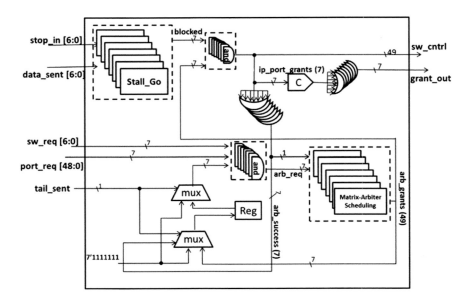

**Fig. 5.6** Switch allocator architecture

### 5.4.4 Stall-Go Flow Control Architecture

Like the other flow control schemes, *Stall-Go* module manages the case of the buffer overflow. When the buffer exceeds its limitation on hosting flits (if the number of flits waiting for process are greater than the depth of the buffer), a flow control has to be considered to prevent from buffer overflow and eventually from packet dropping. Thus, allocating available resources to packets as they progress along their route. We chose *Stall-Go* flow control since it proves to be a low-overhead efficient design choice showing remarkable performance comparing to the other flow control schemes such us *ACK-NACK* or *Credit based* flow control.

Like the other flow control schemes, *Stall-Go* module manages the case of the buffer overflow. When the buffer exceeds its limitation on hosting flits (if the number of flits waiting for process are greater than the depth of the buffer), a flow control has to be considered to prevent from buffer overflow and eventually from packet dropping. Thus, allocating available resources to packets as they progress along their route. We chose *Stall-Go* flow control since it proves to be a low-overhead efficient design choice showing remarkable performance comparing to the other flow control schemes such us *ACK-NACK* or *Credit based* flow control (Pullini 2005).

Code 5.7 Verilog HDL of the state machine decision.

```
   always @(posedge clk) begin

if (!reset) begin
 if ((state=='GO) && stop_in && data_sent)
  state <= 'SENT1;
 if (state=='SENT1) begin
  if (stop_in && !data_sent)
   state <= 'GO;
  if (!stop_in && data_sent)
   state <= 'STOP;
 end

if ((state=='STOP) && stop_in) // stop_in = nearly_full
 state <= 'GO;
   end else
 state <= 'GO;
end

   assign blocked = ( ((state=='STOP) && !stop_in) || ((state=='SENT1) && !
      stop_in && data_sent) );
```

*Stall-Go* module, where the mechanism is represented in Fig. 5.7, uses two control signals: *nearly-full* and *data-sent*. *nearly-full* signal is sent to the upstream node indicating that the input-buffer is almost full and only one slot is still available to host one last flit. After receiving this signal, the *FIFO* buffers suspend sending flits. The *data-sent* signal is issued when the flit is transmitted. Figure 5.8 represents the *Stall-Go* flow control state machine which aims to generate the *nearly-full* and *data-sent* signals. State *GO* indicates that the buffer is still able to host two or more flits. State *SENT* indicates that the buffer can host only one more flit, and finally when we move to state *STOP*, it means that the buffer can not store anymore flits. The state machine is generated as indicated in Code 5.7 that shows

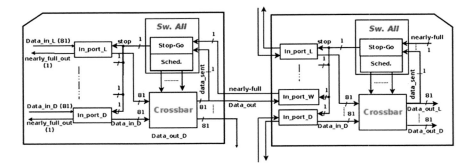

**Fig. 5.7** Stall-Go flow control mechanism

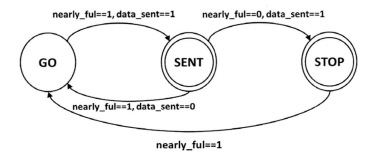

**Fig. 5.8** Stall-Go flow control finite state machine

the Verilog-HDL code explaining the main state transitions using *nearly-full* and *data-sent* signals.

### 5.4.5 Matrix-Arbiter Scheduling Architecture

The second component is the scheduling module. As shown in Fig. 5.9, the input signals *sw-req* and *port-req* indicate the input-ports demanding the access, and which output-ports are they requesting respectively. Depending on these requests, the arbiter allocates the convenient output-port to its demander. Since 3D-ONoC transmits only one flit in every clock cycle, then when two input-ports or more are competing for the same output-port, the presence of a scheduling scheme is required in order to prevent from any possible conflict. The switch allocator in our design employs a least recently served priority scheme via the packet transmit layer. Thus, it can treat each communication as a partially fixed transmission latency (Gold 2004; Fu 2010). Matrix arbiter is used for a least recently served priority scheme.

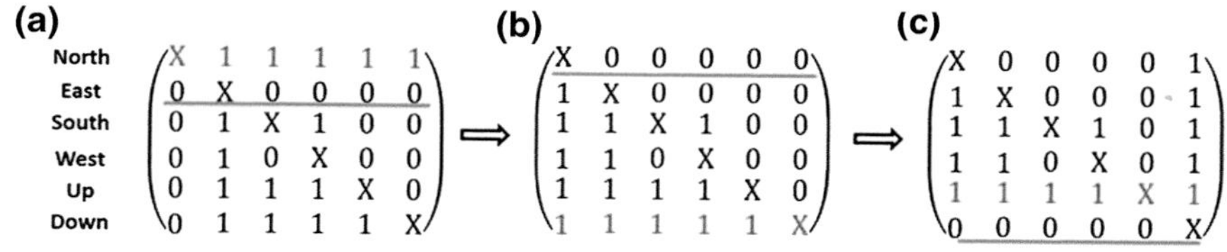

**(a)**

|        | X | 1 | 1 | 1 | 1 | 1 |
|--------|---|---|---|---|---|---|
| North  | X | 1 | 1 | 1 | 1 | 1 |
| East   | 0 | X | 0 | 0 | 0 | 0 |
| South  | 0 | 1 | X | 1 | 0 | 0 |
| West   | 0 | 1 | 0 | X | 0 | 0 |
| Up     | 0 | 1 | 1 | 1 | X | 0 |
| Down   | 0 | 1 | 1 | 1 | 1 | X |

$\Longrightarrow$

**(b)**

| X | 0 | 0 | 0 | 0 | 0 |
|---|---|---|---|---|---|
| 1 | X | 0 | 0 | 0 | 0 |
| 1 | 1 | X | 1 | 0 | 0 |
| 1 | 1 | 0 | X | 0 | 0 |
| 1 | 1 | 1 | 1 | X | 0 |
| 1 | 1 | 1 | 1 | 1 | X |

$\Longrightarrow$

**(c)**

| X | 0 | 0 | 0 | 0 | 1 |
|---|---|---|---|---|---|
| 1 | X | 0 | 0 | 0 | 1 |
| 1 | 1 | X | 1 | 0 | 1 |
| 1 | 1 | 0 | X | 0 | 1 |
| 1 | 1 | 1 | 1 | X | 1 |
| 0 | 0 | 0 | 0 | 0 | X |

**Fig. 5.9** Scheduling-matrix priority assignment

In order to adopt Matrix arbiter scheduling for 3D-ONoC, we implemented a $6\times6$ scheduling-matrix. The scheduling module accepts all the requests from the different connected input-ports and their requested output-ports. Then it assigns priority for each request. In order to give the grant to the convenient input-port, the scheduling module verifies the scheduling-matrix, compares the priorities of the input-ports competing for the same output-port, and gives the grant to the one possessing the highest priority in the matrix. Following this basis, the scheduling module should make the input-port, which got the last grant to use the competed output-port, the lowest priority for the next round of arbitration, and then increases the priority of the rest of the remaining ports. When there are no requests, the priority is unchanged. Based on these assumptions, we are sure that every input-port will be served and get the grant to use the output-port in a fair way.

Figure 5.9 illustrates a simple example of how our scheduling mechanism works. Each row of the matrix represents the competing input requests and their priorities. The scheduling-module starts by examining the priorities of each input-port request. After the highest priority input is served, the arbiter updates the scheduling-matrix by making the request which got the last grant, the lowest priority for the next round of arbitration, by inversing its row and column.

The matrix shown in Fig. 5.9a illustrates the initial scheduling-matrix where *North*, *Up* and *Down* input-ports are asking the grant to eject their flits to the *Local* port. Observing this figure, the *North* request (highlighted in red) has higher priorities compared with the remaining two requests. As a result the Arbiter gives the grant to the *North* request. Then *North* becomes the lowest priority (as it is underlined by a green line) and the remaining two requests priorities are incremented. In the next round (Fig. 5.9b), *Down* seems to have a higher priority than the *Up* request. The arbiter then gives the grant to *Down* and make its priority the lowest. Finally, as it is shown in Fig. 5.9c, the *Up* request having the highest priority among the others, is giving the grant to eject its data to the requested output port. Code 5.8 depicts the Verilog HDL code for the implementation for the Matrix arbiter.

## Code 5.8 Matrix Arbiter code.

```
generate
for (i=0; i<SIZE; i=i+1) begin:ol1
 for (j=0; j<SIZE; j=j+1) begin:il1
  if (j==i)
   assign pri[i][j]=request[i];
  else
  if (j>i)
   assign pri[i][j]=!(request[j]&&state[j*SIZE+i]);
  else
  assign pri[i][j]=!(request[j]&&!state[i*SIZE+j]);
  end
     assign grant[i]=&pri[i];
end
endgenerate

generate
for (i=0; i<SIZE; i=i+1) begin:ol2
 for (j=0; j<SIZE; j=j+1) begin:il2
  assign new_state[j*SIZE+i]=(success&&((state[j*SIZE+i]&&!grant[j])||(grant[i
     ]))||(!success&&state[j*SIZE+i]);
     end
end
endgenerate

always@(posedge clk) begin
 if (reset) state<=-1;
 else begin
 if (|request) state<=new_state;
 end
end
```

## Code 5.9 Code for Crossbar circuit.

```
//crossbar.v
generate
 for (i=0;i<NOUT;i=i+1) begin:output_loop
 mux_out #(NIN, WIDTH) cbar_mux(.cntrl(cntrl_reg[NIN*(i+1)-1:NIN*i]), .data_in(
     data_in), .data_out(data_out[WIDTH*(i+1)-1:WIDTH*i]));
 end
endgenerate

//mux_out
generate
 //loop over each bit of data
 for (i=0;i<WIDTH;i=i+1) begin:bit_loop
  assign data_out[i] = mux(cntrl, data_bits[i]);
  //loop over each input channel
  for (j=0;j<n_in;j=j+1) begin:input_loop
   assign data_bits[i][j] = data_in[WIDTH*j+i];
  end
 end
endgenerate

function mux;
 input [n_in-1:0] cntrl;
 input [n_in-1:0] data_in;
 integer i;

begin
 mux = 0;
 for (i=0; i<n_in; i=i+1) begin
  if(cntrl[i] == 1'b1) mux = data_in[i];
 end
end
endfunction // mux
```

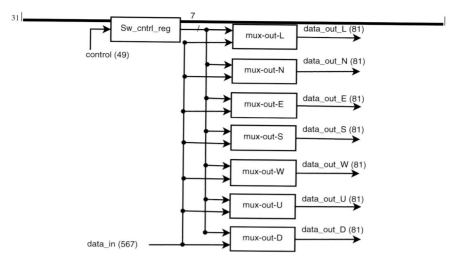

**Fig. 5.10** Crossbar circuit

## 5.4.6 Crossbar Design

The switch allocator, sends the issued *control* signal to the crossbar circuit to complete the third and final Crossbar Traversal pipeline stage (CT), where information about the selected input port and the *Next-Port* are embedded, and then stored in the *sw-cntrl-reg* register as it is shown in Fig. 5.10. After that, the crossbar fetches these information, receives the data from the FIFO buffer of the selected input-port. Then, it allocates the appropriate channel for transmission to the decoded *Next-Port*. Finally, the crossbar sends the flit to its destination as illustrated in Fig. 5.10. When all the flits are transmitted, the *tail* bit informs the switch allocator via a *tail-sent* signal that the packet transmission is completed and can free the used channel so it can be exploited by another packet. Code 5.9 depicts the Verilog HDL code for the implementation for the Crossbar circuit.

## 5.5 Network Interface Architecture

In order to enable real applications to be run on 3D-ONoC system, a Network Interface (NI) was added to every router as a medium interface between the different PEs (cores, memory, I/O, etc.). JPEG encoder application (Rosethal 2006) was used for evaluating the system performance. For this, both *Transmitter* and *Receiver* NI in every switch are designed. The packet size is set to 99-bit (3-bit flits). Each flit contains 17 bits defining the routing information (*xdst*, *ydst*, *zdst*, *Next-Port* and *tail*) and the remaining 16 bits are dedicated for the payload.

Code 5.10 Verilog-HDL sample code for the sending NI.

```verilog
module NI_02_send (clk, rst, enable, data_in, flit);
   input     clk, rst;
   input     enable;
   input  [23:0]  data_in;
   output reg [32:0]   flit;
     always @(state)begin
       case(state)
`f0:begin
     if(cntrl) begin
       next_state <= `f1;
   flit <= 33'hz;
     end
     else next_state <= `f1;
end
`f1:begin
     next_state <= `f3;
      flit[0]    <= `header;
     flit[7:1]   <= `EAST;
     flit[16:8]  <= `dest_03;
     flit[32:17] <= data_in[23:8];
end
`f2:begin
     if(cntrl) begin
     next_state <= `f3;
      flit[0]    <= `header;
     flit[7:1]   <= `EAST;
     flit[16:8]  <= `dest_03;
     flit[32:17] <= data_in[23:8];
     end
     else next_state <= `f2;
end
`f3:begin
     next_state <= `f4;
     flit[0]     <= `header;
     flit[7:1]   <= `EAST;
     flit[11:8]  <= `dest_03;
     flit[24:17] <= data_in[7:0];
     flit[32:25] <= 0;
end
`f4:begin
     next_state <= `f2;
     flit[0]     <= `tail;
     flit[7:1]   <= `EAST;
     flit[16:8]  <= `dest_03;
     flit[17]    <= enable;
     flit[32:18] <=  0;
end
default:next_state <= `f0;
     endcase
   end
```

Figure 5.11 shows the architecture of the *Transmitter-NI* and Fig. 5.12 shows the architecture of the *receiver-NI*.

The NI receives a 32 bits data from the JPEG module that will be divided into two portions representing the payload of the two first flits of the packet. The payload of the third flit contains the 10 bits control signal from the JPEG module, and the remaining six bits are unused.

As shown in Fig. 5.11, a *Control Module* manages the fits generation. It adds the convenient destination addresses and *Next-Port* direction to each flit, and marks the end of the packet by adding the (*tail* bit to the third final flit. The generated flits are then injected into the network. The Verilog HDL implementation of the *Transmitter-NI* is depicted in Code 5.10.

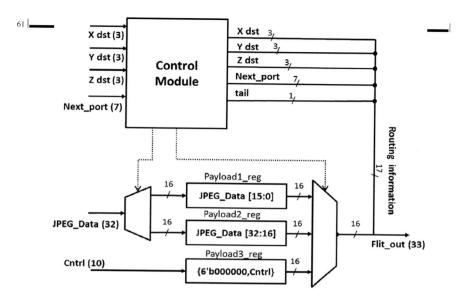

**Fig. 5.11** Network interface architecture: transmitter side

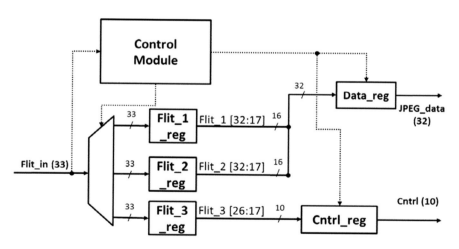

**Fig. 5.12** Network interface architecture: receiver side

Code 5.11 Verilog-HDL sample code for the receiving NI.

```verilog
module NI_03_rec (clk, rst, flit, data_out, enable);

//input output
   input     clk, rst;
   input [32:0]    flit;
   output reg [23:0]    data_out;
   output reg    enable;
   //reg
   reg [15:0]    data_high;
   reg [7:0]    data_low;
   reg       ena;

   reg [1:0]    state;
   reg [1:0]    next_state;
   reg [32:0]    preflit;

 reg [23:0]    pre_data_out;
   //state
   always @(posedge clk)begin
       if(rst==1)state <= 'f0;
       else begin
 preflit <= flit;
 state <= next_state;
       end
     end

   //state
   always @(state or flit)begin
       case(state)

'f0:begin
    if(flit!=preflit)begin
       next_state <= 'f1;
       data_high <= 0;
       data_low <= 0;
    end
    else next_state <= 'f1;
end
'f1:begin
    if(flit!=preflit)begin
       next_state <= 'f2;
       data_high <= flit[32:17];
    end
    else next_state <= 'f1;
end
'f2:begin
    if(flit!=preflit)begin
       next_state <= 'f3;
       data_low <= flit[24:17];
    end
    else next_state <= 'f2;
end
'f3:begin
    if(flit!=preflit)begin
       next_state <= 'f1;
       ena <= flit[17];
 pre_data_out <= {data_high, data_low};
    end
    else next_state <= 'f3;
end
default:next_state <= 'f0;
       endcase
     end
```

On the other side, the *Receiver-NI* receives the incoming three flits of each packet ejected from the network, and then stores them into three temporary registers. After that the 16 bits payload of the first and second flit are fetched form the temporary registers, reassembled together and finally stored in the *Data-reg* register. Controlled by another *Control Module*, the complete 32 bits resulted Data and the 10 bits control signals, are fetched the sent to their attached JPEG module after the complete packet is received.

The Verilog HDL implementation of the *Transmitter-NI* is depicted in Code 5.11. Based on this network interface, another one has been designed to satisfy the requirements of another application that we used for evaluating 3D-ONoC, which is Matrix-Multiplication. We chose the matrix multiplication as one of our evaluating target, since it is wildly used in scientific application. Due to its large multi-dimensional data array, it is extremely demanding in computation power and meanwhile it is potential to achieve its best performance in a parallel architecture and does not involve synchronization (Mandal 2009). All of these reasons make the Matrix-Multiplication a very suitable application to evaluate 3D-ONoC and show its outperforming performance against 2D-ONoC.

## 5.6 3D-ONoC Architecture Design Evaluation

In this section we evaluate the hardware complexity of 3D-ONoC in terms of area utilization, power consumption (static and dynamic) and clock frequency. JPEG encoder (Rosethal 2006) and Matrix-multiplication (Mandal 2009) applications were used. Execution time, the number of hops, and also the number of stall after the execution of the both of the application are also analyzed. Comparison research is also performed with 2D-NoC architecture.

### 5.6.1 JPEG Encoder on 3D-ONoC

JPEG encoder application is a well-known application and is widely used for evaluating systems which expose a lot of parallelism. For instance, we took into consideration the tasks implementation shown in Fig. 5.13. For additional analysis, we made further divisions to the *Y:d-q-h*, *Cb:d-q-h*, *Cr:d-q-h* and *FIFO* modules, and the resulted task graph is illustrated in Fig. 5.14. This extension aims to increase the network size and deploy more parallel execution of the different modules of the application, and then can take advantage of the scalability and the reduced number of hops in the design.

As we analyze the modified task graph represented in Fig. 5.14, we noticed that the communication bandwidth between *DCT*, *Quantization* and *Huffman* modules are very high (640 bits) compared with those found between the different other modules of the application (8, 24 and 32 bits). This bandwidth gap will cause unbalanced traffic distribution especially when implemented on hardware, since we will increase the link size in addition to the size and number of flits in the packet format, causing higher latency and thermal power problem. All these

**Fig. 5.13** Task graph of the
JPEG encoder

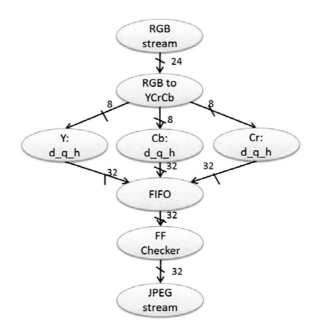

factors, will eventually decrease the overall performance of the system, instead of enhancing it.

For all the reasons previously stated, we will implement the first task graph represented in Fig. 5.13 and we randomly (for simplicity) map the tasks on 2D-ONoC (2×4) and 3D-ONoC (2×2×2) as shown in Figs. 5.15 and 5.16 respectively.

### 5.6.2 Matrix Multiplication on 3D-ONoC

First we assume that an $i{\times}k$ matrix $A$ has $i$ rows and $k$ columns, where $A_{ik}$ is an element of $A$ at the $i$-th row and $k$-th column. As it demonstrated in Fig. 5.17, an $i{\times}k$ matrix $A$ can be multiplied by a $k{\times}j$ matrix $B$ to obtain an $i{\times}j$ matrix $R$. Figure 5.18 presents how the matrix $R$ can be obtained according to Formula 5.1.

$$R_{i,j} = \sum_{n=0}^{k-1} A_{i,n}.B_{n,k} \tag{5.1}$$

When implemented onto 3D-ONoC, and for seek of convenience or without loss in generality, we can assume that all the matrices are square and having $n{\times}n$

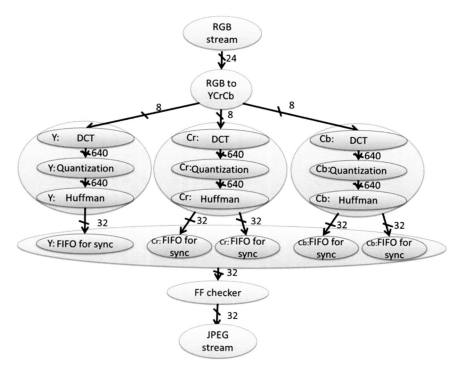

**Fig. 5.14** Extended task graph of the JPEG encoder

size. In 3D-ONoC, each element of the three matrices is assigned to a computation module which is connected to one router. As a result the number of routers connected to the network is the sum of all the elements of three matrices which is equal to $3n^2$. Each element of the matrix $B$ receives $n$ flits from $n$ different elements of the matrix $A$ in order to make the multiplication. Then, each element of

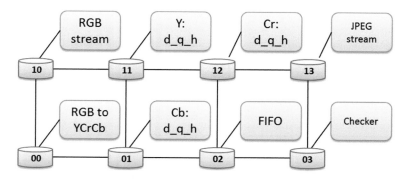

**Fig. 5.15** JPEG encoder mapped on $2 \times 4$ 2D-ONoC

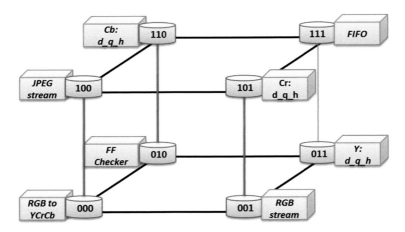

**Fig. 5.16** JPEG encoder mapped on: 2×2×2 3D-ONoC

$$\begin{pmatrix} A11 & \cdots & A1k \\ \vdots & \ddots & \vdots \\ Ai1 & \cdots & Aik \end{pmatrix} X \begin{pmatrix} B11 & \cdots & B1j \\ \vdots & \ddots & \vdots \\ Bk1 & \cdots & Bkj \end{pmatrix} = \begin{pmatrix} R11 & \cdots & R1j \\ \vdots & \ddots & \vdots \\ Ri1 & \cdots & Rij \end{pmatrix}$$

**Fig. 5.17** Matrix multiplication example: the multiplication of an $i \times k$ matrix $A$ by a $k \times j$ matrix $B$ results in an $i \times j$ matrix $R$

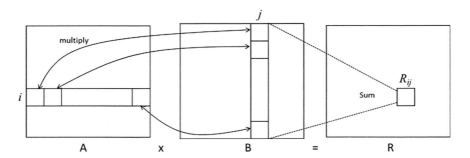

**Fig. 5.18** Simple example demonstrating the matrix multiplication calculation

the matrix $B$ sends $n$ flits to $n$ different elements of the matrix $R$ where all the received values are summed then the final resulted value is outputted. In total $2n^3$ flits travel the network for a $n \times n$ square matrix multiplication.

As we previously stated at the beginning of this section, we want to evaluate the number of hops traversed by all the flits generated by the Matrix application. For this matter we define:

$$3D\_Hops_i = |x\_dest_i - x\_src_i| + |y\_dest_i - y\_src_i| + |z\_dest_i - z\_src_i| \quad (5.2)$$

where $3D\_Hops_i$ is the number of hops consumed for one single flit $i \in \{0, 1, 2, \ldots, 2n^3 - 1\}$ (the set of all flits), traveling from one source node (where the address is defined by $x\_dest$, $y\_dest$ and $z\_dest$) to its destination node ($x\_src$, $y\_src$ and $z\_src$). As a result, we can say that the number of hops consumed by an $nxn$ square matrix multiplication can be defined by:

$$3D\_Total\_Hops = \sum_{k=0}^{2n^3-1} 3D\_Hops_k \tag{5.3}$$

According to Formulas 5.2 and 5.3, the number of hops for 2D-ONoC can be then extracted and defined as shown in Formulas 5.4 and 5.5.

$$2D\_Hops_i = |x\_dest_i - x\_src_i| + |y\_dest_i - y\_src_i| \tag{5.4}$$

$$2D\_Total\_Hops = \sum_{k=0}^{2n^3-1} 2D\_Hops_k \tag{5.5}$$

For the evaluation, we took the case of 3×3, 4×4 and finally a 6×6 matrix multiplication. For each one of these three cases, two mapping approaches has been taken into consideration. For instance, we take the example of 3×3 matrix multiplication. We randomly mapped the elements of the three matrices into 2D-ONoC (3×9) and 3D-ONoC (3×3×3) using an optimistic mapping approach as presented in Fig. 5.19a. In this mapping we tried to make the communication distance as close as possible, in order to reduce the number of hops which eventually will lead to decrease the latency. Figure 5.19b, on the other hand, illustrates a pessimistic task mapping approach. The second approach tries to increase the communication path of the different flits traversing the network.

In order to obtain an easier and more accurate evaluation both of 3D-ONC is implemented in Verilog HDL. We evaluated and compared the hardware complexity in terms of area, power consumption (static and dynamic) and clock frequency and also the performance in term execution time, the number of hops, and also we counted the number of *stop-signal* generated from our *Stall-Go* flow control mechanism. All the evaluation results obtained for 3D-ONoC are than compared to 2D-ONoC system.

We chose the Stratix III FPGA as a target device and then the synthesis was done by the Quartus II software, which both are provided by Altera. We used *PowerPlay Power Analyzer* tool in QuartusII in order to evaluate the power consumption generated. This design approach results in more accurate speed, area and power consumption evaluation. The use of FPGA is a very convenient choice for our design, thanks to its simplicity and the ability of reconfigurability. In addition to that, it provides faster simulation than the traditional software emulation while maintaining a cheaper cost than implementing with real processors. Table 5.1 presents the parameters used for the synthesis of 3D-ONoC design.

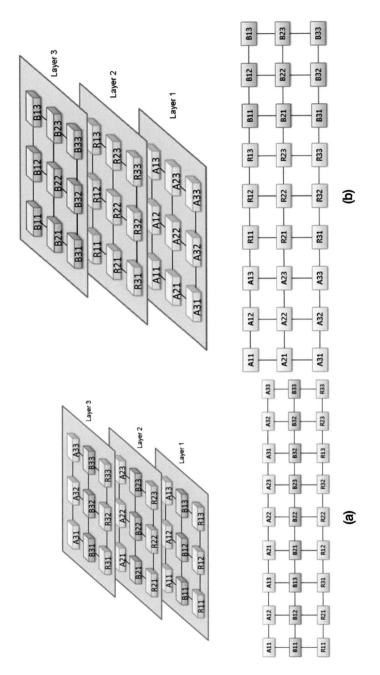

**Fig. 5.19** 3×3 matrix multiplication using (**a**) optimistic and (**b**) pessimistic mapping approaches

**Table 5.1** Simulation parameters

| Parameters | | 2D-ONoC | 3D-ONoC |
|---|---|---|---|
| Network size (Mesh) | JPEG | 2×4 | 2×2×2 |
| | Matrix (3×3) | 3×9 | 3×3×3 |
| | Matrix (4×4) | 6×8 | 4×4×3 |
| | Matrix (6×6) | 9×12 | 6×6×3 |
| Packet size | JPEG | 3 flits | 3 flits |
| | Matrix | 1 flit | 1 flit |
| Flit size | JPEG | 30 bits | 33 bits |
| | Matrix | 35 bits | 30 bits |
| Header size | JPEG | 12 bits | 17 bits |
| | Matrix | 14 bits | 17 bits |
| Payload size | JPEG | 16 bits | 16 bits |
| | Matrix | 21 bits | 21 bits |
| Buffer depth | | 4 | 4 |
| Switching | | Wormhole-like | Wormhole-like |
| Flow control | | Stall-Go | Stall-Go |
| Scheduling | | Matrix-Arbiter | Matrix-Arbiter |
| Routing | | LA-XY | LA-XYZ |
| Target device | | Altera Stratix III | Altera Stratix III |

## 5.6.3 Evaluation Results

The goal of this section is to provide a hardware evaluation for the 3D-ONoC including area, power consumption, and clock frequency when simulated with both JPEG encoder and Matrix multiplication applications. Table 5.2 illustrates the hardware evaluation results obtained. The results show that the logic utilization of 3D-ONoC is increased by an average of 37 % compared to the 2D design. The increased number of ALUTs can be explained by the fact that the 3D-ONoC router has two additional ports and a larger crossbar than 2D-ONoC. The additional number of ports incurs additional buffers, which is costly in term of area.

In term of clock speed 3D ONoC under-performs the 2D-ONoC architecture by 16 % on average due to the increased hardware complexity. While the power static consumption is increased with 3D-ONoC with almost 14 % for the same additional hardware reasons, the dynamic power on the other hands is decreased in

**Table 5.2** 3D-ONoC hardware complexity compared with 2D-ONoC

| Apps | Area (ALUTs) | | Power (mW) | | | | | | F (MHz) | |
|---|---|---|---|---|---|---|---|---|---|---|
| | 2D | 3D | 2D | | | 3D | | | 2D | 3D |
| | | | S | D | Total | S | D | Total | | |
| JPEG | 28.401 | 30.382 | 811.63 | 4.27 | 815.9 | 769.13 | 4.01 | 773.14 | 193.8 | 160.72 |
| M3×3 | 18.012 | 30.954 | 969.84 | 332 | 1301.84 | 1032.14 | 260 | 1292.14 | 158.73 | 130.01 |
| M4×4 | 36.393 | 61.157 | 1073.52 | 495.2 | 1568.72 | 1055.65 | 410 | 1452.65 | 146.56 | 101.41 |
| M6×6 | 89.576 | 144.987 | 1113.29 | 580 | 1693.29 | 1051.06 | 450.2 | 1501.26 | 98.85 | 98.1 |

average of 16 % while executing JPEG and the two mapping approaches foe each of the three matrix multiplications. As a conclusion, the total power consumption is decreased with nearly 1.4 %.

Many factors affect the dynamic power in FPGA, such us capacitance charging, supply voltage and clock frequency. Since the first two factors are the same for both 3D and 2D ONoC designs, and only the clock frequency is different between them, we can say that the reduction of the clock frequency had an impact on the reduction of the dynamic power. Besides that the clock frequency reduction, we believe that the reduction of number of hops (that will be explained in the next section) also plays an important role in the reduction of dynamic power. In fact, when the number of hops is reduced it means that the flit has less hops, shorter path which eventually means less buffering, routing and scheduling. All these factors lead to reduce the dynamic power when using 3D-ONoC when compared with 2D system.

## 5.6.4 Performance Analysis Evaluation

For the performance evaluation, we run each of the four applications. Then we evaluated the execution time, the number of hops and the number of *stop-signal* of each one of them after verifying the correctness of the resulted data. Starting with the execution time, we run each of the four applications on 3D-ONoC and 2D-ONoC. Figure 5.20 demonstrates the execution time results. Taking a closer look at the JPEG application results, we may see that there is a slight improvement of 1.4 % with 3D-ONoC when compared with the 2D architecture. This slight improvement can be explained by many reasons. First, JPEG is a small application which we could map into only eight nodes. That is a quiet small number to exploit the benefits of a 3D-NoC. Seconds, when observing the task graph of JPEG (previously shown in Fig. 5.13), JPEG has indeed some tasks working in parallel (*Y:d-q-h*, *Cb:d-q-h* and *Cr:d-q-h*), but at the same time we can see that *FIFO* module is dependent of those three tasks. Another reason is, the JPEG computation modules involve heavy computation. This leads to decrease the clock frequency of

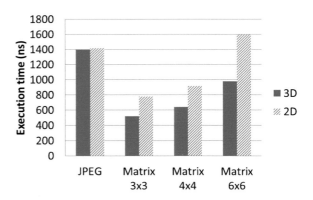

**Fig. 5.20** Execution time comparison between 3D and 2D ONoC

the entire system in a very inconvenient way for 3D-ONoC. The performance of 3D-ONoC is then hided and can't be taken advantage of. All of those reasons have an important impact on the performance of the 3D-ONoC. JPEG might be a very appropriate application to show the out performance of NoC over the traditional interconnect systems (such us bus-based system or P2P), but when we talk about 3D-ONoC that is targeted for hundreds of cores which is dedicated to a large number of cores with higher parallelism tasks.

On the other part, when evaluated with the Matrix multiplication application, 3D-ONoC shows a greater performance and decreases the execution time for about 35, 33 and 41 % for each of 3×3, 4×4 and 6×6 matrix respectively. In total 3D-ONoC reduces the execution time for one single Matrix multiplication to up to 36 % when compared with 2D-ONoC. As we stated previously, due to the fact that the Matrix multiplication has a larger data array, higher number of parallel tasks with less dependency between them, Matrix multiplication shows greater performance than JPEG. While the JPEG is mapped onto 8 nodes only, the matrix multiplication can reach the 108 nodes for the 6×6 matrix size. These factors are very suitable to show the performance enhancement when adopting 3D-ONoC. This enhancement can be related to the reduction of number of hops that offers 3D-ONoC.

Code 12: Verilog-HDL code for hops number count.

```
   for (i=1;i<=3;i=i+1)begin
   for (j=1;j<=3;j=j+1)begin
   for (k=1;k<=3;k=k+1)begin
      #200000
// ***************Hop count from A to B***************
     if ((A_adress [i][j][2:0])>(B_adress [j][k][2:0]))
     Total_hops= Total_hops+ ((A_adress [i][j][2:0])-(B_adress [j][k][2:0]));
     else
     Total_hops= Total_hops+ ((B_adress [j][k][2:0])-(A_adress [i][j][2:0]));

     if ((A_adress [i][j][5:3])>(B_adress [j][k][5:3]))
     Total_hops= Total_hops+ ((A_adress [i][j][5:3])-(B_adress [j][k][5:3]));
     else
     Total_hops= Total_hops+ ((B_adress [j][k][5:3])-(A_adress [i][j][5:3]));

     if ((A_adress [i][j][8:6])>(B_adress [j][k][8:6]))
     Total_hops= Total_hops+ ((A_adress [i][j][8:6])-(B_adress [j][k][8:6]));
     else
     Total_hops= Total_hops+ ((B_adress [j][k][8:6])-(A_adress [i][j][8:6]));

// ***************Hop count from B to R***************
     if ((B_adress [i][j][2:0])>(R_adress [k][j][2:0]))
     Total_hops= Total_hops+ ((B_adress [i][j][2:0])-(R_adress [k][j][2:0]));
     else
     Total_hops= Total_hops+ ((R_adress [k][j][2:0])-(B_adress [i][j][2:0]));

     if ((B_adress [i][j][5:3])>(R_adress [k][j][5:3]))
     Total_hops= Total_hops+ ((B_adress [i][j][5:3])-(R_adress [k][j][5:3]));
     else
     Total_hops= Total_hops+ ((R_adress [k][j][5:3])-(B_adress [i][j][5:3]));

     if ((B_adress [i][j][8:6])>(R_adress [k][j][8:6]))
     Total_hops= Total_hops+ ((B_adress [i][j][8:6])-(R_adress [k][j][8:6]));
     else
     Total_hops= Total_hops+ ((R_adress [k][j][8:6])-(B_adress [i][j][8:6]));
   end
  end
 end
```

Figures 5.21, 5.22, and 5.23 show the variation of the number of hops between 3D-ONoC and 2D-ONoC with 3×3, 4×4 and 6×6 matrix multiplications using pessimistic and optimistic mapping. The number of hops can be calculated using the Verilog code depicted in Code 5.12. This portion of code is added to the test bench that performs the calculation. When we analyze this figure, we may see that 3D-ONoC reduces the number of hops compared with the 2D system with an average percentage of 42, 31 and 47 % 3×3, 4×4 and 6×6 matrices respectively

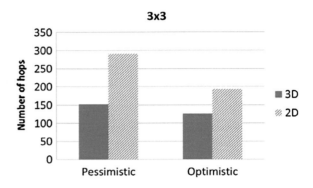

**Fig. 5.21** Average number of hops comparison for both pessimistic and optimistic mapping on 3×3 network size

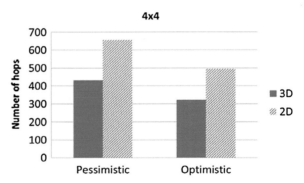

**Fig. 5.22** Average number of hops comparison for both pessimistic and optimistic mapping on 4×4 network size

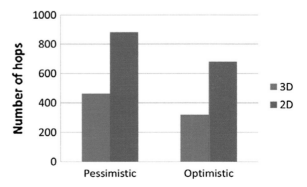

**Fig. 5.23** Average number of hops comparison for both pessimistic and optimistic mapping on 6×6 network size

having a total number of hops reduction of 40 % over the 2D architecture. This can significantly reduce the execution time, since flits have fewer hops to traverse to reach their destination.

Another reason contributing on the performance of 3D-ONoC is the reduction of the traffic congestion. This can be seen by observing the *Stall-Go* flow control and the number of *stop-signal* generated by each Matrix Multiplication. To execute this calculation, we added a small portion of code (Code 5.13) at the end at the end of the 3D-ONoC module, that uses the *net-stop-out* signal issued from the flow control and calculates the total stall count.

Code 5.13: Verilog-HDL code for stall count.

```
// 3D-ONoC top module: network.v

...
...

always @(reset) begin
if (reset) count <= 0;
end


always  @(net_stop_out)
begin : stop
  for (j=0;j<Y_WIDTH;j=j+1)begin
   for (k=0;k<X_WIDTH;k=k+1)begin
    for (l=0;l<NOUT;l=l+1)begin
    if (net_stop_out[k][j][l]) count = count+1;
    end
   end
  end
end
```

As a matter of fact when observing Fig. 5.24, we can see that the stall count increase linearly when we increase the matrix which is related to the number of flits traveling the network. Even 3D-ONoC can reach up to 77 % of stall count reduction over the 2D design with 6×6 Matrix multiplication, the stall count impact cannot be clearly seen with 3×3 and 4×4 calculation. This can simply explained by the fact that we are calculating a single matrix multiplication which generates only 54 and 128 flits for 3×3 and 4×4 matrix size respectively. This

**Fig. 5.24** Stall average count comparison between 3D and 2D ONoC

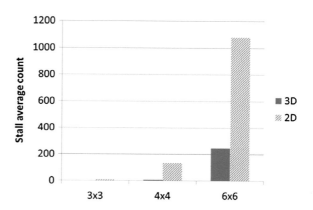

small number of flits was not enough to cause any traffic congestions in 3D-ONoC. For that reason, we decide to extend the evaluation to calculate not only one Matrix multiplication but also to calculate 2, 3 and 4 different matrices at the same. This aims to increase the number of flits traveling the network at the same time to cause congestion. Then we evaluate again the average stall count.

Figure 5.25, depicts the average stall count of both 3D and 2D ONoC when implemented with 1, 2, 3 and 4 matrix multiplications. When analyzing this figure, the stall count has been dramatically decreased to 94, 67 and 59 % in average for 3×3, 4×4 and 6×6 matrix Multiplication respectively. In total 3D-ONoC reduces the stall count to up to 74 %. After calculating the stall number, we want to see the impact of increasing the traffic congestion on the execution time. So evaluate again the execution time of each Matrix size when performing 1, 2, 3 and 4 matrix multiplications. The result obtained are shown in Fig. 5.26 reduces the execution time to 36, 39 and 47 % for 3×3, 4×4 and 6×6 matrix Multiplication respectively. Then improving the total execution time reduction from 36 %, obtained in the first experience with one matrix multiplication, to more than 41 % when evaluated with heavier traffic load.

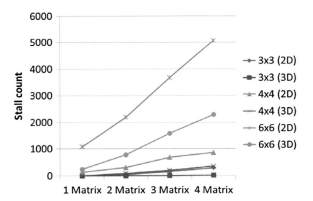

**Fig. 5.25** Stall average count comparison between 3D and 2D ONoC with different traffic loads

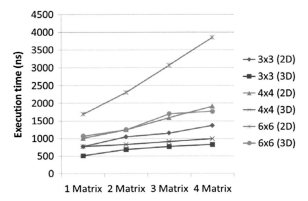

**Fig. 5.26** Execution time comparison between 3D and 2D ONoC with different traffic loads

As the results mentioned above, 3D-ONoC take advantage of its ability to reduce the number of hops to enhance the performance. In addition, since 3D-ONoC router has two additional input-output ports, flits traveling the network have better routing choices which eventually will decrease the congestion that can be caused when using 2D-ONoC, having an important impact on the overall performance of the system. Not forget to mention, this will improve the traffic balance along the whole network which plays a very crucial role on the thermal power dissipated from the design.

## 5.7   Conclusion

Future applications are getting more and more complex, demanding a good architecture to ensure a sufficient bandwidth for any transaction between memories and cores as well as communication between different cores on the same chip. 2D-NoC architecture is efficient for medium scale multicore SoC systems. However, soon it will not be probably a good candidate for large scale heterogeneous many-core systems consisting of more than a thousand cores.

With the emergence of 3D integration technologies, a new opportunity emerges for chip architects by porting the 2D-NoC to the third dimension. In 3D integration technologies, multiple layers of active devices are stacked above each other and vertically interconnected using through-silicon via (TSV). As compared to 2D-IC designs, 3D ICs allow for performance enhancements even in the absence of scaling because of the reduced interconnect lengths. In addition, package density is increased, power consumption is reduced, and the system is more immune to noise. This chapter presented architecture, design and evaluation of a 3D-NoC including complete hardware design details about the main components of the 3D-NoC system.

# Chapter 6
# Network Interface Architecture
# and Design for 2D/3D NoCs

In Network-on-Chip architectures, the network interface (NI) plays and important role ofacting as interface between IP cores and the communication infrastructure. In general, a NIincludes a front-end and a back-end sub-modules. The front-end module implements thecommunication protocol adopted by the core and the back-end module is in charge of implementingbasic communication services, such as packetization/depacketization, controlflow and routing related functions.

The NI must provide low area overhead because NoC designs are generally constrainedby area and power. In addition, a good NI design must provide throughput and/or latencyguarantees, which are essential for the design of NoC based complex multicore SoCs.This chapter complements the previous two chapters about 2D and 3D NoC architectures.It presents a real architecture, design, and evaluation of a simple network interface.

## 6.1 Introduction

Deep sub-micron technologies have enabled the implementation of new application-specific embedded multicore SoC architectures that integrate multiple software programmable processors and dedicated hardware components together onto a single chip. Recently, these application-specific architectures are emerging as a key design solution for today's design challenges, which are being driven by emerging applications in the areas of: wireless communication, broadband/distributed networking, distributed computing, and multimedia computing. Despite these new opportunities, designers of these systems are currently confronted with the enormously difficult task of designing these complex heterogeneous multi-core architectures.

NoC designs have been mainly focusing more on issues related to router architectures, control flow schemes, routing algorithms, and low power and fault tolerance designs. Comparatively, less focus has been put on the design of the Network Interface (NI) which is also a very important component in an NoC based

A. Ben Abdallah, *Multicore Systems On-Chip: Practical Software/Hardware Design*, Atlantis Ambient and Pervasive Intelligence 7, DOI: 10.2991/978-94-91216-92-3_6, © Atlantis Press and the author 2013

multicore SoC system. The NI separates communication (network) from computation (PEs). This feature increases the hardware design efficiency. In the rest of
this section, we will describe the basics of typical NI architecture.

## 6.2  Network Interface Basics

Whether it is used in on-chip network on off-chip network, the NI's main job is to
convert messages to packets and packets to messages. In NoC architecture, a core
is connected to router through the NI and it communicates within the network
using packets. Design of the NI needs to consider the I/O structure of the core and
the protocols used in the NoC at physical, data link and network layers.

The NI functionality can be divided into two parts: the *Core part*, and the
*Network part* as illustrated in Fig. 6.1. The *Network part* handles interface to the
router; wile the *Core part* is connected with core and it deals with the data and
address bus width, and control signals. There are generally two types of NIs: (1)
Network interface for source routing, and (2) Network interface for distributed
routing. Bellow, we will describe both of these architectures. However, this
chapter only focuses on the design of the distributed routing NI type.

### 6.2.1  Source Routing Network Interface

As the name indicates, in source routing the information about packet route is
embedded in the packet's header at the source end. In this way, the source node
makes all routing decisions before the packet is transmitted into the network
(NoC). The NI contains a routing table filled with routing information. The
sender's NI selects route path from the its table and places this information in the

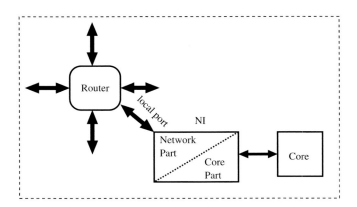

**Fig. 6.1** Network interface

packet header. Then, packet are transmitted in the network through the NI. When a given packet reaches an intermediate router, the route path is read from the packet's header and forwarded to the corresponding neighbor router until it reaches its destination.

## 6.2.2  Distributed Routing Network Interface

In distributed routing NI, a destination address is added in the packet's header. Unlike source routing NI, it does not have a path information table. So, the circuit size is relatively smaller than the source routing NI's one.

In distributed routing protocol, the routing functions are implemented in each NoC router. The header, which is generally compact, carries the destination address and some control bits. In this way, each router contains information about the neighbor routers. When the packet arrives at the input port of the downstream router, the route path is selected either by looking up the routing table or calculating the routing path in hardware.

The advantage of the distributed routing is that it can be easily expended to support adaptive routing. The disadvantage is the large additional hardware for execution of routing logic, and the extra memory unit used to store routing tables. Distributed routing is suitable for regular topologies, such as mesh topology (described in Chap. 4).

# 6.3  Overview of OASIS NoC Architecture

As was described in Chap. 4, OASIS NoC (ONoC) is a $4 \times 4$ mesh network and adopts wormhole switching. Data path of one single router is shown in Fig. 6.2. The input is 76-bit flit and a stop signal for each input-port. The router has 5 input/output ports (local, east, west, north, and south).

In the input port, data flits are fetched and decoded to determine new *next-port* direction which is needed for the next router in the downstream node. The *Next-port* information is transmitted from the input port to the router allocator, and the appropriate output port is granted to the corresponding packet. Finally, the crossbar sends packet to the next appropriate router input (Ben-Abdallah 2006; Mori 2009).

Wormhole switching and virtual cut through forwarding methods are both employed in the used OASIS NoC system. The forwarding method that is chosen in a given instance is dependent on the level of packet fragmentation. In ONoC, each router has buffers which can store four flits.

When a packet is larger than four flits, ONoC chooses wormhole switching. Otherwise, virtual cut through is used. In other words, when buffer size is greater than or equal to the number of flits, virtual cut through is used, and when buffer

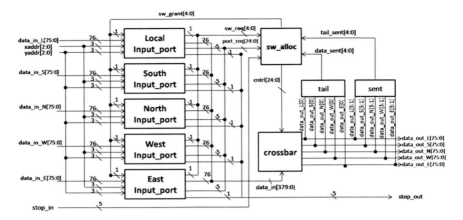

**Fig. 6.2**  One router data-path

**Fig. 6.3**  4 × 4 OASIS NoC
mesh topology

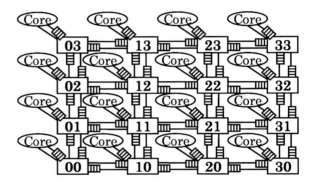

size is less than or equal to the number of flits, wormhole switching is used (Mori 2010). ONoC is a 4 × 4 mesh architecture as shown in Fig. 6.3. Each router has X-Y coordinates which are called node addresses. It is based on simple X-Y routing scheme.

## 6.4  Architecture, and Design Decision for Distributed Routing NI

The block diagram of the designed NI is given in Fig. 6.4. FPGA and Quartus II software design tools were used for the prototyping of this interface. The used core is a Nios II processor (NiosII 2012), which is a configurable 32-bit RISC soft core processor.

As shown in the figures, the NI has different internal blocks, including Buffers, Flitizer, Deflitizer and Controllers. The controller is the main module of the NI and

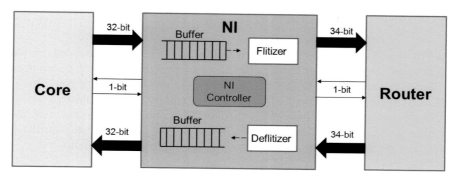

**Fig. 6.4** Distributed routing NI architecture block diagram

it controls packet transmission from core to router and from router to core. When a core wants to send a packet to another core, it first stores the packet in the buffer of the NI. When the router is ready to receive the packet, the NI converts the packet into flits and sends the flits to the router. Similarly, when the NI receives flit(s) from the router, the NI converts them/it into a packet and stores it/them in the buffer. Then, when the core is ready to receive the packet, the NI transfers the packet to the core. Some control signals are used for the communication between core and NI and NI and router. A wormhole switching technique is used in the packet transmission from NI to router and from router to NI.

Before we start talking about the actual design of the NI, we need first to make several design decisions. We mainly need to decide: (1) Network size, (2) Packet size, (3) Buffer size, (4) Communication Protocol, (5) Packet buffering, and (6) Packet/flit format.

## 6.4.1 Network Size Decision

Network (NoC) size is a very important decision which we need to make. The network size depends mainly on the target application and on how much parallelize we have. In other words, after mapping the application (task-graph) to the NoC architecture (refer to Chap. 3), we are able to know the number of needed cores. If, for example, after several simulations and profiling, we found that we need 62 cores to run a given application, the network size should be, then, 8 × 8 (64 cores). Notice that with this size, there will be unused routers since we have only 62 cores (1 router for each core).

For our network interface, we assumed the NoC size of 8 × 8. Thus, 6-bit are needed to represent one destination address direction. Since we have two directions (X-Y coordinates) we need 12-bit for the complete address. The 12-bit will be embedded in the header of the packet.

## 6.4.2 Packet Size Decision

Packets in a given NoC system can be of different sizes. The size depends on the application, target platform, and available hardware resources. Therefore, we need to decide the packet size so that we can decide the maximum buffer size. This is also very important because NoC design is area and power constrained.

In this design and in order to keep the design simple, we assume that the maximum size of the packet will be 512-bit, i.e., $16 \times 32$-bit flits. In distributed routing, a packet can have, then, 1 flit minimum and 16 flit maximum.

## 6.4.3 Buffer Size Decision

The role of a buffer in the NI is to temporarily store the packets while they are transferred from the source core to the destination core. The size of the buffer in the NI should be equal or larger than the packet size. The ideal is to have the maximum size of the buffer at least equal to the maximum size of a packet. Since our packet size is fixed to 512-bit, the buffer size is also 512-bit.

## 6.4.4 Communication Protocol and Flow Control Decisions

We used *Ready-to-Receive* (RTR) based scheme as a communication protocol between core and NI and between NI and router. In this scheme, two 1-bit signals and 1 WR signal are used for handshaking signals. We assume that *phit* size is the same as *flit* size.

This NI design will be tested with Altera Nios II core which can be connected with various external peripherals. Nios II support 32-bit PIO width. Thus, it can send/receive 32-bits of data at a time.

## 6.4.5 Packet Format Decision

As we mentioned, the maximum size of a packet is fixed to 512-bits. The packet is divided into three parts: HEADER, BODY, and END. The packet's HEADER contains the first 32-bits of the packet. The last 32-bits is the END of the packet and the remaining bits of the packet are reserved for the payload (BODY). The packet format for the distributed routing NI is shown in Fig. 6.5.

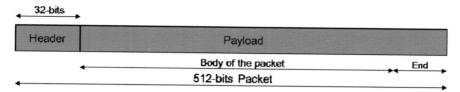

**Fig. 6.5**  Packet format

### 6.4.5.1 Packet Header Format

The size of the packet's HEADER is 32-bits. Since the maximum size of the NoC is $8 \times 8$, a minimum 6-bits are required to represent the node address in the network. In the HEADER, the first 6-bits represent the *Destination Address* of the core in the network. The next 6-bits represent the *Packet Size*, which helps tracking the arrival of the whole packet. The next 4-bits carry the *Packet-Sequence-Number*. This number is used to rearrange the packet in correct order at the destination core. The next 8-bits are *Unused* and are reserved for future extension. The remaining 8-bits are for *Payload* data field. The HEADER format is shown in Fig. 6.6. The formats of the BODY and END flits are shown in Fig. 6.7.

## *6.4.6 Flit-Level Decision*

### 6.4.6.1 Flit Size

After receiving a packet from the core, the NI converts the packet into flits. This process is called *Flitization*. A packet can have minimum 1 flit and maximum 16 flits. The size of a flit is kept fixed and is equal to 34-bits.

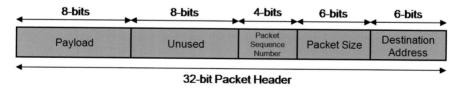

**Fig. 6.6**  Packet HEADER format

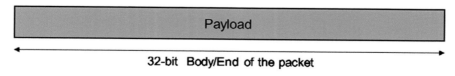

**Fig. 6.7**  BODY and END format

**Table 6.1** Flit types and coding

| Flit type | Code |
|---|---|
| Single flit with full payload | 00 |
| HEADER flit | 01 |
| Body flit | 10 |
| End flit | 11 |

#### 6.4.6.2 Flit Types

First 2-bits of each flit indicate *Flit Type*. Each type of flit is encoded as shown in Table 6.1.

#### 6.4.6.3 Flit Format After Flitization

*HEADER Flit*: The HEADER flit is the first flit of a packet that enters into the network through the NI. In distributed routing, this flit carries first 24-bits as control information and next 2-bits are unused while the rest 8-bits are payload. HEADER flit is used for locking the path for the following body flits and a end flit while traversing through the network.

Two bits are used to decode the type of HEADER flits. Code 00 is used when the original packet from the core is only 32-bits including the packet header. In this case, there will be only 1 flit that corresponds to the original packet and there will be no BODY and END flits.

When the code is 01, this means that the original packet is more than 32-bits. In this case, the packet can have both BODY and END flits or just an END flit. The HEADER flit format is shown in Fig. 6.8. *BODY Flit*: The BODY flit always follows the HEADER flit and carries the payload. After flitization, a packet may have a minimum of 0 BODY flit and maximum of 14 BODY flits, depending on the payload size in the original packet. The BODY flit is represented by code 10 and its format is shown in Fig. 6.9. *END Flit*: The END flit is the last flit in the group flits corresponding to a particular packet. It follows the last BODY flit. It unlocks the path for the packet to which it belongs. It should be noted here that the path was locked by the HEADER flit of the same group of flits. The END flit format is shown in Fig. 6.10.

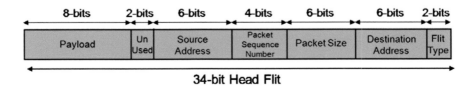

**Fig. 6.8** HEADER flit format

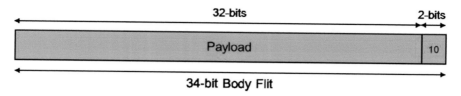

Fig. 6.9  BODY flit format

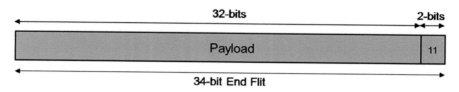

Fig. 6.10  END flit format

#### 6.4.6.4  Flit Format After Deflitization

The process of converting the flits into a packet is called *Deflitization*. The *Deflitization* process starts after receiving the 34-bits HEADER flit from a router and continues until the END flit is received. *Deflitization* is needed for all cores in the network.

*HEADER Flit*: When the NI receives the 34-bits HEADER flit from the router, it removes the *Flit Type* and the *Destination Address* bits from the above flit. After that, the *Source Address* bits are shifted to the most right position. The *Packet Size* and *Packet Sequence Number* bits are also shifted to LSB (Least Significant Bit) side by 2-bits. The next 8-bits are unused and the remaining 8-bits are payload. The new created 32-bits packet HEADER (see Fig. 6.11) is stored in the NI buffer.

*BODY and END Flits*: Both BODY and END flits are deflitized by removing the *Flit Type* bits and the rest 32-bits payload is transferred to the buffer in the NI. The formats of both BODY and END flits after deflitization are the same and shown in Fig. 6.12.

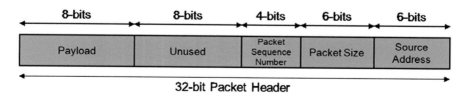

Fig. 6.11  Format of packet header after deflitization

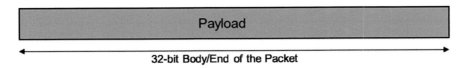

Fig. 6.12 Format of BODY/END flits after deflitization

Table 6.2 Summary of decisions for distributed routing NI

| Maximum NoC size | Maximum packet size (Bits) | Buffer size (Bits) | | Flit size (Bits) |
|---|---|---|---|---|
| | | Buffer 1 | Buffer 2 | |
| $8 \times 8$ | 512 | 512 | 512 | 34 |

## 6.4.7 Summary of all Decisions

The design decisions at all levels for the distributed routing NI are shown in Table 6.2.

## 6.5 Distributed Routing Network Interface Design

The detailed internal structure of the NI for distributed routing is shown in Fig. 6.13. It consists of 6 internal blocks: C2R-Buffer, Flitizer, C2R-Controller,

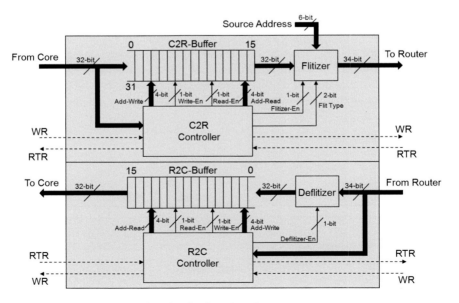

Fig. 6.13 Internal structure of NI for distributed routing

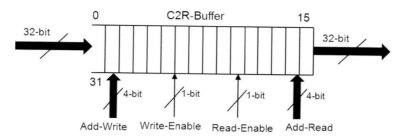

**Fig. 6.14**  C2R-Buffer

R2C-Buffer, Deflitizer, and R2C-Controller. Each block performs its defined specific job.

The NI has different blocks and control signals as shown in Fig. 6.13.

### 6.5.1  Core-to-Router (C2R) Buffer

C2R-Buffer is a FIFO structure which is connected to the input port of the NI from the core side. The C2R buffer has $16 \times 32$ entries. Whenever the above buffer receives the "Write-Enable" signal from the C2R-Controller, it stores a packet coming from the core at a particular location specified by the "Add-Write" signal from C2R-Controller. Similarly, whenever it receives the "Read-Enable" signal from C2R-Controller, it sends the chunk from the address location which is specified by the "Add-Read" signal (Fig. 6.14).

### 6.5.2  Flitizer Module Architecture

As we mentioned earlier, the process of converting a packet into flits is called *flitization*. The input and output signals to the flitizer module are illustrated in Fig. 6.15. When the "Flitizer-Enable" signal arrives from the C2R-Controller, the flitizer module starts working on the flitization process; it reads the 32-bits of a packet from the C2R-Buffer. If the "Flit Type" value is "00", it means the packet contains only 1 flit. In this case, no BODY and END flits are present in the packet. If the "Flit Type" value is "01", it means the packet contains more than 1 flit.

The flitizer circuit adds 2-bits flit type in the "Flit Type" field and 6-bits source address in the packet header, i.e., from bit numbers 18 to 23, and creates a 34-bits HEADER flit. When it receives the "Flit Type" signal ("10" or "11"), it assumes that the incoming packet from the C2R-Buffer is BODY or END of the packet respectively. In this situation, the flitizer just adds the "Flit Type" to the flit at the field, creates a 34-bits BODY or END flits. After the flitization process completes, flits are transferred to the router.

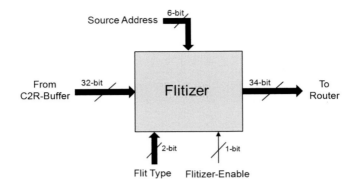

**Fig. 6.15**  Flitizer module architecture

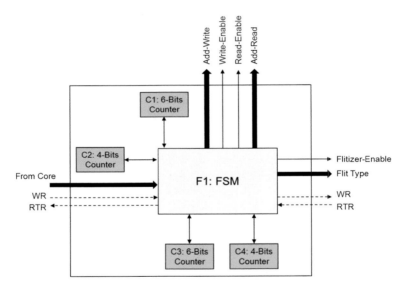

**Fig. 6.16**  Core-to-Router (C2R) controller architecture

### 6.5.3  Core-to-Router (C2R) Controller

The Core-to-Router (C2R) is also a very important block in the NI since it generates several important control signals. The C2R controller consists of several modules as shown in Fig. 6.16. The C1 counter is a 6-bits counter and is used to count the total number of payload bytes of the packet coming from a given core to the NI. Initially, C1 is set to "000000". When a packet header arrives from the core, the corresponding bits in the packet header, which represents the size of payload bytes, will be stored in this counter.

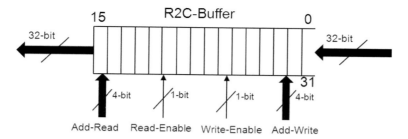

**Fig. 6.17** Router-to-Core (R2C) buffer

The C2 counter is 4-bits counter and is used to locate the address of C2R-Buffer to store the received packet from the core. Initially its value is also set to "0000". The C2 value is incremented by 1 whenever a new chunk of the packet is stored in the C2R-Buffer.

The C3 counter counts the total number of payload bytes (packet size) that has been transferred to router from C2R-Buffer. Initially its value is also set to "000000". Similar to C1 counter, when a packet header is received from the core, the corresponding bits in the packet header will be stored in C3 counter.

The C4 counter is used to locate the address of the C2R-Buffer from where the chunk of the packet has to be transferred to flitizer. Whenever a chunk of the packet is sent from C2R-Buffer to flitizer, the counter value will be incremented by 1.

### 6.5.4 Router-to-Core (R2C) Buffer

The Router-to-Core (R2C) has a 16 entries FIFO buffer connected to the output port of the NI (see Fig. 6.17). Whenever it receives the "Write Enable" signal (high state) from R2C-Controller, it stores the flit (coming from deflitizer) at a specified address location. The address location is specified by the "Add-Write" signal from R2C-Controller. Similarly, whenever it receives the "Read-Enable" signal, it sends the stored flit from the specified address location of R2C-Buffer to the core (Nios II core in our case).

### 6.5.5 Deflitizer Module Architecture

The deflitization process starts whenever Deflitizer receives the "Deflitizer-Enable" signal from the R2C-Controller and then it reads a 34-bits flit from a router's port (see Fig. 6.18). It should first checks the "Flit Type" bits. If it is "00" or "01", the Deflitizer simply removes the "Flit Type" and "Destination Address" bits from the flit and shifts the "Source Address" bits to the "Destination Address" field and creates a 32-bits packet header. The created packet HEADER should exactly

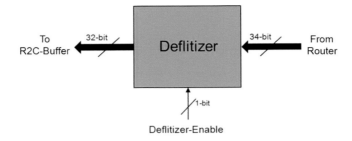

**Fig. 6.18** Deflitizer module architecture

match the one that was created at the source. We have to note that only "Destination Address" bits are replaced by "Source Address" bits and the rest of the header bits remains the same. As soon as the deflitization process is completed, the created packet HEADER will be sent to R2C-Buffer.

### 6.5.6 Router-to-Core (R2C) Controller

The Router-to-Core (R2C) module is responsible for controlling the communications from the router to the core. This module consists of different components, including a finite-state-machine (FSM) component. The block diagram of the R2C module is shown in Fig. 6.19.

## 6.6 Evaluation

The NI is designed in Verilog HDL, analyzed and synthesized with Altera Quartus II, and simulated with ModelSim-Altera. The NI was also prototyped with Altera FPGA board.

### 6.6.1 RTL and Gate Level Simulation

As we mentioned, the designed NI is simulated (RTL and Gate levels) and implemented on an Altera FPGA board. For RTL and Gate level evaluations, simulation results of data flow from core to router and from router to core are provided.

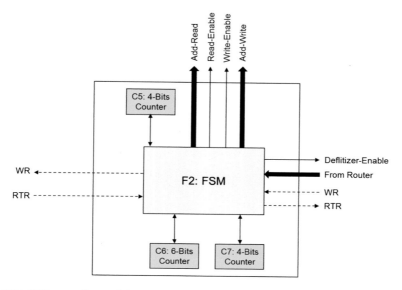

**Fig. 6.19** R2C controller module architecture

## 6.6.1.1 RTL Simulation Results

The results of the RTL simulation and the wave forms of the simulation for data from core to router and from router to core are also performed.

*Data Flow from Core to Router*: The RTL view of CER path is shown in Fig. 6.20. A test-bench file, written in Verilog HDL, is used for the simulation which generates 16 packets including a HEADER, 14 BODIE, and 1 END flits. The wave form of the RTL simulation is shown in Fig. 6.21. At the first line, the *WR* signal from core is high and the packet HEADER is inputted. The *WR* signal to router is high and the HEADER flit is outputted at the second one. The following packets are inputted, flitized, and finally sent to the router.

*Data Flow from Router to Core*: The RTL view of R2C path is shown in Fig. 6.22.

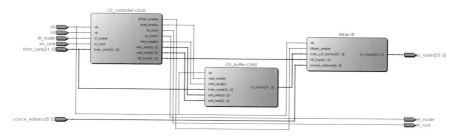

**Fig. 6.20** RTL view of C2R module

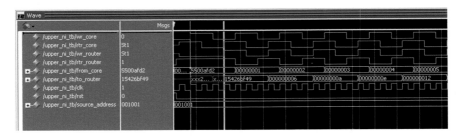

**Fig. 6.21** Wave form of RTL simulation for C2R

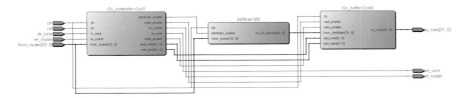

**Fig. 6.22** RTL view of R2C module

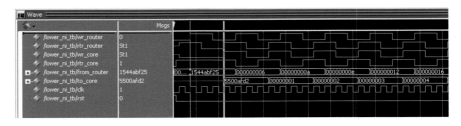

**Fig. 6.23** Wave form of RTL simulation for R2C

In this simulation, a test-bench file generates 16 flits: 1 HEADER flit, 14 BODY flits, and 1 END flit. The wave form of the RTL simulation is shown in Fig. 6.23. A HEADER flit is inputted when the *WR* signal from router becomes high. After several clocks, when the *WR* signal to core becomes high, deflitized packet is sent to the output port. The following flits are also inputted, deflitized and transferred to the core.

### 6.6.1.2 Gate Level Simulation Results

In this evaluation, results of the Gate Level simulation for data flow from core to router and from router to core are given.

*Data Flow from Core to Router*: The RTL view of C2R path was shown in Fig. 6.20. For the RTL simulation, 16 packets, including 1 HEADER, 14 BODY

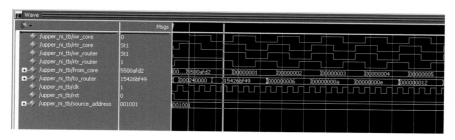

**Fig. 6.24** Waveform of gate level simulation for C2R

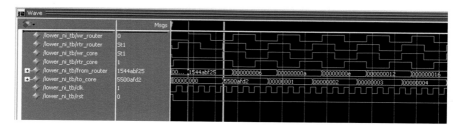

**Fig. 6.25** Waveform of gate level simulation for R2C

flits, and 1 END flit are transferred from the input port to the output port of the NI. The waveform of the Gate Level simulation is shown in Fig. 6.24.

*Data Flow from Router to Core*: The RTL view of R2C path was shown in Fig. 6.22. In this simulation, 16 flits (1 HEADER, 14 BODY, and 1 END) are generated and sent from the input port to the output port. The waveform of the Gate Level simulation is shown in Fig. 6.25.

## 6.6.2 Hardware Prototyping

To test our distributed routing NI, we implemented a complete system on Altear DE2 board with Nios II core, on-chip RAM, 6 PIOs, and Avalon bus. The target FPGA device family is Cycle II EP2C35F672C6 and on-board 50 MHz clock frequency is used. The prototyped system is shown in Fig. 6.26.

### 6.6.2.1 Data Flow from Core to Router

The RTL view of the implemented system is shown in Fig. 6.27. Data flow from core to router, which is the conversion of a packet into flits is verified. The Nios II processor core sends packets to the dummy router through the NI. The dummy router just receives flits from the NI and sends them to the output decoder which

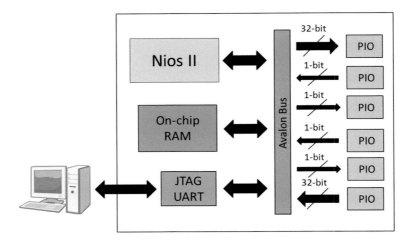

**Fig. 6.26** Nios II system architecture

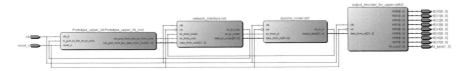

**Fig. 6.27** C2R architecture

displays the flits on 8 seven-segment displays (for data except flit type) and 2 red LEDs (for flit type) on the DE2 FPGA board. A C program is written with Nios II IDE to generate packets and control signals from the Nios II processor. The program makes the Nios II core send packets to the dummy router 16 times. The packet size (found in HEADER) decides the number of packets which the Nios II core sends to the router. The Nios II core sends a single packet in the first time, a packet HEADER and END flits in the second time, and so on, until the end of the loop. Four examples of output results are shown in Figs. 6.28, 6.29, 6.30 and 6.31.

### 6.6.2.2  Data Flow from Router to Core

In this phase, the conversion of flits into a packet, i.e., deflitization is verified. The RTL view of the implemented circuit is shown in Fig. 6.32. The circuit mainly consists of a clock generator (clock-gen), Nios II, NI, dummy router, and output decoder blocks. This time, the router sends flits to the Nios II core. The packets which the Nios II core receives from the router are displayed on 8 seven-segment

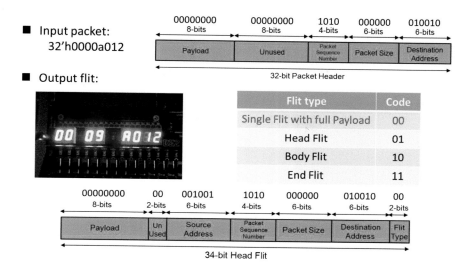

Fig. 6.28 Single-packet to single-flit

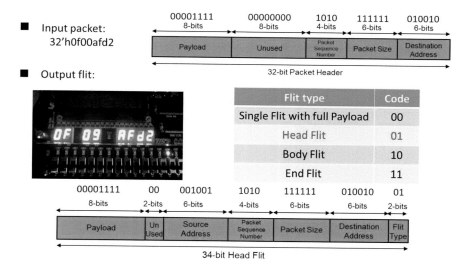

Fig. 6.29 Packet HEADER to flit HEADER

displays. The clock-gen block generates 1 s clock cycle. In the same way, a C program is written to make the Nios II processor receive packets from the dummy router. The received packets can be seen in the Nios II IDE console. Four examples of the output results are shown in Figs. 6.33, 6.34, 6.35 and 6.36.

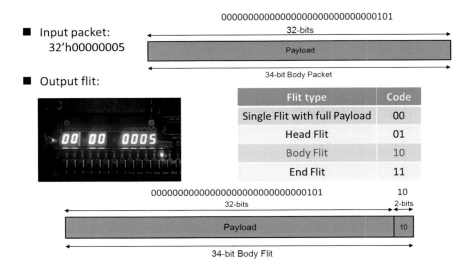

**Fig. 6.30**  Packet BODY to flit BODY

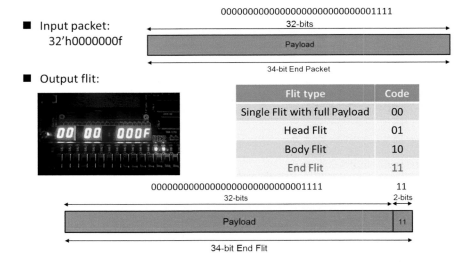

**Fig. 6.31**  Packet END to flit END

### 6.6.2.3  Data Flow from Core to Core

In this simulation, we want to verify that data from core to core via the NI is correct. The RTL view of the core to core path is shown in Fig. 6.37. The module

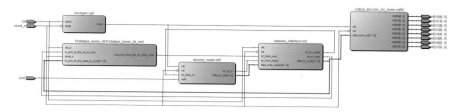

**Fig. 6.32**  Router to core architecture

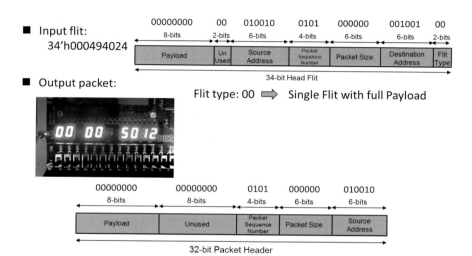

**Fig. 6.33**  Single-flit to single-packet

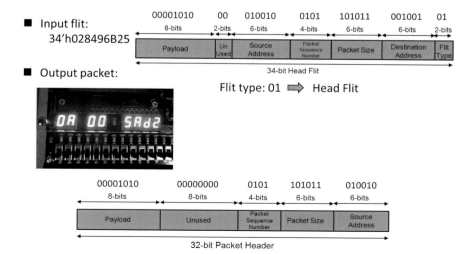

**Fig. 6.34**  Flit HEADER to packet HEADER

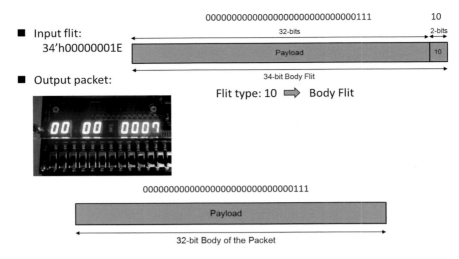

Fig. 6.35  Flit BODY to packet BODY

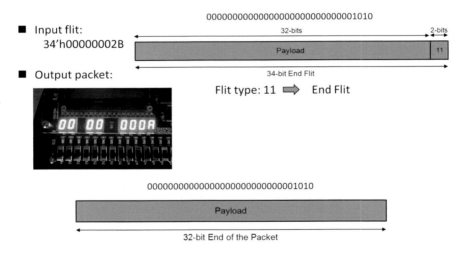

Fig. 6.36  Flit END to packet END

includes dummy memory, NI for the memory, memory-side dummy router, Nios II-side dummy router, NI for Nios II core, and Nios II.

### 6.6.2.4 Packet Transfer from Nios II Core to Dummy Memory

Packet transfer from Nios II core to dummy memory is verified. The RTL view of the implemented circuit is shown in Fig. 6.38. This circuit consists of a Nios II core,

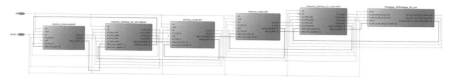

**Fig. 6.37**   Core to core architecture

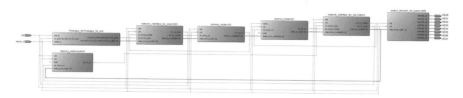

**Fig. 6.38**   Nios II core to dummy memory RTL view

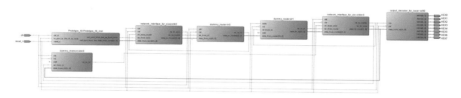

**Fig. 6.39**   RTL view of the dummy memory to Nios II core module

dummy memory, 2 NIs, 2 dummy routers, and output decoder blocks. A C program is also used to generate packets from the Nios II core. It is the same code as the one used in the previous subsection. The packets which the Nios II core sends to the memory can be seen in the Nios II IDE console.

### 6.6.2.5   Packet Transmission from Dummy Memory to Nios II Core

In this verification, we verified the packet transmission from dummy memory to Nios II core. The RTL view of the implemented circuit is shown in Fig. 6.39. This circuit has Nios II system, dummy memory, 2 NIs, 2 dummy routers, output decoder and clock-gen blocks. The Nios II core receives packets from the memory through NI and router. The memory initially has packets in its buffers and sends them to the Nios II core. The memory-side router receives flits from the neighboring NI and transfers them to another one. The C program which was used in the previous simulations is again used. The packets that the core receives from the memory can be seen in the Nios II IDE console. The results of core to memory and memory to core are combined and shown in Figs. 6.40, 6.41, 6.42 and 6.43.

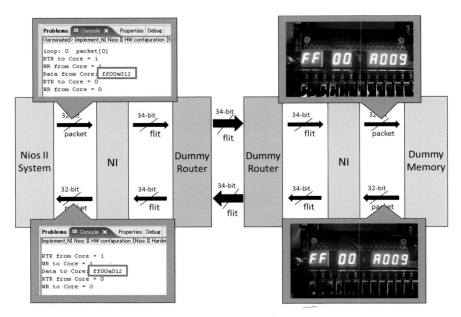

**Fig. 6.40**  Core-memory: single packet

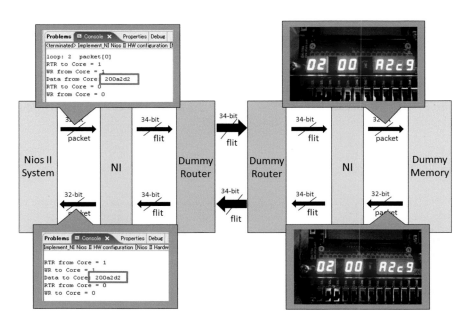

**Fig. 6.41**  Core-memory: packet HEADER

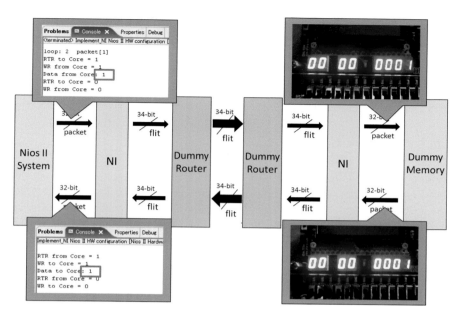

**Fig. 6.42**   Core-memory: packet BODY

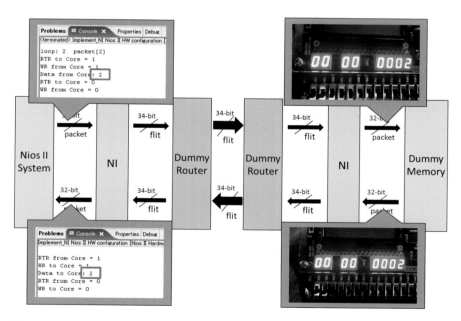

**Fig. 6.43**   Core-memory: packet END

**Table 6.3** Hardware complexity

|  | Area (Total logic elements) | Speed (Fmax) (MHz) | Power (mW) |
|---|---|---|---|
| NI | 229/33,216 ($<1\%$) | 231.75 | 156.83 |
| Core to router | 1,696/33,216 (5 %) | 73.02 | 188.16 |
| Router to core | 1,700/33,216 (5 %) | 69.41 | 185.51 |
| Core to core | 1,968/33,216 (6 %) | 75.71 | 135.49 |

### 6.6.3 Hardware Complexity

Table 6.3 shows the hardware complexity details of the prototyped NI. From the above table, it is clear to see that the NI is less than 1 % of the Cyclone II FPGA. The area utilization is small enough to not really affect the overall complexity of the NoC architecture. The delay of the packet transfer through the NI is $3 + 4(N-1)$ clock cycles/packet. Where N is the number of flits.

## 6.7 Conclusion

The network interface plays and important role of acting as interface between IP cores and the communication infrastructure. The NI includes a front-end and a back-end sub-modules and must provide low area overhead because NoC designs are generally constrained by area and power. Also, a good NI design must provide throughput and/or latency guarantees, which are essential for the design of NoC based complex multicore SoCs. This chapter presented architecture, design, and evaluation of a simple NI tragedy for NoC architectures.

# Chapter 7
# Parallelizing Compiler for Single and Multicore Computing

To overcome challenges from high power densities and thermal hot spots in microprocessors, multicore computing platforms have emerged as the ubiquitous computing platform from servers to embedded systems. But, providing multiple cores does not directly translate into increased performance for most applications. The burden is placed on software developers to find and exploit coarse-grain parallelism to effectively make use of the abundance of computing resources provided by the systems. With the rise of multicore systems and many-core processors, concurrency becomes a major issue in the daily life of a programmer. Thus, compiler and software development tools will be critical to help programmers create high performance software. This chapter covers software issues of a so called parallelizing queue compiler targeted for future single and multicore embedded systems.

## 7.1 Instruction Level Parallelism

Instruction level parallelism (ILP) is the key to improve the performance of modern architectures. ILP allows the instructions of a sequential program to be executed in parallel on multiple data paths and functional units. Data and control independent instructions determine the groups of instructions that can be issued together while keeping the program correctness (Muchnick 1997).

A good scheduling is crucial to achieve high performance. An effective scheduling for the exploitation of ILP depends greatly on two factors: the processor features, and the compiler techniques. In superscalar processors, the compiler exposes ILP by rearranging instructions. However, the final schedule is decided at run-time by the hardware (Hennessy 1990). In VLIW machines, the scheduling is decided at compile-time by aggressive static scheduling techniques (Allen 2002; Muchnick 1997).

Sophisticated compiler optimizations have been developed to expose high amounts of ILP in loop regions (Wolfe 1996) where many scientific and multimedia programs spend most of their execution time. The purpose of some loop transformations such as loop unrolling is to enlarge basic blocks by combining instructions called in multiple iterations to a single iteration. A popular loop

A. Ben Abdallah, *Multicore Systems On-Chip: Practical Software/Hardware Design*,     153
Atlantis Ambient and Pervasive Intelligence 7, DOI: 10.2991/978-94-91216-92-3_7,
© Atlantis Press and the author 2013

scheduling technique is modulo scheduling (Rau 1994; Lam 1988) where the iterations of a loop are parallelized in such a way that a new iteration initiates before the previous iteration has completed execution.

These static scheduling algorithms improve greatly the performance of the applications at the cost of increasing the register pressure (Loca 1998). When the schedule requires more registers than those available in the processor, the compiler must insert spill code to fit the application in the available number of architected registers (Printer 1993). Many high performance architectures born in the last decade (Sparc 1992; Kane 1992; Kessler 1999) were designed on the assumption that applications could not make effective use of more than 32 registers (Mahlke 1992). Recent studies have shown that the register requirements for the same kind of applications using the current compiler technology demands more than 64 registers (Postiff 2000).

High ILP register requirements has direct impact in the processor performance as a large number of registers need to be accessed concurrently. The number of ports to access the register file affect the access time and the power consumption. In order to maintain clock speed and low power consumption, high performance embedded, and digital signal processors have implemented partitioned register banks (Janssen 1995) instead of a large monolithic register file. Several software solutions for the compiler have been proposed to reduce the register requirements of modulo schedules (Salamea 2004), and other studies have focused on the compilation issues for partitioned register files (Jang 1998; Huang 2001). A hardware/compiler technique to alleviate register pressure is to provide more registers than allowed by the instruction encoding. In Fernandes (1997) and Tyson (2001) the usage of queue register files has been proposed to store the live variables in a software pipelined loop schedule while minimizing the pressure on the architected registers. The work in Ravindran (2205) proposes the use of register windows to give the illusion of a large register file without affecting the instruction set bits.

An alternative to hide the registers from the instruction set encoding is by using a queue machine. A queue machine uses a first-in first-out structure, called the operand queue, as the intermediate storage location for computations. Instructions read and write the operand queue implicitly. Not having explicit operands in the instructions make instructions short improving code density. Also false dependencies disappears from programs eliminating the need for register renaming logic that reduces circuitry and improves power consumption (Kucuk 2003).

Queue computers have been studied in several works. Bruno (Preiss 1985) investigated the possibility of evaluating expression trees and highlighted the problems of evaluating directed acyclic graphs (DAG) in an abstract queue machine.

In Okamoto (1999), Okamoto presented some design issues of a superscalar queue machine. Schmit et al. (2002) use a queue machine as the execution layer for reconfigurable hardware. They transform the program's data flow graph (DFG) into a spatial representation that can be executed in a simple queue machine. This transformation inserts extra special instructions to guarantee correct execution by allowing every variable to be produced and consumed only once. Their experiments show that the execution of programs in their queue machine have the potential of exploiting high levels of parallelism while keeping code size less than a RISC instruction set.

In Ben-Abdallah (2006) and Sowa (2005), a 32-bit QueueCore processor with a 16-bit instruction set format was designed. The approach is to allow variables to be produced only once but can be consumed multiple times. We sacrifice some bits in the instruction set for an offset reference to indicate the relative location of a variable to be reused. The goal is to allow DAGs to be executed without transformations that increase the instruction count while keeping reduced instructions that generate dense programs.

Ideas about compiling for queue machines have been discussed in the previous work in an abstract way. Some problems have been clearly identified but no algorithms have been proposed. Before, we explored the possibility of using a retargettable code generator for register machines to map register code into the queue computation model (Canedo 2006). The resulting compiler mapped the operand queue in terms of a large number general purpose registers in the machine description file that is used by the code generator in order to avoid spill code. This approach led to complex algorithms to map register programs into queue programs, excessively long programs, poor parallelism, and poor code quality.

This chapter presents a code generation scheme implemented in a compiler for the QueueCore processor. The compiler generates assembly code from C programs and is suitable for singlecore and multicore platforms. The queue compiler exposes *natural* ILP from the input programs to the QueueCore processor. Experimental results show that the compiler can extract more parallelism for the QueueCore than an ILP compiler for a RISC machine, and also generates programs with lower code size.

## 7.2 Parallel Queue Compiler

The Queue Computation Model (QCM) is the abstract definition of a computer that uses a first-in first-out data structure as the storage space to perform operations. Elements are inserted, or en-queued, through a write pointer named QT that references the rear of the queue. And elements are removed, or dequeued, through a read pointer named QH that references the head of the queue.

### 7.2.1 Queue Processor Overview

The QueueCore is a 32-bit processor with a 16-bit wide producer order QCM instruction set architecture based on the produced order parallel QCM (Sowa 2005). The instruction format reserves 8-bit for the opcode and 8-bit for the operand. The operand field is used in binary operations to specify the offset reference value with respect of QH from which the second source operand is dequeued, QH $-N$. Unary operations have the freedom to dequeued their only

source operand from QH −N. Memory operations use the operand field to represent
the offset and base register, or immediate value. For cases when 8-bit is not enough
to represent an immediate value or an offset for a memory instruction, a special
instruction named "covop" is inserted before the conflicting memory instruction.
The "covop" instruction extends the operand field of the following instruction.

QueueCore defines a set of specific purpose registers available to the programmer
to be used as the frame pointer register ($fp), stack pointer register ($sp), and
return address register ($ra). Frame pointer register serves as base register to access
local variables, incoming parameters, and saved registers. Stack pointer register is
used as the base address for outgoing parameters to other functions.

## 7.2.2 Compiling for 1-Offset QueueCore Instruction Set

The instruction sequence to correctly evaluate a given expression is generated
from a level-order traversal of the expressions' parse tree (Preiss 1985). A level-
order traversal visits all the nodes in the parse tree from left to right starting from
the deepest level towards the root as shown in Fig. 7.1a.

The generated instruction sequence is shown in Fig. 7.1b. All nodes in every
level are independent from each other and can be processed in parallel. Every node
may consume and produce data. For example, a load operation produces one
datum and consumes none, a binary operation consumes two data and produces
one. A QSTATE is the relationship between all the nodes in a level that can be
processed in parallel and the total number of data consumed and produced by the
operations in that level. Figure 7.1c shows the production and consumption
degrees of the QSTATEs for the sample expression.

Although the instruction sequence from a directed acyclic graph (DAG) is
obtained also from a level-order traversal, there are some cases where the basic
rules of en-queueing and dequeueing are not enough to guarantee correctness of
the program (Preiss 1985). Figure 7.2a shows the evaluation of an expression's
DAG that leads to incorrect results. In Fig. 7.2c, notice that at QSTATE 1 there are
three operands produced, and at QSTATE 2 the operations consume four operands.
The add operation in Fig. 7.2b consumes two operands, a, b, and produces one,
the result of the addition a + b. The sub operation consumes two operands that
should be b, c, instead it consumes operands c, a + b.

In our previous work (Sowa 2005) we have proposed a solution for this
problem. We give flexibility to the dequeueing rule to get operands from any
location in the operand queue. In other words, we allow operands to be consumed
multiple times. The desired operand's location is relative to the head of the queue
and it is specified in the instruction as an offset reference, QH −N. As the
en-queueing rule, *production* of data, remains fixed at QT, we name this model
the *Producer Order Queue Computation Model*.

Figure 7.1 shows the code for this model that solves the problems in Fig. 7.2.
Notice that add, sub, div instructions have offset references that indicate the

**Fig. 7.1** Instruction
sequence generation from the
parse tree of expression
$x = \frac{a+b}{b-c}$. **a** Parse tree.
**b** Instruction sequence.
**c** QSTATEs

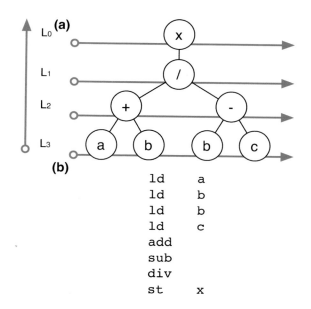

(b)

```
ld    a
ld    b
ld    b
ld    c
add
sub
div
st    x
```

(c)

| QSTATE | Level | Consume | Produce |
|---|---|---|---|
| 1 | L3 | 0 | 4 |
| 2 | L2 | 4 | 2 |
| 3 | L1 | 2 | 1 |
| 4 | L0 | 1 | 0 |

place relative to QH where the operands should be taken. The "sub − 1, 0"
instruction now takes operand $b$ from QH −1, and operand $c$ from QH itself,
QH +0. We name the code for this model *P-Code*. This nontraditional computation
model requires new compiler support to statically determine the value of the offset
references.

Correct evaluation of binary instructions whose both source operands are away
from QH using QueueCore's one operand instruction set is not possible. To ensure
correct evaluation of this case, a special instruction has been implemented in the
processor. The dup instruction takes a variable in the operand queue and places a
copy in QT. The compiler is responsible of placing dup instructions to guarantee that
binary instructions will have their first operand available always at QH, and the
second operand may be taken from an arbitrary position in the operand queue by
using QueueCore's one operand instruction set. Let the expression $x = -a/(a + a)$
be evaluated using QueueCore's one offset instruction set, its DAG is shown in
Fig. 7.2a. Notice that the level $L_3$ produces only one operand, $a$, that is consumed by
the following instruction, neg. The add instruction is constrained to take its first
source operand directly from QH, and its second operand has freedom to be taken
from QH −$N$. For this case, the dup instruction is inserted to make a copy of

**Fig. 7.2** Instruction
sequence generation from
DAG of expression $x = \frac{a+b}{b-c}$.
**a** DAG. **b** Instruction
sequence. **c** QSTATEs

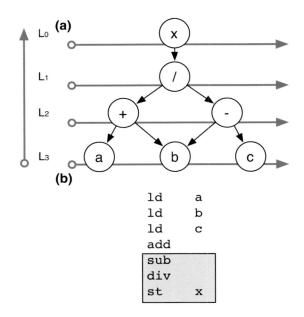

(c)

| QSTATE | Level | Consume | Produce |
|--------|-------|---------|---------|
| 1 | $L_3$ | 0 | 3 |
| 2 | $L_2$ | 4 | 2 |
| 3 | $L_1$ | 2 | 1 |
| 4 | $L_0$ | 1 | 0 |

*a* available as the first source operand of instruction `add` as shown with the dashed
line in Fig. 7.2b. Notice that level $L_3$ in Fig. 7.2b produces two data instead of one.
The instruction sequence using QueueCore's one offset instruction set is shown in
Fig. 7.2c. This mechanism allows safe evaluation of binary operations in a DAG
using one offset instruction set at the cost of the insertion of `dup` instructions. The
QueueCore's instruction set format was decided from our design space exploration
(Canedo 2006). We found that binary operations that require the insertion of `dup`
instructions are rare in program DAGs. We believe that one operand instruction set is
a good design to keep a balance between compact instructions and program
requirements.

## 7.3 Parallelizing Compiler Framework

There are three tasks the parallelizing queue compiler must do that make it different from traditional compilers for register machines:

(1) constrain all instructions to have at most one offset reference,
(2) compute offset reference values, and
(3) schedule the program expressions in level-order manner.

We developed a C compiler for the QueueCore that uses GCC's 4.0.2 front-end and middle-end. The C program is transformed into abstract syntax tree (AST) by the front-end. Then the middle-end converts the ASTs into a language and machine independent format called GIMPLE (Novillo 2004). A set of tree transformations and optimizations to remove redundant code and substitute sequences of code with more efficient sequences is optionally available from the GCC's middle-end for this representation. Although these optimizations are available in our compiler, until this point our primary goal was to develop the basic compiler infrastructure for the QueueCore and we have not validated the results and correctness of programs compiled with these optimizations enabled. We wrote a custom back-end that takes GIMPLE intermediate representation and generates assembly code for the QueueCore processor. Figure 7.3 shows the phases and intermediate representations of the queue compiler infrastructure. The uniqueness of our compiler is from the 1-offset code generation algorithm implemented as the first and second phases in the back-end. This algorithm transforms the data flow graph to assure that the program can be executed using a one-offset queue instruction set. The algorithm then statically determines the offset values for all instructions by measuring the distance of QH relative position with respect of each instruction. Each offset value is computed once and remains the same until the final assembly code is generated. The third phase of the back-end converts our middle-level intermediate representation into a linear one-operand low level intermediate code, and at the same time, schedules the program in a level-order manner. The linear low level code facilitates the extraction of natural ILP done by the fourth phase. Finally, the fifth phase converts the low level representation of the program into assembly code for the QueueCore. The following subsections describe in detail the phases, the algorithms, and the intermediate representations utilized by our queue compiler to generate assembly code from any C program.

## 7.3.1 1-Offset P-Code Generation Phase

GIMPLE is a three address code intermediate representation used by GCC's middle-end to perform optimizations. Three address code is a popular intermediate representation in compilers that expresses well the instructions for a register machine, but fails to express instructions for the queue computation model. The first task of our back-end is to expand the GIMPLE representation into QTrees. QTrees are ASTs without limitation in the number of operands and operations.

GIMPLE's high-level constructs for arrays, pointers, structures, unions, subroutine calls, are expressed in simpler GIMPLE constructs to match the instructions available in a generic queue hardware.

**Fig. 7.3** Parallelizing
compiler infrastructure

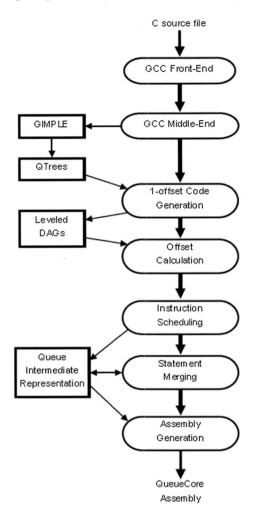

The task of the first phase of our back-end, 1-offset P-Code Generation, is to constrain the binary instructions in the program to have at most one offset reference. This phase detects the cases when dup instructions need to be inserted and it determines the correct place. The code generator takes as input QTrees and generates leveled directed acyclic graphs (LDAGs) as output. A leveled DAG is a data structure that binds the nodes in a DAG to a levels (Heath 1999). We chose LDAGs as data structure to model the data dependencies between instructions and QSTATEs.

The algorithm works in two stages. The first stage converts QTrees to LDAGs augmented with *ghost nodes*. A ghost node is a node without operation that serves as a mark for the algorithm. The second stage takes the augmented LDAGs and remove all ghost nodes by deciding whether a ghost node becomes a dup instruction or is removed.

### 7.3.1.1 Augmented LDAG Construction

QTrees are transformed into LDAGs by a post-order depth-first recursive traversal over the QTree. All nodes are recorded in a look-up table when they first appear, and are created in the corresponding level of the LDAG together with its edge to the parent node. Two restrictions are imposed over the LDAGs for the 1-offset P-Code QCM.

**Definition 7.3.1**   A level is an ordered list of elements with at least one element.

**Definition 7.3.2**   The sink of an edge must be always in a deeper or same level than its source.

**Definition 7.3.3**   An edge to a ghost node spans only one level.

When an operand is found in the look-up table the Definition 7.3.2 must be kept. Line 5 in Algorithm 7.1 is reached when the operand is found in the look-up table and it has a shallower level (closer to the root) than the new level. The function dag_ghost_move_node() moves the operand to the new level, updates the look-up table, converts the old node into a ghost node, and creates an edge from the ghost node to the new created node.

The function insert_ghost_same_level() in Line 8 is reached when the level of the operand in the look-up table is the same to the new level. This function creates a new ghost node in the new level, makes an edge from the parent node to the ghost node, and an edge from the ghost node to the element matched in the look-up table. These two functions build LDAGs augmented with ghost nodes that obey Definitions 7.3.2 and 7.3.3.

### 7.3.1.2 dup Instruction Assignment and Ghost Nodes Elimination

The second and final stage of the 1-offset P-Code generation algorithm takes the augmented LDAG and decides what ghost nodes are assigned to be a dup node or eliminated from the LDAG. The only operations that need a dup instruction are those binary operations whose both operands are away from QH. The augmented LDAG with ghost nodes facilitate the task of identifying those instructions. All binary operations having ghost nodes as their left and right children need to be transformed as follows.

---

**Algorithm 7.1** dag_levelize_ghost (tree $t$, level)

---

  1: nextlevel $\Leftarrow$ level + 1
  2: match $\Leftarrow$ lookup ($t$)
  3: **if** match $\neq$ null **then**
  4:     **if** match.level < nextlevel **then**
  5:         relink $\Leftarrow$ dag_ghost_move_node (nextlevel, $t$, match)
  6:         **return** relink
  7:     **else if** match.level = lookup ($t$) **then**
  8:         relink $\Leftarrow$ insert_ghost_same_level (nextlevel, match)
  9:         **return** relink
 10:     **else**
 11:         **return** match
 12:     **end if**
 13: **end if**
 14: /* Insert the node to a new level or existing one */
 15: **if** nextlevel > get_Last_Level() **then**
 16:     new $\Leftarrow$ make_new_level ($t$, nextlevel)
 17:     record (new)
 18: **else**
 19:     new $\Leftarrow$ append_to_level ($t$, nextlevel)
 20:     record (new)
 21: **end if**
 22: /* Post-Order Depth First Recursion */
 23: **if** $t$ is binary operation **then**
 24:     lhs $\Leftarrow$ dag_levelize_ghost ($t$.left, nextlevel)
 25:     make_edge (new, lhs)
 26:     rhs $\Leftarrow$ dag_levelize_ghost ($t$.right, nextlevel)
 27:     make_edge (new, rhs)
 28: **else if** $t$ is unary operation **then**
 29:     child $\Leftarrow$ dag_levelize_ghost ($t$.child, nextlevel)
 30:     make_edge (new, child)
 31: **end if**
 32: **return** new

---

The ghost node in the left children is substituted by a dup node, and the ghost node in the right children is eliminated from the LDAG. For those binary operations with only one ghost node as the left or right children, the ghost node is eliminated from the LDAG. Algorithm 7.2 describes the function dup_assignment ().

---

**Algorithm 7.2** dup_assignment (Node $i$)

---

```
 1: if isBinary (i) then
 2:     if isGhost (i.left) and isGhost (i.right) then
 3:         dup_assign_node (i.left)
 4:         dag_remove_node (i.right)
 5:     else if isGhost (i.left) then
 6:         dag_remove_node (i.left)
 7:     else if isGhost (i.right) then
 8:         dag_remove_node (i.right)
 9:     end if
10:     return
11: end if
```

---

## 7.3.2 Offset Calculation Phase

Once the LDAGs including dup instructions have been built, the next step is to calculate the offset reference values for the instructions. Following the definition of the producer order QCM, the offset reference value of an instruction represents the distance, in number of queue words, between the position of QH and the operand to be dequeued.

The main challenge in the calculation of offset values is to determine the QH relative position with respect of every operation. We define the following properties to facilitate the description of the algorithm to find the position of QH with respect of any node in the LDAG.

**Definition 7.3.4** An $\alpha$-node is the first element of a level.

**Definition 7.3.5** The QH position with respect of the $\alpha$-node of Level-j is always at the $\alpha$-node of the next level, Level-(j+1).

**Definition 7.3.6** A level-order traversal of a LDAG is a walk of all nodes in every level (from the deepest to the root) starting from the $\alpha$-node.

**Definition 7.3.7** The distance between two nodes in a LDAG, $\delta(u,v)$, is the number of nodes found in a level-order traversal between $u$ and $v$ including $u$.

**Definition 7.3.8** A hard edge is a dependence edge between two nodes that spans only one level.

Let $p_n$ be a node for which the QH position must be found. QH relative position with respect of $p_n$ is found after a node in a traversal $P_i$ from $p_{n-1}$ to $p_0$ ($\alpha$-node) meets one of two conditions. The first condition is that the node is the $\alpha$-node, $P_i = p_0$. From Definition 7.3.5, QH position is at $\alpha$-node of the next level $lev(p) + 1$. The second condition is that $P_i$ is a binary or unary operation and has a hard edge to one of its operands $q_m$. QH position is given by $q_m$'s following node as a result of a level-order traversal. Notice that $q_m$'s following node can be $q_{m+1}$, or the $\alpha$-node of $lev(q_m) + 1$ if $q_m$ is the last node in $lev(q_m)$. The proposed algorithm is described in Algorithm 7.3.

After the QH position with respect of $p_n$ has been found, the only operation to calculate the offset reference value for each of $p_n$'s operands is to measure the distance $\delta$ between QH's position and the operand's position as described in Algorithm 7.4.

In brief, for all nodes in a LDAG $w$, the offset reference values to their operands are calculated by determining the position of QH with respect of every node, and measuring the distance to the operands. Every edge is annotated with its offset reference value.

---

**Algorithm 7.3** qh_pos (LDAG $w$, Node $u$)

1:   $I \Leftarrow$ getLevel $(u)$
2:   **for** $i \Leftarrow u.prev$ to $I.\alpha$-node **do**
3:     **if** isOperation $(i)$ **then**
4:       **if** isHardEdge $(i.right)$ **then**
5:         $v \Leftarrow$ BFS_nextnode $(i.right)$
6:         **return** $v$
7:       **end if**
8:       **if** isHardEdge $(i.left)$ **then**
9:         $v \Leftarrow$ BFS_nextnode $(i.left)$
10:         **return** $v$
11:       **end if**
12:     **end if**
13: **end for**
14: $L \Leftarrow$ getNextLevel $(u)$
15: $v \Leftarrow L.\alpha$-node
16: **return** $v$

---

**Algorithm 7.4** OpOffset (LDAG $w$, Node $v$, Operand $r$)

1:   offset $\Leftarrow \delta(\text{qh\_pos}(w,v),r)$
2:   **return** offset

---

## 7.3.3 Instruction Scheduling Phase

The instruction scheduling algorithm of our compiler is a variation of basic block scheduling (Muchnick 1997) where the only difference is that instructions are generated from a level-order topological order of the LDAGs. The input of the algorithm is an LDAG annotated with offset reference values. For every level in the LDAG, from the deepest level to the root level, all nodes are traversed from left to right and an equivalent low level intermediate representation instruction is selected for every visited node.

Instruction selection was simplified by having one low level instruction for every high level instruction in the LDAG representation. The output of the instruction scheduling is a QIR list. QIR is a single operand low level intermediate representation capable to express the instruction set of the QueueCore. The only operand is used for memory operations and branch instructions. Offset reference values are encoded as attributes in the QIR instructions. Figure 7.4 shows the QIR list for the LDAG. The QIR includes annotations depicted in Fig. 7.4 with the prefix QMARK_*.

A extra responsibility of this phase is to check code correctness of the 1-offset P-Code generation algorithm by comparing with zero the value of the offset reference for the first operand of binary instructions based on the assumption that the 1-offset P-Code generation algorithm constrains all instructions to have at most one offset reference. For every compiled function this phase also inserts the QIR instructions for the function's prologue and epilogue.

## 7.3.4 Natural Instruction Level Parallelism Extraction: Statement Merging Transformation

Statement merging transformation reorders the instructions of a sequential program in such a way that all independent instructions from different statements are in the same level an can be executed in parallel following the principle of the QCM. This phase makes a dependence analysis on individual instructions of different statements looking for conflicts in memory locations. Statements are considered the transformation unit. Whenever an instruction is reordered, the

**Fig. 7.4** QIR code fragment

```
(QMARK_BBSTART (B1))

(QMARK_STMT)
    (QMARK_LEVEL)
        (PUSH_Q (i))
        (PUSH_Q (4))
    (QMARK_LEVEL)
        (LOAD_ADDR_Q (a))
        (MUL_Q)
    (QMARK_LEVEL)
        (ADD_Q)
    (QMARK_LEVEL)
        (SLOAD_Q)
    (QMARK_LEVEL)
        (POP_Q (x))

(QMARK_STMT)
    (QMARK_LEVEL)
        (PUSH_Q (x))
        (PUSH_Q (4))
    (QMARK_LEVEL)
        (LOAD_ADDR_Q (a))
        (MUL_Q)
    (QMARK_LEVEL)
        (ADD_Q)
        (PUSH_Q (7))
    (QMARK_LEVEL)
        (STORE_Q)

(QMARK_STMT)
    (GOTO_Q (L2))
```

entire data flow graph of the statement to where it belongs is reordered to keep its original shape. In this way, all offsets computed by the offset calculation phase remain the same, and the data flow graph is not altered.

The data dependence analysis looks for two accesses to the same memory location whenever two instructions have the same offset with respect of the base register. Instructions that may alias memory locations are merged safely using a conservative approach to guarantee correctness of the program. Statements with branch instructions and function calls are non-mergeable.

Figure 7.5a shows a program with three statements $S_1$, $S_2$, $S_3$. The original sequential scheduling of this program is driven by a level-order scheduling as

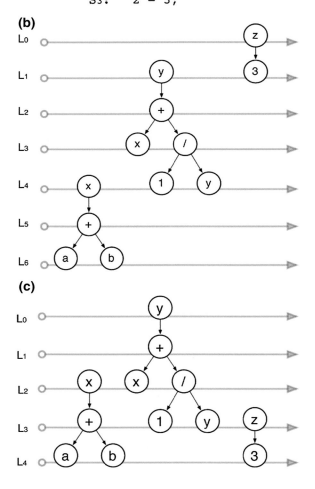

**Fig. 7.5** Statement merging transformation

**(a)**

```
S1:    x = a + b;
S2:    y = x + (1 / y);
S3:    z = 3;
```

shown in Fig. 7.5b. When the statement merging transformation is applied to this program a dependency analysis reveals a flow dependency for variable $x$ in $S_1$, $S_2$ in levels $L_4$, $L_3$. Instructions from $S_2$ can be moved one level down and the flow dependency on variable $x$ is kept as long the store to memory happens before the load. Statement $S_3$ is independent from the previous statements, this condition allows $S_3$ to be pushed to the bottom of the data flow graph. Figure 7.5c shows the DFG for the sample program after the statement merging transformation. For this example, the number of levels in the DFG has been reduced from seven to five.

From the QCM principle, the QueueCore is able to execute the maximum parallelism found in DAGs as no false dependencies occur in the instructions. This transformation merges statements to expose all the available parallelism (Wall 1991) within basic blocks. With the help of the compiler, QueueCore is able to execute *natural* instruction level parallelism as it appears in the programs. Statement merging is available in the queue compiler as an optimization flag which can be enabled upon user request.

## 7.3.5 Assembly Generation Phase

The last stage of the queue compiler is the assembly code generation for the QueueCore processor. It is done by a one-to-one translation from QIR code to assembly code. The assembly generator is in charge of inserting covop instructions to expand the operand field of those instructions that have operands beyond the limits of the operand field bits.

Figure 7.6a shows the generated assembly code and Fig. 7.6b shows the assembly code with natural parallelism exposed for the C program. Notice that the original assembly code and the assembly code after statement merging contain exactly the same instructions with the only difference that the order the instructions change. All instructions have one operand. Depending on the instruction type the only operand has different meaning. The highlighted code fragment in Fig. 7.6a shows the assignment of an array element indexed by variable to another variable, in C language "x=a[i]". The first instruction loads the index variable into the queue, its operand specifies the base register and the offset to obtain the memory location of the variable.

The operand in the second instruction specifies the immediate value to be loaded, if the value is greater than the instruction bits the assembly phase inserts a covop instruction to extend the immediate value. The operand in the third instruction works is used to compute the effective address of the first element of the array. The next two arithmetic instructions use their operand as the offset reference and help to compute the address of the array element indexed by a variable. For this example, both are binary instructions and take their first operand implicitly from QH and the second operand from QH +1. The lds instruction loads into the queue the value of a computed address taken the operand queue as

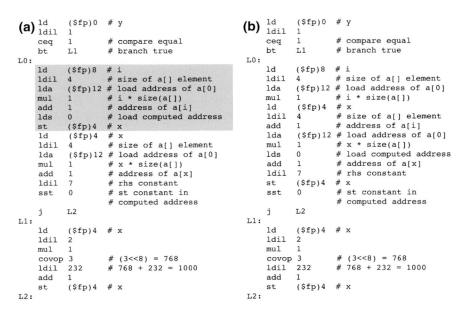

**Fig. 7.6** Assembly output for QueueCore processor **a** Original QueueCore assembly code **b** ILP exposed for QueueCore assembly processor

an offset reference given by its only operand. The last instruction stores the value pointed by QH to memory using base addressing.

To demonstrate the efficiency of our one-offset queue computation model, we developed a C compiler that targets the QueueCore processor. For a set of numerical benchmark programs, we evaluated the characteristics of the resulting queue compiler. We measured the effectiveness of statement merging optimization for improving ILP, we analyzed the quality of the generated code in terms of the distribution of instruction types, and we demonstrate the effectiveness of the queue compiler as a design space exploration tool for our QueueCore by analyzing the maximum offset value required by the chosen numerical benchmarks.

To show the potential of our technique for a high-performance processor, we compared the compile-time exposed ILP from our compiler against the ILP exposed by an optimizing compiler for a typical RISC processor. And to highlight the low code size features of our design, we also compare the code size to the embedded versions of two RISC processors.

The chosen benchmarks are well known numerical programs: radix-8 fast Fourier transform, livermore loops, whetstone loops, single precision linpack, and quake benchmark. To compare the extracted ILP, we compiled the programs using our queue compiler with statement merging transformation. For the RISC-like processor, we compiled the benchmarks using GCC 4.0.2 with classical and ILP optimizations enabled (−O3) targeting the MIPS I (Kane 1992) instruction set. The ILP for the QueueCore is measured directly from the DDG in the compiler.

The ILP for the MIPS I is measured from the generated assembly based on the register and memory data dependencies and control flow, assuming no-aliasing information.

Code size was measured from the text segment of the compiled programs. MIPS16 (Kissel 1997) and ARM/Thumb (Goudge 1996) were chosen for the RISC-like embedded processors. GCC 4.0.2 compiler for MIPS16 and ARM/Thumb architectures was used with full optimizations enabled (−O3) to generate the object files. For the QueueCore, the queue compiler was used with statement merging transformation.

## 7.4  Parallelizing Compiler Development Results

The resulting back-end for the QueueCore consists of about 8,000 lines of C code. Table 7.1 shows the number of lines for each phase of the back-end.

### 7.4.1  Queue Compiler Evaluation

First, we analyze the effect of the statement merging transformation on boosting ILP in our compiler. Figure 7.7 shows the improvement factor of the compiled code with statement merging transformation over the original code without statement merging, both scheduled using the level-order traversal.

All benchmarks show an improvement gain ranging from 1.73 to 4.25. The largest ILP improvement is for the fft8g program because it contains very large loop bodies without control flow where the statement merging transformation can work most effectively. Statement merging is a code motion transformation and does not insert or eliminate instructions.

To evaluate the quality of the generated code of our compiler, we organized the QueueCore instructions into five categories: memory, ALU, move data, control

**Table 7.1**  Lines of C code for each phase of the queue compiler's back-end

| Phase | Lines of code | Description |
| --- | --- | --- |
| 1-offset P-code generation | 3000 | Code generation algorithm, QTrees and LDAGs infrastructure |
| Offset calculation | 1500 | Algorithm to find the location of QH and distance to each operation |
| Instruction scheduling | 1500 | Level-order scheduling, lowering to QIR, and QIR infrastructure |
| Statement merging | 1000 | Natural ILP exploitation and data dependency analysis |
| Assembly generation | 1000 | Assembly code generation from QIR |
| Total | 8000 | |

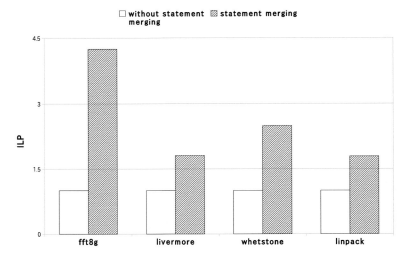

**Fig. 7.7** Effect on ILP of statement merging transformation in the queue compiler

flow, and covop. Memory instructions are to load and store to main memory including loading immediate values; ALU includes comparison instructions, type conversions, integer and floating point arithmetic-logic instructions; move data includes all data transfer between special purpose registers; control flow includes conditional and unconditional jumps, and subroutine calls; and covop includes all covop instructions to extend memory accesses and immediate values.

Table 7.2 shows the distribution of the instruction categories in percentages for the compiled programs. From the table we can observe that memory operations account for about 50 % of the total number of instructions, ALU instructions about 40 %, move data less than 1 %, control flow less about 8 %, and covop about 2 %. These results point a place for future improvement of our compiler infrastructure. We believe that classical local and global optimizations (Aho 1986) may improve the quality of the generated code by reducing the number of memory operations.

The developed queue compiler is a valuable tool for the QueueCore's architecture design space exploration since it gives us the ability to automatically generate assembly code and extract characteristics of the compiled programs that affect the processor's parameters. To emphasize the usage of the queue compiler as

**Table 7.2** Instruction category percentages for the compiled benchmarks for the QueueCore

| Benchmark | Memory | ALU | Move data | Control flow | Covop |
|---|---|---|---|---|---|
| fft8g | 48.60 | 47.55 | 0.32 | 2.90 | 0.63 |
| Livermore | 58.55 | 33.29 | 0.20 | 5.95 | 4.01 |
| Whetstone | 58.73 | 26.73 | 1.11 | 13.43 | 0.00 |
| Linpack | 48.14 | 41.59 | 0.58 | 8.16 | 1.52 |
| Equake | 44.52 | 43.00 | 0.56 | 7.76 | 3.5 |

a design tool, we measured the maximum offset value required by the compiled benchmarks.

Table 7.3 shows the maximum offset value for the given programs. These compiling results show that the eight bits reserved in the QueueCore's instruction format (Ben-Abdallah 2006) for the offset reference value are enough to satisfy the demands of these numerical calculation programs.

## 7.4.2 Comparison of Generated QueueCore Code with Optimized RISC Code

The graph in Fig. 7.8 compares the ILP improvement of the queue compiler over the optimizing compiler for MIPS processor. For all the analyzed programs, the queue compiler exposed more natural parallelism to the QueueCore than the optimizing compiler for the RISC machine. The improvement of parallelism comes from the natural parallelism found in the level-order scheduled data flow graph with merged statements.

QueueCore's instruction set benefits from this transformation and scheduling as no register names are present in the instruction format. The RISC code, on the other hand, is limited by the architected registers. It depends on the good judgment of the compiler to make effective use of the registers to extract as much parallelism as possible, and whenever the register pressure exceeds the limit then spill registers to memory. The loop bodies in livermore, whetstone, linpack, and equake benchmarks consist of one or few instructions with many operands and operations. The improvement of our technique in these programs comes mainly from the level-order scheduling of these "fat" statements since the statement merging has no effect across basic blocks.

The greatest improvement on these benchmarks was for the fft8g program which is dominated by manually unrolled loop bodies where the statement merging takes full advantage. In average, our queue compiler is able to extract more parallelism than the optimizing compiler for a RISC machine by a factor of 1.38.

Figure 7.9 shows the normalized code size of the compiled benchmarks for MIPS16, ARM/Thumb and QueueCore using the MIPS I as the baseline. For most of the benchmarks our design achieves denser code than the baseline and the

| **Table 7.3** QueueCore's program maximum offset reference value | Benchmark | Maximum offset |
|---|---|---|
| | fft8g | 29 |
| | Livermore | 154 |
| | Whetstone | 31 |
| | Linpack | 174 |
| | Equake | 89 |

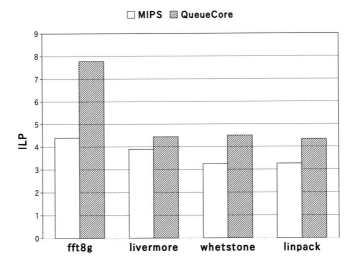

**Fig. 7.8** Instruction level parallelism improvement of queue compiler over optimizing compiler for a RISC machine

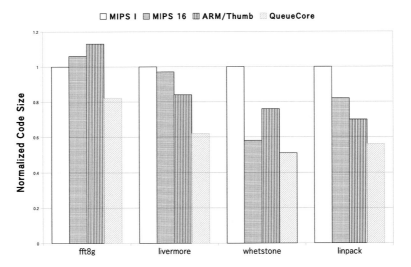

**Fig. 7.9** Normalized code size for two embedded RISC processors and QueueCore

embedded RISC processors. Except for the equake program where the MIPS16 achieved lower code size than the QueueCore.

A closer inspection to the object file revealed that the QueueCore program has about two times more instructions than the MIPS and MIPS16 code. This is due to the effect of local optimizations such as constant folding, common sub expression elimination, dead code removal, etc. that are applied in the RISC compilers and not in the queue compiler. In average, our design achieves 31 % denser code than

MIPS I, 20 % denser code than the embedded MIPS16, and 26 % denser code than the ARM/Thumb processor.


## 7.5  Conclusion

With the rise of multi-core systems and many-core processors, concurrency becomes a major issue in the daily life of a programmer. Thus, compiler and software development tools will be critical to help programmers create high performance software.

This chapter described design and evaluation of a parallelizing compiler targeted for single and multicore computing. The design eliminates the register pressure by hiding completely the register file from the instruction set while maintaining a short instruction format with one operand reference. The queue compiler takes advantage of this design and it is capable to expose the maximum natural parallelism available in the data flow graph by means of a statement merging transformation. We evaluated the design by comparing the compile-time extracted parallelism against an optimizing compiler for a traditional RISC machine for a set of numerical benchmarks.

# Chapter 8
# Power Optimization Techniques for Multicore SoCs

Power dissipation continues to be a primary design constraint in single and multicore systems. Increasing power consumption not only results in increasing energy costs, but also results in high die temperatures that affect chip reliability, performance, and packaging cost. Energy conservation has been largely considered in the hardware design in general and also in embedded multicore systems' components, such as CPUs, disks, displays, memories, and so on. Significant additional power savings can be also achieved by incorporating low-power methods into the design of network protocols used for data communication (audio, video, etc.). This chapter investigates in details power reduction techniques at components and the network protocol levels.

## 8.1 Introduction

Computation and communication have been steadily moving toward embedded multicore devices. With continued miniaturization and increasing computation power, we see ever growing use of powerful microprocessors running sophisticated, intelligent control software in a vast array of devices including pagers, cellular phones, laptop computers, digital cameras, video cameras, video games, etc. Unfortunately, there is an inherent conflict in the design goals behind these devices: as mobile systems, they should be designed to maximize battery life, but as intelligent devices, they need powerful processors, which consume more energy than those in simpler devices, thus reducing battery life.

In spite of continuous advances in semiconductor and battery technologies that allow microprocessors to provide much greater computation per unit of energy and longer total battery life, the fundamental trade-offs between performance and battery life remains critically important (Martin 1999; Gregory 1995; Kravets and Krishnan 2000; Lorch 1995).

Multimedia applications and mobile computing are two trends that have a new application domain and market. Personal mobile or ubiquitous computing is playing a significant role in driving technology. An important issue for these devices will be the user interface—the interaction with its owner. The device needs

A. Ben Abdallah, *Multicore Systems On-Chip: Practical Software/Hardware Design*,     175
Atlantis Ambient and Pervasive Intelligence 7, DOI: 10.2991/978-94-91216-92-3_8,
© Atlantis Press and the author 2013

to support multimedia tasks and handles many different classes of data traffic over a limited bandwidth wireless connection, including delay sensitive, real-time traffic such as video and speech.

Wireless networking greatly enhances the utility of a personal computing device. It provides mobile users with versatile communication, and permits continuous access to services and resources of the land-based network. A wireless infrastructure capable of supporting packet data and multimedia services in addition to voice will bootstrap on the success of the Internet, and in turn drives novel networked applications and services. However, the technological challenges to establishing this paradigm of personal mobile computing are non-trivial. In particular, these devices have limited battery resources. While reduction of the physical dimensions of batteries is a promising solution, such effort alone will reduce the amount of charge retained by the batteries. This will in turn reduce the amount of time a user can use the computing device. Such restrictions tend to undermine the notion of mobile computing. In addition, more extensive and continuous use of network services will only aggravate this problem since communication consumes relatively much energy. Unfortunately, the rate at which battery performance improves is very slow, despite the great interest created by the wireless business.

The energy efficiency is an issue involving all layers of the system, its physical layer, its communication protocol stack, its system architecture, its operating system, and the entire network (Kravets and Krishnan 2000). This implicates several mechanisms that can be used to attain a high-energy efficiency. There are several motivations for energy-efficient design. Perhaps the most visible driving source is the success and growth of the portable consumer electronic market.

In its most abstract form, a networked system has two sources of energy drain required for its operation:

(1) Communication, due to energy spent by the wireless interface and due to the internal traffic between various parts of the system, and
(2) Computation, due to processing for applications, tasks required during communication, and operating system.

Thus, minimizing energy consumption is a task that will require minimizing the contributions of communication and computation.

From another hand, power consumption has become a major concern because of the ever-increasing density of solid-state electronic devices, coupled with an increasing use of mobile computers and portable communication devices. The technology has thus far helped to build low power systems. The speed-power efficiency has indeed gone up since 1990 by 10 times each 2.5 years for general-purpose processors and digital signal processors (DSPs) (Gregory 1995).

Design for low-energy consumption is certainly not a challenging research field, and yet remains one of the most difficult as future mobile multicore SoC system designers attempt to pack more capabilities such as multimedia processing and high bandwidth radios into battery operated portable miniature packages. Playing times of only a few hours for personal audio, notebooks, and cordless phones are clearly not very consumer friendly. Also, the required batteries are voluminous and heavy, often leading to bulky and unappealing products (Rulnick and Bambos 1996).

The key to energy efficiency in future mobile multicore SoCS will be, then, designing higher layers of the mobile system, their functionality, their system architecture, their operating system, and the entire network, with energy efficiency in mind.

## 8.2 Power Aware Technological-Level Design Optimizations

### 8.2.1 Factors Affecting CMOS Power Consumption

Most components in a mobile system are currently fabricated using CMOS technology. Since CMOS circuits do not dissipate power if they are not switching, a major focus of low power design is to reduce the switching activity to the minimal level required to perform the computations (Najm 1994; Pedram 1996).

The sources of energy consumption on a CMOS chip can be classified as static and dynamic power dissipation. The average power is given by:

$$P_{avg} = P_{static} + P_{dynamic} \qquad (8.1)$$

The static power consumption is given by:

$$P_{static} = P_{short-circuit} + P_{leak} = I_{sc} \cdot V_{dd} + I_{leak} \cdot V_{dd} \qquad (8.2)$$

and the dynamic power consumption is given by:

$$P_{dynamic} = \alpha_{0 \to 1} C_L \cdot V_{dd}^2 \cdot f_{clk} \qquad (8.3)$$

The three major sources of power dissipation are, then, summarized in the following equation:

$$P_{avg} = \alpha_{0 \to 1} C_L \cdot V_{dd}^2 \cdot f_{clk} + I_{sc} \cdot V_{dd} + I_{leak} \cdot V_{dd} \qquad (8.4)$$

The first term of Formula (8.4), represents the switching component of power, where $\alpha_{0 \to 1}$ is the node transition activity factor (the average number of times the node makes a power consuming transition in one clock period), $C_L$ is the load capacitance and $f_{clk}$ is the clock frequency. The second term is due to the direct-path short circuit current, $I_{sc}$, which arises when both the NMOS and PMOS transistors are simultaneously active, conducting current directly from supply ground. The last term, $I_{leak}$ (leakage current), which can arise from substrate injection and sub-threshold effects, is primarily determined by fabrication technology.

$\alpha_{0\to1}$ is defined as the average number of times in each clock cycle that a node with capacitance, $C_L$, will make a power consuming transition resulting in an average switching component of power for a CMOS gate to be simplified to:

$$P_{\text{switch}} = \alpha_{0\to1} C_L \cdot V_{\text{dd}}^2 \cdot f_{\text{clk}} \tag{8.5}$$

Since the energy expended for each switching event in CMOS circuits is $C_L \cdot V_{\text{dd}}^2 \cdot f_{\text{clk}}$, it has the extremely important characteristics that it becomes quadratically more efficient as the high transition voltage level is reduced.

It is clear that operating at the lowest possible voltage is most desirable, however, this comes at the cost of increased delays and thus reduced throughput. It is also possible to reduce the power by choosing an architecture that minimizes the effective switched capacitance at a fixed voltage: through reductions in the number of operations, the interconnect capacitance, internal bit widths and using operations that require less energy per computation. We will use Formula (8.4) and (8.5) to discuss the energy reduction techniques and trade-offs that involve energy consumption of digital circuits. From these formulas, we can see that there are four ways to reduce power:

(1) reduce the capacity load $C$,
(2) reduce the supply voltage $V$,
(3) reduce the switching frequency $f$, and
(4) reduce the switching activity.

## 8.2.2 Reducing Voltage and Frequency

Supply voltage scaling has been the most adopted approach to power optimization, since it normally yields considerable savings thanks to the quadratic dependence of $P_{\text{switch}}$ on $V_{\text{dd}}$ (Najm 1994). The major shortcoming of this solution, however, is that lowering the supply voltage affects circuit speed. As a consequence, both design and technological solutions must be applied in order to compensate the decrease in circuit performance introduced by reduced voltage. In other words, speed optimization is applied first, followed by supply voltage scaling, which brings the design back to its original timing, but with a lower power requirement.

It is well known that reducing clock frequency $f$ alone does not reduce energy, since to do the same work the system must run longer. As the voltage is reduced, the delay increases. A common approach to power reduction is to first increase the speed performance of the module itself, followed by supply voltage scaling, which brings the design back to its original timing, but with a lower power requirements (Pedram 1996).

A similar problem, i.e., performance decrease, is encountered when power optimization is obtained through frequency scaling. Techniques that rely on reductions of the clock frequency to lower power consumption are thus usable under the constraint that some performance slack does exist. Although this may seldom occur for designs considered in their entirety, it happens quite often that some specific units in a larger architecture do not need peak performance for some clock/machine cycles. Selective frequency scaling (as well as voltage scaling) on such units may thus be applied, at no penalty in the overall system speed.

## 8.2.3  Reducing Capacitance

Energy consumption in CMOS circuitry is proportional to capacitance C. Therefore, a path that can be followed to reduce energy consumption is to minimize the capacitance. A significant fraction of a CMOS chip's energy consumption is often contributed to driving large off-chip capacitances, and not to core processing. Off-chip capacitances are in the order of five to tens of pF. For conventional packaging technologies, pins contribute approximately 13–14 pF of capacitance each (10 pF for the pad and 3–4 pF for the printed circuit board) (Borkar 1999).

From our earlier discussion, Eq. (8.5) indicates that energy consumption is proportional to capacitance; I/O power can be a significant portion of the overall energy consumption of the chip. Therefore, in order to save energy, use few external outputs, and have them switch as infrequently as possible. Packaging technology can have a impact on the energy consumption. For example, in multi-chip modules where all of the chips of a system are mounted on a single substrate and placed in a single package, the capacitance is reduced. Also, accessing external memory consumes much energy. So, a way to reduce capacitance is to reduce external accesses and optimize the system by using on-chip resources like caches and registers.

### 8.2.3.1  Chip Layout

There are a number of layout-level techniques that can be applied. Since the physical capacitance of the higher metal layers are smaller, there is some advantage to select upper level metals to route high-activity signals. Furthermore, traditional placement involves reducing area and delay, which in turn translates to minimizing the physical capacitance of wires. Placement that incorporates energy consumption, concentrates on minimizing the activity-capacitance product rather than capacitance alone. In general, high-activity wires should be kept short and local. Tools have been developed that use this basic strategy to achieve about 18 % reduction in energy consumption.

The capacitance is an important factor for the energy consumption of a system. However, reducing the capacity is not the distinctive feature of low-power design, since in CMOS technology energy is consumed only when the capacitance is switched. It is more important to concentrate on the switching activity and the number of signals that need to be switched. Architectural design decisions have more impact than solely reducing the capacitance.

### 8.2.3.2 Technology Scaling

Scaling advanced CMOS technology to the next generation improves performance, increases transistor density, and reduces power consumption. Technology scaling typically has three main goals:

(1) Reduce gate delay by 30 %, resulting in an increase in operating frequency of about 43 %;
(2) Double transistor density; and
(3) Reduce energy per transistor by about 65 %, saving 50 % of the power.

These are not ad hoc goals; rather, they follow scaling theory (Borkar 1999).

As the Semiconductor Industry Association road-map (SIA) indicates, the trend of process technology improvement is expected to continue for years (SIA 1997). Scaling of the physical dimension involves reducing all dimensions: thus transistors widths and lengths are reduced; interconnection length is reduced, etc. Consequently, the delay, capacitance and energy consumption will decrease substantially.

Another way to reduce capacitance at the technology level is to reduce chip area. For example, an energy efficient architecture that occupies a larger area can reduce the overall energy consumption, e.g., by exploiting locality in a parallel implementation.

## 8.3 Power Aware Logic-Level Design Optimizations

Logic-level power optimization has been extensively researched in the last few years. While most traditional power optimization techniques for logic cells focus on minimizing switching power, circuit design for leakage power reduction is also gaining importance (Ye et al. 1998). As a result, logic-level design can have a high impact on the energy-efficiency and performance of the system. Issues in the logic level relate to for example state-machines, clock gating, encoding, and the use of parallel architectures.

### 8.3.1 Clock Gating

Several power minimization techniques work especially well at the logic level. Most of them rely on switching frequency. The best example of which is the use of clock gating (Benini and de Micheli 1999). Clock gating provides a way to selectively stop the clock, and thus force the original circuit to make no transition, whenever the computation to be carried out by a hardware unit at the next clock cycle is useless. In other words, the clock signal is disabled to shut down some modules of the chip, that are inactive. This saves on clock power, because the local clock line is not toggling all the time.

For example the latency for the CPU of the TMS320C5x DSP processor (Benini et al. 2001) to return to active operation from the IDLE3 mode takes around 50 μs, due to the need of the on-chip PLL circuit to lock with the external clock generator. With the conventional scheme, the register is clocked all the time, whether new data is to be captured or not. If the register must hold the old state, its output is fed back into the data input through a multiplexer whose enable line (ENABLE) controls whether the register clocks in new data or recycles the existing data. However, with a gated clock, the signal that would otherwise control the select line on the multiplexer now controls the gate. The result is that the energy consumed in driving the register's clock input (CLK) is reduced in proportion to the decrease in average local clock frequency. The two circuits function identically, but utilization of the gated clock reduces the power consumption (Fig. 8.1).

### 8.3.2 Logic Encoding

The power consumption can be also reduced by carefully minimizing the number of transitions. The designer of a digital circuit often has the freedom of choosing the encoding scheme. Different encoding implementations often lead to different

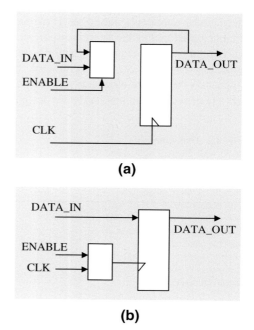

**Fig. 8.1** Clock gating example: **a** conventional, **b** gated clock

area, power, and delay trade-offs. An appropriate choice of the representation of the signals can have a big impact on the switching activity.

The frequency of consecutive patterns in the traffic streams is the basis for the effectiveness of encoding mechanisms. For example, a program counter in a processor generally uses a binary code. On average two bits are changed for each state transition (Ben-Abdallah et al. 2005). Using a Gray-code (single bit changes) can give interesting energy savings. However, a Gray-code incremental requires more transistors to implement than a ripple carry incrementer (Ben-Abdallah et al. 2005). Therefore, a combination can be used in which only the most frequently changing LSB bits use a Gray code.

## 8.3.3 Data Guarding

Switching activity is the major cause of energy dissipation in most CMOS digital systems. Therefore, to reduce power consumption, switching activities that do not contribute to the actual communication and computation should be eliminated. The basic idea is to identify logical conditions at some inputs to a logic circuit that is invariant to the output. Since those input values do not affect the output, the input transitions can be disabled.

Data logic-guarding technique (Tiwari et al. 1998), is an efficient method used to guard not useful switching activities to propagate further inside the system. The technique is based on reducing the switching activities by placing transparent latches/registers with an enable signal at the inputs of each block of the circuit that needs to be selectively turned off. If the module is to be active in a clock cycle, the enable signal makes the latch transparent, permitting normal operation. If not, the latch retains its previous state and no transitions propagate through the inactive module (see Fig. 8.2). As a summary, the logic-level design can have a high impact on the energy-efficiency and the performance of a given system. Even with the use of state of the arts hardware design language (i.e., Verilog HDL), there are

**Fig. 8.2** Dual Operation ALU with Guard Logic. The multiplexer does the selection only after both units have completed their evaluation. The evaluation of one of the two units is avoided by using a guard-logic; two latches (L1 and L2) are placed with enable signals (s1 and s2) at the inputs of the shifter and the adder respectively

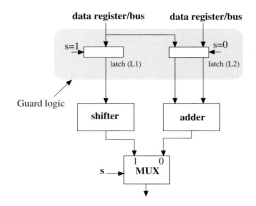

still many optimizations techniques that should be explored by the designers to reduce the energy consumption at the logic-level. The most effective technique used at this level is the reduction of switching activities.

## 8.4 Power-Aware System Level Design Optimizations

In the previous sections we have explored sources of energy consumption and showed the low level—technology and circuit levels, design techniques used to reduce the power dissipation. In this section, we will concentrate on the energy reduction techniques at the architecture and system level.

### 8.4.1 Hardware System Architecture Power Consumption Optimizations

The implementation dependent part of the power consumption of a system is strongly related to the number of properties that a given system or algorithm may have. The component that contributes a significant amount of the total energy consumption is the communication channels or interconnects.

Experiments have already been made in designs and proved that about 10–40 % of the total power may be dissipated in buses, multiplexers and drivers (Liang et al. 2004; Abnous and Rabaey 1996). This amount can increase dramatically for systems with multiple chips due to large off-chip bus capacitance.

The energy consumption of the communication channels is largely dependent on algorithm and architecture-level design decisions. Regularity and locality are two important properties of algorithms and architectures for reducing the energy consumption due to the communication channels. The idea behind regularity is to capture the degree to which common patterns appear in an algorithm. Common patterns enable the design of less complex architecture and therefore simpler interconnect structure and less control hardware. Simple measures of regularity include the number of loops in the algorithm and the ratio of operations to nodes in the data flow graph. The statistics of the percentage of operations covered by sets of patterns is also indicative of an algorithm's regularity. Quantifying this measure involves first finding a promising set of patterns, large patterns being favored. The core idea is to grow pairs of as large as possible isomorphic regions from corresponding pairs of seed nodes (Rabaey et al. 1995).

Locality relates to the degree to which a system or algorithm has natural isolated clusters of operation or storage with few interconnections between them. Partitioning the system or algorithm into spatially local clusters ensures that the majority of the data transfers take place within the clusters and relatively few between clusters. The result is that the local buses with a low electrical capacity are shorter and more frequently used than the longer highly capacitive global buses. Locality of reference can be used to partition memories. Current high-level synthesis tools are targeted to area minimization or performance optimization. However, for power reduction it is better to reduce the number of accesses to long global buses and have the local buses be accessed more frequently.

In a direct implementation targeted at area optimization, hardware sharing between operations might occur, destroying the locality of computation. An architecture and implementation should preserve the locality and partition and implement it such that hardware sharing is limited. The increase in the number of functional units does not necessarily translate into a corresponding increase in the overall area and energy consumption since the localization of interconnect allows a more compact layout and also fewer access to buffers and multiplexers are needed.

### 8.4.1.1 Hierarchical Memory System

Efficient use of an optimized custom memory hierarchy to exploit temporal locality in the data accesses can have a very large impact on the power consumption in data dominated applications. The idea of using a custom memory hierarchy to minimize the power consumption is based on the fact that memory power consumption depends primarily on the access frequency and the size of the memory. For on-chip memories, memory power increases with the memory size. In practice, the relation is between linear and logarithmic depending on the memory library. For off chip memories, the power is much less dependent on the size because they are internally heavily partitioned. Still they consume more energy per access than the smaller on-chip memories. Hence, power savings can be obtained by accessing heavily used data from smaller memories instead of from large background memories (Su and Despain 1995).

As most of the time only a small memory is read, the energy consumption is reduced. Memory considerations must also be taken into account in the design of any system. By employing an on-chip cache significant power reductions together with a performance increase can be gained. Apart from caching data and instructions at the hardware level, caching is also applied in the file system of an operating system (Su and Despain 1995). The larger the cache is, the better performance is achieved. Energy consumption is reduced because data is kept locally, and thus requires less data traffic. Furthermore, the energy consumption is reduced because less disk and network activity is required.

The compiler also has impact on power consumption by reducing the number of instructions with memory operands. It also can generate code that exploits the characteristics of the machine and avoids expensive stalls. The most energy can be saved by a proper utilization of registers. In Mehta et al. (1997), a detailed review of some compiler techniques that are of interest in the power minimization arena is also presented.

Secondary Storage

Secondary storage in modern mobile systems generally consists of a magnetic disk supplemented by a small amount of DRAM used as a disk cache; this cache may be in the CPU main memory, the disk controller, or both (Doughs et al. 1994; Li et al. 1994; Douglis et al. 1994). Such a cache improves the overall performance of secondary storage. It also reduces its power consumption by reducing the load on the hard disk, which consumes more power than the DRAM.

Energy consumption is reduced because data is kept locally, and thus requires less data traffic. In addition, the energy consumption is reduced because less disk and network traffic is required. Unfortunately, there is trade-off in size of the cache memory since the required amount of additional DRAM can use as much as energy as a conventional spinning hard disk (Erik et al. 1995).

A possible technology for secondary storage is an integrated circuit called flash memory (Douglis et al. 1994). Like a hard disk, such memory is non-volatile and can hold data without consuming energy. Furthermore, when reading or writing, it consumes only 0.15–0.47 W, far less than a hard disk. It has a read speed of about 85 ns per byte, quite like DRAM, but write speed of about 410 μs per byte, about 10–100 times slower than hard disk. However, since flash memory has no seek time, its overall write performance is not that much worse than a magnetic disk; in fact, for sufficiently small random writes, it can actually be faster. Since flash is practically as fast as DRAM at reads, a disk cache in no longer important for read operation. The cost per megabyte of flash is about 7–40 times more expensive than guard disk, but about 2–5 times less expensive than DRAM. Thus, flash memory might also be effective as a second level cache bellow the standard DRAM disk cache (Douglis et al. 1994; Doughs et al. 1994).

### 8.4.1.2 Processor

In general, the power consumption of the CPU is related to the clock rate, the supply voltage, and the capacitance of the devices being switched (Benini and de Micheli 1999; Lorch and Smith 1996; Weiser et al. 1994; Govil et al. 1995). One power-saving feature is the ability to slow down the clock. Another is the ability to selectively shut off functional units, such as the floating-point unit; this ability is generally not externally controllable. Such a unit is usually turned off by stopping the clock propagated to it. Finally, there is the ability to shut down processor operation altogether so that it consumes little or no energy. When this last ability is used, the processor typically returns to full power when the next interrupt occurs. A time energy consumption relation ships is given in Fig. 8.3.

Turning off a processor has little downside; no excess energy is expended turning the processor back on, the time until it comes back on is barely noticeable, and the state of the processor is unchanged from it turning off and on, unless it has a volatile cache (Benini and de Micheli 1999). Therefore, reducing the power consumption of the processor can have a greater effect on overall power savings

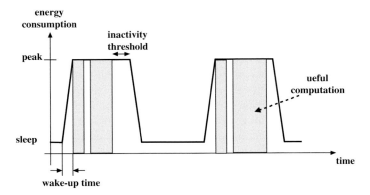

**Fig. 8.3** Power consumption in typical processor core

than it might seem from merely examining the percentage of total power attributable to the processor.

### 8.4.1.3  Display and Back-Light

The display and back-light have very few energy-saving features. This is unfortunate, since they consume a great deal of power in their maximum-power states; for instance, on the Duo 280c, the display consumes a maximum of 0.75 W and the back-light consumes a maximum of 3.40 (Lorch 1995; Lorch and Smith 1998). The back-light can have its power reduced by reducing the brightness level or by turning it off, since its power consumption is roughly proportional to the luminance delivered. The display power consumption can be reduced by turning the display off. It can also be reduced slightly by switching from color to monochrome or by reducing the update frequency, which reduces the range of shades or colors of Gray for each pixel, since such shading is done by electrically selecting each pixel for a particular fraction of its duty cycle. Generally, the only disadvantage of these low-power modes is reduced readability. However, in the case of switches among update frequencies and switches between color and monochrome, the transitions can also cause annoying flashes.

## 8.4.2  Operating System Power Consumption Optimization

Software and algorithmic considerations can also have a severe impact on energy consumption (Lorch and Smith 1998; Liang et al. 2004; Tiwari et al. 1994; Wolf 2002; Mehta et al. 1997; Lorch 1995). Digital hardware designers have promptly reacted to the challenge posed by low-power design. Designer skills, technology improvements and CAD tools have been successful in reducing the energy consumption. Unfortunately, software engineers and system architects are often less "energy-aware" than digital designers, and they also lack suitable tools to estimate the energy consumption of their designs. As a result, energy-efficient hardware is often employed in a way that does not make optimal use of energy saving possibilities. In this section we will show several approaches to reduce energy consumption at the operating system level and to the applications (Table 8.1).

A fundamental OS task is efficient management of host resources. With energy as the focus, the question becomes how to make the basic interactions of hardware and software as energy efficient as possible for local computation. One issue observed in traditional performance-centric resource management involves latency hiding techniques. A significant difference and challenge in energy-centric resource management is that power consumption is not easy to hide.

As one instance of power-aware resource management, we consider memory management. Memory instructions are among the more power-hungry operations on embedded processors (Tiwari et al. 1994), making the hardware/software of memory management a good candidate for optimization. Intel's guidelines for mobile power (Intel 1998, 2001) indicate that the target for main memory should be approximately 4 % of the power budget. This percentage can dramatically increase in systems with low power processors, displays, or without hard disks. Since many small devices have no secondary storage and rely on memory to retain data, there are power costs for memory even in otherwise idle systems. The amount of memory available in mobile devices is expanding with each new model to support more demanding applications (i.e., multimedia) while the demand for longer battery life also continues to grow significantly.

Scheduling is needed in a system when multiple functional units need to access the same object. In operating systems scheduling is applied at several parts of a system for processor time, communication, disk access, etc. Currently scheduling is performed on criteria like priority, latency, time requirements etc. Power consumption is in general only a minor criterion for scheduling; despite the fact that much energy could be saved.

**Table 8.1** Operating system functionality and corresponding techniques for optimizing energy utilization

| CPU scheduling | Idle power mode, voltage scaling |
|---|---|
| Operating system functionality | Energy efficient techniques |
| Memory allocation | Adaptive placement of memory blocks, switching of hardware energy reduction modes |
| Application/OS interaction | Agile content negotiation trading fidelity for power, APIs |
| Resource Protection and allocation | Fair distribution of battery life among both local and distributed tasks, locking battery for expensive operations |
| Communication | Adaptive network polling, energy-aware routing, placement of distributed computation, and server binding |

Subsystems of a computer, such as the CPU, the communication device, and storage system have small usage duty cycles. That is, they are often idle and wait for the user or network interaction. Furthermore, they have huge differences in energy consumption between their operating states.

Recent advances in ad hoc networks allow mobile devices to communicate with one another, even in the absence of pre-existing base-stations or routers. All mobile devices are able to act as routers, forwarding packets among devices that may otherwise be out of communication range of one another. Important challenges include discovering and evaluating available routes among mobile devices and maintaining these routes as devices move, continuously changing the "topology" of the underlying wireless network. In applications with limited battery power, it is important to minimize energy consumption in supporting this ad-hoc communication.

There are numerous opportunities for power optimizations in such environments, including:

(i)   reducing transmission power adaptively based on the distance between sender and receiver,
(ii)  adaptively setting transmission power in route discovery protocols,
(iii) balancing hop count and latency against power consumption in choosing the "best" route between two hosts, and
(iv)  choosing routes to fairly distribute the routing duties (and the associated power consumption) among nodes in an ad-hoc network (Havinga and Smit 2001).

## 8.4.3 Application, Compilation Techniques and Algorithm

In traditional power-managed systems, the hardware attempts to provide automatic power management in a way that is transparent to the applications and users. This has resulted in some legendary user problems such as screens going blank during video or slide-show presentations, annoying delays while disks spin up unexpectedly, and low battery life because of inappropriate device usage. Because the applications have direct knowledge of how the user is using the system to perform some function, this knowledge must penetrate into the power management decision-making system in order to prevent the kinds of user problems described above. This suggests that operating systems ought to provide application programming interfaces so that energy-aware applications may influence the scheduling of the system's resources.

The switching activity in a circuit is also a function of the present inputs and the previous state of the circuit. Thus it is expected that the energy consumed during execution of a particular instruction will vary depending on what the previous instruction was. Thus an appropriate reordering of instructions in a program can result in lower energy. Today, the cost function in most compilers is either speed or code size, so the most straightforward way to proceed is to modify the objective function used by existing code optimizers to obtain low-power versions of a given software program. The energy cost of each instruction must be considered during code optimization. An energy aware compiler has to make a trade-off between size and speed in favor of energy reduction.

At the algorithm level functional pipelining, re-timing, algebraic transformations and loop transformations can be used (Tiwari et al. 1994). The system's essential power dissipation can be estimated by a weighted sum of the number of operations in the algorithm that has to be performed. The weights used for the different operations should reflect the respective capacitance switched. The size and the complexity of an algorithm (e.g., operation counts, word length) determine the activity. Operand reduction includes common sub-expression elimination, dead code elimination etc. Strength reduction can be applied to replace energy consuming operations by a combination of simpler operations (for example by replacing multiplications into shift and add operations).

## 8.4.4 Energy Reduction in Network Protocols

Up to this point we have mainly discussed the techniques that can be used to decrease the energy consumption of digital systems and focused on the computing components of a mobile host. In this subsection we will discuss some techniques that can be used to reduce the energy consumption that is needed for the communication external of the mobile host.

We classify the sources of power consumption, with regard to network operations, into two types: (1) communication related and (2) computation related.

Communication involves usage of the transceiver at the source, intermediate (in the case of ad hoc networks), and destination nodes. The transmitter is used for sending control, route request and response, as well as data packets originating at or routed through the transmitting node. The receiver is used to receive data and control packets—some of which are destined for the receiving node and some of which are forwarded. Understanding the power characteristics of the mobile radio used in wireless devices is important for the efficient design of communication protocols.

The computation mainly involves usage of the CPU, main memory, the storage device and other components. Also, data compression techniques, which reduce packet length, may result in increased power consumption due to increased computation. There exists a potential trade-off between computation and communication costs. Techniques that strive to achieve lower communication costs may result in higher computation needs, and vice-versa. Hence, protocols that are developed with energy efficiency goals should attempt to strike a balance between the two costs.

Energy reduction should be considered in the whole system of the mobile and through all layers of the protocol stack. The following discussion presents some general guidelines that may be adopted for an energy efficient protocol design.

### 8.4.4.1 Protocol Stack Energy Reduction

Data communication protocols dictate the way in which electronic devices and systems exchange information by specifying a set of rules that should a consistent, regular, and well-understood data transfer service. Mobile systems have strict constraints on the energy consumption, the communication bandwidth available, and are required to handle many classes of data transfer over a limited bandwidth wireless connection, including real time traffic such as speed and video. For example, multimedia applications are characterized by their various media streams with different quality of service requirements.

In order to save energy an obvious mode of operation of the mobile host will be a sleep mode (Sivalingam et al. 2000). To support such mode the network protocols need to be modified. Store-and-forward schemes for wireless networks, such as the IEEE 802.11 proposed sleep mode, not only allow a network interface to enter a sleep mode but can also perform local retransmissions not involving the higher network protocol layers.

There are several techniques used to reduce the power consumption in all layers within the protocol stack. In Fig. 8.4, we list areas in which conservation mechanisms are efficient.

Collisions should be eliminated as much as possible within the media access layer (MAC) layer, a sub layer of the data link layer, since they result in retransmissions. Retransmissions lead to unnecessary power consumption and to possibly unbounded delays. Retransmissions cannot be completely avoided in a wireless network due to the high error-rates. Similarly, it may not be possible to fully eliminate collisions in a wireless mobile network. This is partly due to user mobility and a constantly varying set of mobiles in a cell.

For example, new users registering with the base station may have to use some form of random access protocol. In this case, using a small packet size for registration and bandwidth request may reduce energy consumption. The EC-MAC protocol (Sivalingam et al. 2000) is one example that avoids collisions during reservation and data packet transmission. This is the default mechanism used in the IEEE 802.11 wireless protocol in which the receiver is expected to keep track of channel status through constant monitoring. One solution is to broadcast a schedule that contains data transmission starting times for each mobile as in Sivalingam et al. (2000). Another solution is to turn off the transceiver whenever the node determines that it will not be receiving data for a period of time.

Physical Layer

As shown in Fig. 8.4, the lowest level of the protocol stack is the physical layer. This layer consists of radio frequency (RF) circuits, modulation, and channel coding systems. At this level, we need to use an energy-efficient radio that can be in various operating modes (like variable RF power and different sleep modes) such that it allows a dynamic power management (Akyildiz et al. 2002). Energy

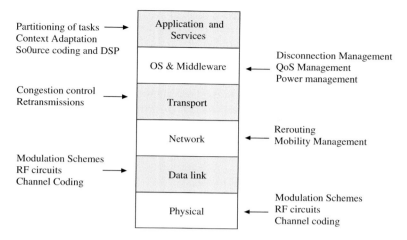

**Fig. 8.4** Protocol stack of a generic wireless network, and corresponding areas of energy efficient possible research

can also be saved if it is able to adapt its modulation techniques and basic error-correction schemes. The energy per bit transmitted or received tends to be lower at higher bit rates. For example, the WaveLAN radio operates at 2 Mb/s and consumes 1.8 W, or 0.9 J/bit.

A commercially available FM transceiver (Radiometrix BIM-433) operates at 40 kb/s and consumes 60 mW, or 1.5 J/bit. This makes the low bit-rate radio less efficient in energy consumption for the same amount of data. However, when a mobile has to listen for a longer period for a broadcast or wake-up from the base station, then the high bit-rate radio consumes about 30 times more energy than the low bit rate radio. Therefore, the low bit-rate radio must be used for the basic signaling only, and as little as possible for data transfer. To minimize the energy consumption, but also to mitigate interference and increase network capacity, the transmit power on the link should be minimized, if possible.

Data Link Layer

The data link layer is thus responsible for wireless link error control, security (encryption/decryption), mapping network layer packets into frames, and packet retransmission. A sub layer of the data link layer, the media access control (MAC) protocol layer is responsible for allocating the time-frequency or code space among mobiles sharing wireless channels in a region.

In an energy efficient MAC protocol the basic objective is to minimize all actions of the network interface, i.e., minimize on-time of the transmitter as well as the receiver. Another way to reduce energy consumption is by minimizing the number of transitions the wireless interface has to make. By scheduling data transfers in bulk, an inactive terminal is allowed to doze and power off the receiver as long as the network interface is reactivated at the scheduled time to transmit the data at full speed.

An example of an energy-efficient MAC protocol is $E^2MaC$ (Havinga et al. 1999). The $E^2MaC$ protocol is designed to provide QoS to various service classes with a low energy consumption of the mobile. In this protocol, the main complexity is moved from the mobile to the base station with plenty of energy. The scheduler of the base station is responsible to provide the connections on the wireless link the required QoS and tries to minimize the amount of energy spend by the mobile. The main principles of the $E^2MaC$ protocol are avoid unsuccessful actions, minimize the number of transitions, and synchronize the mobile and the base-station.

Network Layer

The network layer is responsible for routing packets, establishing the network service type, and transferring packets between the transport and link layers. In a mobile environment this layer has the added responsibility of rerouting packets and mobility management. Errors on the wireless link can be propagated in the protocol stack. In the presence of a high packet error rate and periods of intermittent connectivity of wireless links, some network protocols (such as TCP) may overreact to packet losses, mistaking them for congestion. TCP responds to all losses by invoking congestion control and avoidance algorithms. These measures result in an unnecessary reduction in the link's bandwidth utilization and increases in energy consumption because it leads to a longer transfer time.

The limitations of TCP can be overcome by a more adequate congestion control during packet errors. These schemes choose from a variety of mechanisms to improve end-to-end throughput, such as local retransmissions, split connections and forward error correction.

A comparative analysis of several techniques to improve the end-to-end performance of TCP over lossy, wireless hops is given (Balakrishnan et al. 1997). These schemes are classified into three categories: end-to-end protocols, where loss recovery is performed by the sender; link-layer protocols, that provide local reliability; and split-connection protocols that break the end-to-end connection into two parts at the base station. The results show that a reliable link-layer protocol with some knowledge of TCP provides good performance, more than using a split-connection approach. Selective acknowledgment schemes are useful, especially when the losses occur in bursts.

OS and Middle-Ware Layer

The operating system and middle-ware layer handles disconnection, adaptively support, and power and QoS management within wireless devices. This is in addition to the conventional tasks such as process scheduling and file system management. To avoid the high cost, in terms of performance, energy consumption or money, of wireless network communication is to avoid use of the network when it is expensive by predicting future access and fetching necessary data when the network is cheap. In the higher level protocols of a communication system caching and scheduling can be used to control the transmission of messages. This works in particular well when the computer system has the ability to use various networking infrastructures (depending on the availability of the infrastructure at a certain locality), with varying and multiple network connectivity and with different characteristics and costs. True prescience, of course, requires knowledge of the future. Two possible techniques, LRU caching and hoarding, are for example present in the Coda cache manager. A summary of other software strategies for energy efficiency is presented in (Kistler 1993; Lorch and Smith 1998).

## 8.5  Conclusion

Power dissipation continues to be a primary design constraint in single and multicore based systems. Increasing power consumption not only results in increasing energy costs, but also results in high die temperatures that affect chip reliability, performance, and packaging cost.

This chapter has investigated a number of energy-aware design techniques that can be used into complex multicore systems. In particular, this chapter covered techniques used to design energy-aware systems at the technology, logic, and system levels. The vast majority of the techniques used at the system architectures, are derived from existing uni-processor energy-aware systems.

# Chapter 9
# Soft-Core Processor for Low-Power Embedded Multicore SoCs

Soft-core processors are becoming increasingly common in modern multicore SoCs. A soft-core processor is a programmable processor that can be synthesized to a circuit, typically integrated into a larger multicore SoC. Queue based instruction set architecture processor offers an attractive option in the design of embedded SoC systems. This chapter describes architecture and design results of a low power Soft-core 32-bit QueueCore architecture. This core is an efficient architecture which can be easily programmed and integrated in a multicore SoC platform.

## 9.1 Introduction

Since conventional processors are already capable of starting one operation per cycle, reducing CPI further requires starting more than one operation per cycle. To extract ILP (Instruction Level Parallelism), these processors keep many in-flight instructions, use dynamic scheduling, and register renaming (Smith and Sohi 1995). As results, hardware complexity, power dissipation, and resource under-utilization in these architectures become critical performance limiting factors (Tiwari et al. 1998). There are many efforts in architectures design that address these problems. Thus, computer architects are continuously challenged to bring innovations to design micro-architectures, instruction set, and compilers, which help to keep the balance between performance, complexity and power. Several processors have achieved success as two or four-way Super-scalar implementations. However, adding still more functional units is not useful if the rest of the processor is not capable of supplying those functional units with continuous and independent instructions to perform.

A wish to have simple but still fast machine pushed us to look for alternatives. The research was inspired by several original ideas (Ben-Abdallah 2002; Preiss and Hamacher 1985; Fernandes et al. 1997; Heath et al. 1996), which proposed the usage of queue (first-in-first-out memory) instead of registers (random access memory) as intermediate storage of results. In these architectures, each instruction removes the required amount of data from the head of operand queue (GERG) and then stores the result of computation at the tail of operand queue.

A. Ben Abdallah, *Multicore Systems On-Chip: Practical Software/Hardware Design*,
Atlantis Ambient and Pervasive Intelligence 7, DOI: 10.2991/978-94-91216-92-3_9,
© Atlantis Press and the author 2013

In (Schmit et al. 2002) it was also argued that a queue machine application can be easily mapped to an appropriate hardware. However, no real hardware was proposed or designed and only theoretical techniques were proposed to virtualize the hardware.

A produced order parallel Queue processor (PQP) was presented in Ben-Abdallah et al. (2004, 2005, 2006). The key ideas of the PQP model are the operands and results manipulation schemes. The Queue execution model stores intermediate results in a circular queue-register (QREG). A given instruction implicitly reads its first operand from the head (QH) of the QREG, its second operand from a location explicitly addressed with an offset from the first operand location. The computed result is finally written into the QREG at a position pointed by a queue-tail pointer (QT).

The PQP processor has several promising advantages over register-based machines. First, PQP programs have higher instruction level parallelism because they are constructed using breadth-first algorithm (Ben-Abdallah 2002). Second, instructions of PQP are shorter because they do not need to specify operands explicitly. That is, data is implicitly taken from the head of operand queue and the result is implicitly written at the tail of the operand queue. This makes instruction lengths shorter and independent from the actual number of physical queue words. Finally, PQP instructions are free from false dependencies. This eliminates the need for register renaming (Ben-Abdallah 2002).

The QC-2 core implements all hardware features found in PQP core, supports single precision floating-point accelerator, and uses *QCaEXT* scheme—a novel technique used to extend immediate values and memory instruction offsets that were otherwise not representable because of bit-width constraints in the PQP processor. The aim of the *QCaEXT* technique is to achieve code density that is similar to the PQP code with performance similar to architecture set on 32-bit memory. Moreover, the QC-2 core implements new instructions for controlling the QREG unit (discussed later).

From another hand, known Soft-cores, such as ARM, Tensillica, Microblaze, and Nios, generally provide little support to assist users in customizing a soft-core's parameters to a particular application. Thus, users must manually select and simulate a user-determined set of candidate soft-core configurations to find the best configuration for a particular application. Each such simulation requires long time, limiting the number of candidate configurations that can be studied.

This chapter describes architecture and design results of a low power Soft-core 32-bit QueueCore architecture. This soft core is an efficient architecture which can be easily programmed and integrated in a multicore SoC platform. In addition, we consider the well known prototyping-based emulation approach, that substitutes real time hardware emulation for slow simulator-based execution (Maejima et al. 1997; Takahashi et al. 1997). To achieve good synthesis results for FPGAs implementation with sufficient performance, we have created the synthesizable model of the QC-2 processor for the integer and floating subset of the parallel Queue processor instruction set architecture (Ben-Abdallah et al. 2006). A prototype implementation is produced by synthesizing the high-level model for the Stratix FPGA device (Lewis et al. 2002).

## 9.2  Produced Order Queue Computing Overview

As we mentioned, the produced order queue computing model uses a circular queue-register (also named operand queue) instead of random access registers to store intermediate results. A data is inserted in the QREG in produced order scheme and can be reused. This feature has a profound implication in the areas of parallel execution, program compactness, hardware simplicity and high execution speed (Ben-Abdallah 2002).

This section gives a brief overview about the produced order Queue computation model. We show in Fig. 9.1a, a sample data flow graph for the expressions: $e = ab/c$ and $f = ab(c + d)$. Datum is loaded with load instruction (ld), computed with multiply ($*$), add ($+$), and divide ($/$) instructions. The result is stored back in the data memory with store instruction (st).

In Fig. 9.1a, producer and consumer nodes are shown. For example, $A2$ is a producer node and $A4$ is a consumer node ($A4$ is also a producer to m6 node). The instruction sequence for the queue execution model is correctly generated when we traverse the data flow graph (shown in Fig. 9.1a) from left to right and from the highest to the lowest level (Ben-Abdallah 2002). In Fig. 9.1b, the *augmented* data flow graph that can be correctly executed in the proposed queue execution model is given. The generated instruction sequence from the *augmented* graph is shown in Fig. 9.1c and the content of the QREG at each execution stage is shown in Fig. 9.1d.

A special register, called queue head pointer, points to the first data in the QREG. Another pointer, named queue tail pointer, points to the location of the QREG in which the result data is stored. A live queue head pointer (LQH) is also used to keep used data that could be reused and thus should not be overwritten. These data, which are found between QH and LQH pointers, are called *live-data* (discussed later). The *live-data* entries in the QREG are statically controlled. Two special instructions are used to *stop* or *release* the LQH pointer. Immediately after using the data, the QH is incremented so that it points to the data for the next instruction. QT is also incremented after the result is stored.

The four load instructions load in parallel $a$, $b$, $c$ and $d$ data and place them into the QREG. At this state, QH and LQH point to datum $a$ and the QT points to an empty location as shown in Fig. 9.1d (State 1). The fifth and sixth instructions are also executed in parallel. The *mul* refers $a$ and $b$ then inserts $(a * b)$ into the QREG. QH is incremented by two and the QT is incremented by one. The *add* refers $c$ and $d$ then inserts $(c + d)$ into the QREG. At this state, the QH, QT and LQH are incremented as shown in Fig. 9.1d (State 2). The seventh instruction ($div - 2$) divides the data pointed by QH (in this case $(a * b)$) by the data located at $-2$, negative offset, from QH (in this case c). The QH is incremented and points to $(c + d)$. The eighth instruction multiplies the data pointed by QH (in this case $(c + d)$) with the data located at $-1$ from QH (in this case $(a * b)$). After parallel execution of these two instructions, the QREG content becomes as shown in Fig. 9.1d State 3. The last two instructions store the result back in the data memory. Since the QREG becomes empty, LQH, QH and QT point to the same empty location (State 4).

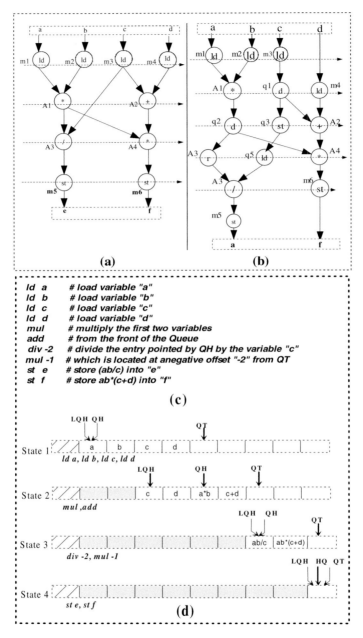

**Fig. 9.1** Sample data flow graph and queue-register contents for the expressions: $e = ab/c$ and $f = ab(c + d)$. **a** Original sample program. **b** Translated (augmented) sample program. **c** Generated instructions sequence. **d** Circular queue-register content at each execution state

## 9.3 QC-2 Core Architecture

### 9.3.1 Instruction Set Design Considerations

The QC-2 supports a subset of the produced order queue processor instruction set architecture (Ben-Abdallah et al. 2006). All instructions are 16-bit wide, allowing simple instructions fetch and decode stages and facilitating pipelining of the processor. The QC-2 integer instruction format is illustrated in Fig. 9.2. Several examples showing the operations of five different instructions are also given in Fig. 9.2a–e.

In the current version of our implementation, we target the QC-2 core for small applications where our concerns focus on the ability to execute Queue programs on a processor core with small die size and low power consumption characteristics when compared to other conventional 32-bit architectures. However, the short instructions may limit the memory addressing space as only 8-bit are left for offset

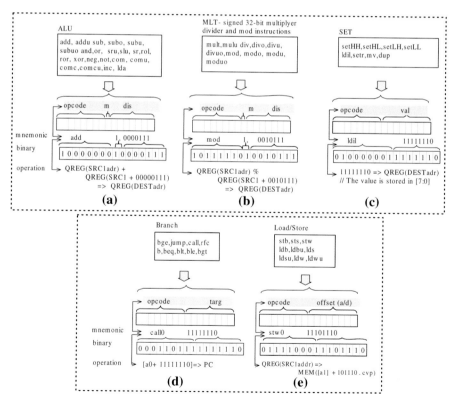

**Fig. 9.2** QC-2 instruction format and computing examples: **a** *add* instruction, **b** *mod* instruction, **c** load immediate (*ldil*) instruction, **d** *call* instruction, and **e** store word (*stw*) instruction

(6-bit) and base address (2-bit—00:a0/d0, 01:a1/d1, 10:a2/d2, and 11:a3/d3). To cope with this shortage, QC-2 core implements *QCaEXT* technique, which uses a special "covop" instruction that extends *load* and *store* instructions offsets and also extends immediate values if necessary.

The Queue processor compiler (Canedo 2006) outputs full addresses and full constants and it is the duty of the QC-2 assembler to detect and insert a "covop" instruction whenever an address or a constant exceeds the limit imposed by the instruction's field sizes. Conditional branches are handled in a particular way since the compiler does not handle target addresses, instead it generates target labels. When the assembler detects a target label, it looks if the label has been previously read and fills the instruction with the corresponding value and "covop" instruction if needed. There is a back-patch pass in the assembler to resolve all missing forward referenced instructions (Canedo 2006).

## 9.3.2  Instruction Pipeline Structure

The execution pipeline operates in six stages combined with five pipeline-buffers to smooth the flow of instructions through the pipeline. The QC-2 block diagram is shown in Fig. 9.3. Data dependencies between instructions are automatically handled by hardware interlocks. Below we describe the salient characteristics of the QC-2 core.

(1) *Fetch (FU)*: The instruction pipeline begins with the fetch stage, which delivers four instructions to the decode unit each cycle. This is the same bandwidth as the maximum execution rate of the functional units. At the beginning of each cycle, assuming no pipeline stalls or memory wait states occur, the address pointer hardware (APH) of the fetched instructions issues a new address to the memory system. This address is the previous address plus 8 bytes or the target address of the currently executing flow-control instruction.

(2) *Decode (DU)*: The DU decodes four instructions in parallel during the second phase and writes them into the decode buffer. This stage also calculates the number of consumed (CNBR) and produced (PNBR) data for each instruction. The CNBR and PNBR are used by the next pipeline stage to calculate the sources (*source1* and *source2*) and destination locations for each instruction. Decoding stops if the queue buffer becomes full or/and a *halt* signal is received from one or more stages following the decode stage.

(3) *Queue computation (QCU)*: Four instructions arrive at the QCU unit each cycle. The QCU calculates the first operand (*source1*) and destination addresses for each instruction. The mechanism used for calculating the *source1* address is given in Fig. 9.4. The QCU unit keeps track of the current value of the QH and QT pointers.

(4) *Barrier*: inserts barrier flags for dependency resolutions.

**Fig. 9.3** QC-2 architecture block diagram. During RTL description, the core is broken into small and manageable modules using modular approach structure for easy verification, debugging and modification

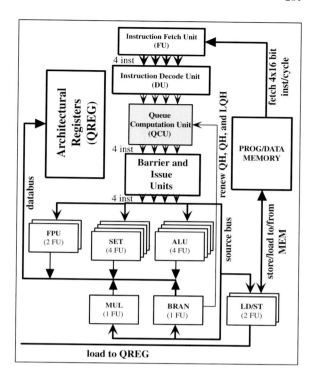

(5) *Issue (IS)*: four instructions are issued for execution each cycle. In this stage, the second operand (*source2*) of a given instruction is first calculated by adding the address *source1* to the displacement that comes with the instruction. The second operand address calculation is performed in the QCU stage. However, for a balanced pipeline consideration, the *source2* is calculated at the beginning of the IS stage. The hardware mechanism used for calculating the *source2* address is shown in Fig. 9.5 (discussed later).

An instruction is ready to be issued if its data and its corresponding functional unit are available. The processor reads the operands from the QREG in the second half of the IS stage and execution begins in the execution stage (stage 6).

(6) *Execution (EXE)*: The macro data flow execution core consists of 4 integer ALU units, 2 floating-point units, 1 branch unit, 1 multiply unit, 4 set-units, and 2 load/store units.

The load and store units share a 16-entry address window (AW), while the integer units and the branch unit share a 16-entry integer window (IW). The floating-point accelerator (FPA) has its own 16-entries floating point window (FW). The load/store units have their own address generation logic. Stores are executed to memory in-order.

**Fig. 9.4** Source 1 (*source1*) address calculation hardware

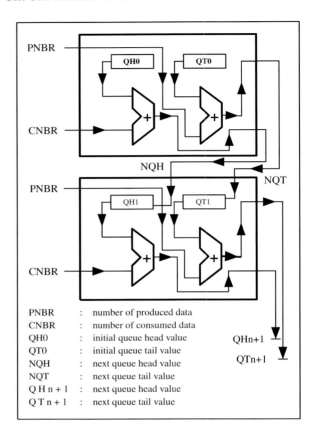

| PNBR | : | number of produced data |
| CNBR | : | number of consumed data |
| QH0 | : | initial queue head value |
| QT0 | : | initial queue tail value |
| NQH | : | next queue head value |
| NQT | : | next queue tail value |
| Q H n + 1 | : | next queue head value |
| Q T n + 1 | : | next queue tail value |

### 9.3.3 Dynamic Operands Addresses Calculation

To execute instructions in parallel, the QC-2 processor must calculate each instruction's operand(s) and destination addresses dynamically. As a result, the "static" Queue data structure (compiler point of view) is regarded dynamically as a circular queue-register structure. Figure 9.5 show block diagrams of the hardware used for calculating *source2*.

To calculate the *source1* address of a given instruction, the number of consumed data (CNBR) field is added to the current queue head value ($QH_n$). The destination address on the next instruction ($INST_{n+1}$) is calculated by adding the PNBR field (8-bit) to the current queue tail value ($QT_n$). Notice that the calculation is performed sequentially. Each QREG entry is written exactly once and it is busy until it is written. If a subsequent instruction needs its value, that instruction must wait until requested data is written. After a given entry in the QREG is written, the corresponding data in the above entry is ready and its ready bit (RDB) is set.

**Fig. 9.5** Source 2 (*source2*) address calculation hardware

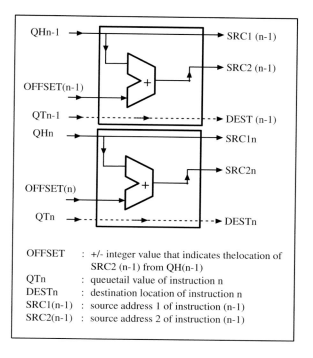

| | |
|---|---|
| OFFSET | : +/- integer value that indicates the location of SRC2 (n-1) from QH(n-1) |
| QTn | : queue tail value of instruction n |
| DESTn | : destination location of instruction n |
| SRC1(n-1) | : source address 1 of instruction (n-1) |
| SRC2(n-1) | : source address 2 of instruction (n-1) |

## 9.3.4 QC-2 FPA Organization

The QC-2 floating-point accelerator is a pipelined structure and implements a subset of the IEEE-754 single precision floating-point standard (IEEE 1985, 1981). The FPA consists of a floating-point ALU (FALU), floating-point multiplier (FMUL), and floating point divider (FDIV). The FALU, FMUL, FDIV and the floating-point queue-register employ 32-wide data paths. Most FPA operations are completed within three execution cycles. The FPA's execution pipelines are simple in design for high speed that the QC-2 core requires. All frequently used operations are directly implemented in the hardware. The FPA unit supports the four rounding modes specified in the IEEE 754 floating point standard: round toward-to-nearest-even, round towards positive infinity, round towards negative infinity, and round towards zero.

### 9.3.4.1 Floating Point ALU Implementation

The FALU does floating-point addition, subtraction, compare and conversion operations. Its first stage subtracts the operands exponents (for comparison), selects the larger operand, and aligns the smaller mantissa. The second stage adds or subtracts the mantissas depending on the operation and the signs of the operands. The result of this operation may overflow by a maximum of 1-bit position.

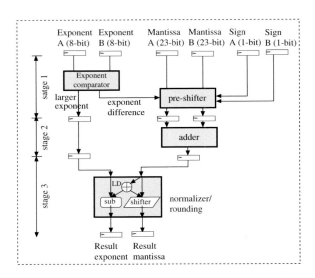

**Fig. 9.6** QC-2's FPA
hardware: adder circuit

Logic embedded in the mantissa adder is used to detect this case, allowing 1-bit normalization of the result on the fly. The exponent data path computes (E+1). If the 1-bit overflow occurred, (E+1) is chosen as the exponent of stage 3; otherwise, E is chosen. The third stage performs either rounding or normalization because these operations are not required at the same time. This may also result in a 1-bit overflow. Mantissa and exponent corrections, if needed, are implemented exactly in this stage, using instantiations of the mantissa adder and exponent blocks. The area efficient FALU hardware is shown in Fig. 9.6. The exponents of the two inputs (Exponent A and Exponent B) are fed into the exponent comparator, which is implemented with a subtracter and a multiplexer. In the pre-shifter, a new mantissa is created by right shifting the mantissa corresponding to the smaller exponent by the difference of the exponents so that the resulting two mantissas are aligned and can be added.

The size of the pre-shifter is about $m * log(m) LUTs$, where $m$ is the bit-width of the mantissa. If the mantissa adder generates a carry output, the resulting mantissa is shifted one bit to the right and the exponent is increased by one. The normalizer transforms the mantissa and exponent into normalized format. It first uses a leading-one detector (LD) circuit to locate the position of the most significant one in the mantissa. Based on the position of the LD, the resulting mantissa is left shifted by an amount subsequently deducted from the exponent. If there is an exponent overflow (during normalization), the result is saturated in the direction of overflow and the overflow flag is set. Underflows are handled by setting the result to zero and setting an underflow flag.

We have to notice that the LD anticipator can be also predicted directly from the input to the adder. This determination of the leading digit position is performed in parallel with the addition step so as to enable the normalization shift to start as soon as the addition completes. This scheme requires more area than a standard adder, but exhibits reduced latency. For hardware simplicity and logic limitation, our FPA hardware does not support earlier LD prediction.

### 9.3.4.2 Floating Point Multiplier Implementation

Figure 9.7 shows the data path of the FMUL unit. As with other conventional architectures, QC-2's FMUL operation is much like integer multiplication. Because floating point numbers are stored in sign-magnitude form, the multiplier needs only to deal with unsigned integer numbers and normalization. Similar to the FALU, the FMUL unit is a three stages pipeline that produces a result on every clock cycle. The bottleneck of this unit was the $24 * 24$ integer multiplications.

The first stage of the floating-point multiplier is the same denormalization module used in addition to insert the implied 1 to the mantissa of the operands. In the second stage, the mantissas are multiplied and the exponents are added. The output of the module is registered. In the third stage, the result is normalized or rounded.

The multiplication hardware implements the radix-8 modified Booth algorithm. Recoding in a higher radix was necessary to speed up the standard Booth multiplications algorithm since greater numbers of bits are inspected and eliminated during each cycle. It effectively reduces the total number of cycles necessary to obtain the product. In addition, the radix-8 version was implemented instead of the radix-4 version because it reduces the multiply array in stage 2.

**Fig. 9.7**  QC-2's FPA
hardware: multiplier circuit

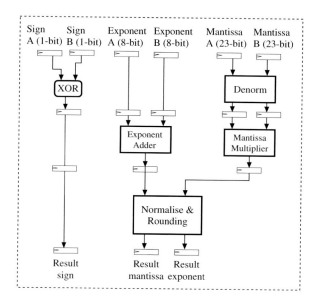

## 9.3.5 Circular Queue-Register Structure

The finite state machine transition for QC-2 pipeline synchronization is shown in Fig. 9.8. The QREG structure is shown in Fig. 9.9. For clarity, only the first sixteen entries ($ENTRY_0$ to $ENTRY_{15}$) are shown. Figure 9.9a shows the QREG initial state. In this state, the QREG is empty and the QH, QT and LQH pointers point to the same location (QREG logical entry 0). When the first data is written into the QREG storage, the QT is incremented by 1. Since no data is consumed yet, the QH and LQH still point to the initial location. This scenario is shown in Fig. 9.9b.

The QH pointer is incremented by 1 after data 1 (*dat1*) is consumed as shown in Fig. 9.9c. Because *dat1* maybe reused again, the LQH pointer still points to $ENTRY_0$, which holds data 1 (*dat1*). A special instruction, named *stplqh* (stop LQH) was implemented to stop the automatic movement of LQH. The automatic LQH movement (default setting) is restored with another special instruction, named *autlqh* (automatic LQH). In some situation the QREG storage may have three types of entries as shown in Fig. 9.9d. These entries are: *dead entries*—data is no longer needed, *live entries*—data can be reused, and (3) *empty entries*—no data in these entries.

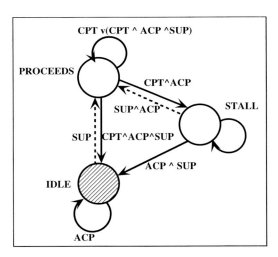

**Fig. 9.8** Finite state machine transition for QC-2 pipeline synchronization. The following conditions are evaluated: next stage can accept data (ACP), previous pipeline stage can supply data (SUP), last cycle of computation (CPT)

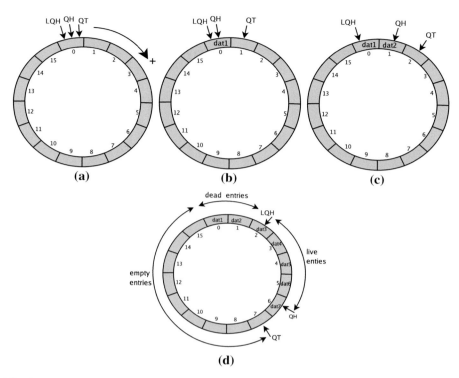

**Fig. 9.9** Circular queue-register (QREG) structure. **a** initial QREG state; **b** QREG state after writing the first 32 bit data (dat1); **c** QREG state after writing the second data (dat2) and consuming the first 32 bit data (dat1); **d** QREG state with LQH pointer update and different regions

## 9.4  Synthesis of the QC-2 Core

### 9.4.1  Design Approach

To make the QC-2 design easy to debug, modify and adapt, we decided to use a high-level description, which was also used by other system designers, such as works in Micheli et al. (2001), Sheliga and Sha (1996), Kim et al. (2003), Maejima et al. (1997), Takahashi et al. (1997). We have developed the QC-2 core in Verilog HDL. After synthesizing the HDL code, the designed processor has characteristics that enable investigation of the actual hardware performance and functional correctness. It also gives us the possibility to study the effect of coding style and instruction set architectures over various optimizations.

For the QC-2 processor to be useful for these purposes, we identified the following requirements:

(1) high-level description: the format of the QC-2 description should be easy to understand and modify;
(2) modular: to add or remove new instructions, only the relevant parts should have to be modified. A monolithic design would make experiments difficult; and
(3) the processor description should be synthesizable to derive actual implementations.

The QC-2 has been designed with a distributed controller to facilitate debugging and future adaptation for specific application requirements since we target embedded applications. This distributed controller approach replaces a monolithic controller which would be difficult to adapt. The distributed controller is responsible for pipeline flow management and consists of communicating state machines found in each pipeline.

In this design, we have decided to break up the unstructured control unit to small, manageable units. Each unit is described in a separate HDL module. That is, instead of a centralized control unit, the control unit is integrated with the pipeline data path. Thus, each pipeline stage is mainly controlled by its own simple control unit.

In this scheme, each distributed state machine corresponds to exactly one pipeline stage, and this stage is controlled exclusively by its corresponding state machine. Overall flow control of the QC-2 processor is implemented by cooperation of the control units in each stage based on communicating state machines. Each pipeline stage is connected to its immediate neighbors, and indicates whether it is able to supply or accept new instructions. Communication with adjacent pipeline stages is performed using two asynchronous signals, *AVAILABLE* and *PROCEED*. When a stage has finished processing, it asserts the *AVAILABLE* signal to indicate that data is available to the next pipeline stage. The next stage will, then, indicate whether it can proceed these data by using the *PROCEED* signal.

Since all fields, necessary to find what actions are to be taken next, are available in the pipeline stage (for example operation status ready bits and synchronization signals from adjacently stages), computing the next stage is simple. This basic state machine is extended to cover the operational requirements of each stage, by dividing the *PROCEED* state into sub states as needed. An example is the implementation of the Queue computation stage, where *PROCEED* is divided into sub states for reading initial addresses values, calculating next addresses values, and addresses fixup (when needed).

We have synthesized the QC-2 core for Stratix FPGAs and HardCopy devices with Altera Quartus II professional edition tool. In order to estimate the impact of the description style on the target FPGAs efficiency, we have explored logic synthesis for FPGAs. The idea of this experiment was to optimize critical design parts for speed or resource optimizations. In this work, our experiments and the results described are based on the Altera Stratix architecture (Lewis et al. 2002).

We selected Stratix FPGAs device because it has good tradeoffs between routability and logic capacity. In addition it has an internal embedded memory that eliminates the need for external memory module and offers up to 10 Mbits of embedded memory through the TriMatrix TM memory feature. We also used Altera Quartus II professional edition for simulation, placement and routing. Simulations were also performed with Cadence Verilog-XL tool.

## 9.5 Results and Discussions

### 9.5.1 Execution Speedup and Code Analysis

Before describing the QC-2 synthesis results, we first present the execution time, speed up and programs size (binaries) evaluation results for several benchmark programs. We obtained these results by using our back-end tool (QC2ESTM) and QueueCore/QC-2 compiler (Canedo 2006; Canedo et al. 2007). The embedded applications are selected from MediaBench (Lee et al. 1997) and MiBench (Matthew et al. 2001) suites. The selected benchmarks include two video compressing applications: H.263, MPEG2; one graph processing algorithm: Susan; two encryption algorithms: AES, Blowfish; and one signal processing: FFT.

Table 9.1 shows the normalized code size of several benchmark programs compiled with a port of GCC 4.0.2 for every target architecture. We selected MIPS I ISA (Kane and Heinrich 1992) as the baseline and include other three embedded RISC processors and a CISC representative. The last column shows the normalized code size for the applications compiled using the QC-2 compiler (Canedo 2006; Canedo et al. 2007). The table shows that the binaries for the QC-2 processor are about 70 % smaller than the binaries for MIPS and about 50 % smaller than ARM (Patankar et al. 1999). Compared to dual-instruction set embedded RISC processors, MIPS16 (Kissel 1997) and Thumb (Goudge and Segars 1996), QC-2 binaries are about 20 and 40 % denser, respectively. When compared to the CISC architecture, Pentium processor (Alpert and Avnon 1993), QC-2 binaries are about 14 % denser.

**Table 9.1** Normalized code sizes for various benchmark programs over different target architectures

| Benchmark | MIPS16 | ARM | Thumb | ×86 | QC-2 |
|-----------|--------|--------|-------|-------|-------|
| H.263 | 58.00 | 83.66 | 80.35 | 57.20 | 41.34 |
| MPEG2 | 53.09 | 78.40 | 69.99 | 53.22 | 36.75 |
| Susan | 47.34 | 80.48 | 77.54 | 46.66 | 35.12 |
| AES | 51.27 | 86.67 | 69.59 | 44.62 | 34.93 |
| Blowfish | 54.59 | 86.38 | 82.76 | 57.45 | 45.49 |
| FFT | 58.09 | 100.74 | 92.54 | 46.27 | 36.77 |
| Average | 53.73 | 86.05 | 78.79 | 50.9 | 36.77 |

**Table 9.2** Execution time and speedup results

| Benchmark | PQP-S | QC-2 | Speedup |
|-----------|-------|------|---------|
| H.263 | 25980 | 11777 | 2.21 |
| MPEG2 | 22690 | 10412 | 2.18 |
| Susan | 11321 | 7613 | 1.49 |
| AES | 5132 | 1438 | 3.57 |
| Blowfish | 5377 | 3044 | 1.77 |
| FFT | 9127 | 5234 | 1.74 |

**Table 9.3** QC-2 Hardware configuration parameters

| Items | Configuration | Description |
|-------|---------------|-------------|
| IW | 16-bit | Instruction width |
| FW | 8 bytes | Fetch width |
| DW | 8 bytes | Decode width |
| SI | 85 | Supported instructions |
| QREG | 256 | Circular queue-register |
| ALU | 4 | Arithmetic logical unit |
| LD/ST | 2 | Load/Store unit |
| BRAN | 1 | Branch unit |
| SET | 4 | Set unit |
| MUL | 1 | Multiply unit |
| FPU | 2 | Floating-point unit |
| GPR | 16 | General purpose registers |
| MEM | 2048 word | PROG/DATA memory |

Table 9.2 shows the execution time in cycles for serial (PQP-S) and parallel (QC-2) architectures. The last column in the table shows the speedup of the parallel execution scheme over serial configuration. This table shows that the queue computation model extracts natural parallelism found in programs speeding up these embedded applications by factors from 1.49 to 3.57.

## 9.5.2 Synthesis Results

Table 9.3 shows the hardware configuration parameters of the designed QC-2 core. Table 9.4 summarizes the synthesis results of the QC-2 for the Stratix FPGA and HardCopy targets. The complexity of each module as well as the whole QC-2 core are given as the number of logic elements (LEs) for the Stratix FPGA device and as the total combinational functions (TCF) count for the HardCopy device (Structured ASIC). The design was optimized for balanced optimization guided by a properly implemented constraint table. We also found that the processor consumes about 95.3 % of the total logical elements of the target device. The achievable throughput of the 32-bit QC-2 core on different execution platforms is shown in Fig. 9.10. For the hardware platforms, we show the processor frequency.

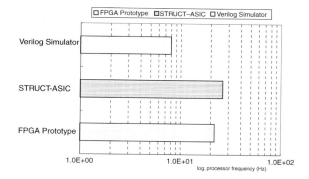

**Fig. 9.10** Achievable frequency is the instruction throughput for hardware implementations of the QC-2 processor. Simulation speeds have been converted to a nominal frequency rating to facilitate comparison

**Table 9.4** QC-2 processor design results: modules complexity as LE (logic elements) and TCF (total combinational functions) when synthesized for FPGAs (with Stratix device) and Structured ASIC (HardCopy II) families

| Descriptions | Modules | LE | TCF |
|---|---|---|---|
| Instruction fetch unit | IF | 633 | 414 |
| Instruction decode unit | ID | 2573 | 1564 |
| Queue compute unit | QCU | 1949 | 1304 |
| Barrier queue unit | BQU | 9450 | 4348 |
| Issue unit | IS | 15476 | 7065 |
| Execution unit | EXE | 7868 | 3241 |
| Queue-register unit | QREG | 35541 | 21190 |
| Memory access | MEM | 4158 | 3436 |
| Control unit | CTR | 171 | 152 |
| QC-2 core | QC-2 | 77819 | 42714 |

For comparison purposes, the Verilog HDL simulator performance has been converted to an artificial frequency rating by dividing the simulator throughput by a cycle count of 1 CPI. This chart shows the benefits which can be derived from direct hardware execution using a prototype when compared to processor simulation. The data used for this simulation are based on event-driven functional Verilog HDL simulation (Ben-Abdallah et al. 2006).

The critical path of the QC-2 core with 16 registers configuration is 44.4 ns, that was 22.5 MHz of clock frequency. For QC-2 core with 256 registers, the critical path is 39.2 ns. The clock frequencies for both configurations are low due to the fact that, we synthesized the processor library to random logic of standard cell. However, the performance may be much more improved by using specific layout generation tools. Figure 9.11 compares two different target implementations for $256 \times 33$ QREG for various optimizations. Depending on the target implementations device, either logic elements (LEs) or total combinational

**Fig. 9.11** Resource usage and timing for 256 × 33 bit QREG unit for different coding and optimization strategies

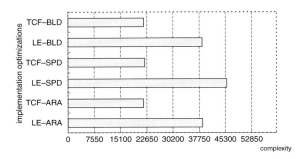

functions (TCF) are generated as storage elements. Implementations based on HardCopy device, which generates TCF functions give almost similar complexity for the three used optimizations—area (ARA), speed (SPD) and balanced (BLD). For FPGA implementation, the complexity for SPD optimization is about 17 and 18 % higher than that for ARA and BLD optimizations respectively.

## 9.5.3  Speed and Power Consumption Comparison with Synthesizable CPU Cores

Queue computing and architecture design approaches take into account performance and power consumption considerations early in the design cycle and maintain a power-centric focus across all levels of design abstraction. In QC-2 processor, all instructions designed are fixed format 16-bit words with minimal decoding effort. As a result, the QC-2 architecture has much smaller programs than either RISC or CISC machines.

As we showed in the previous section, programs sizes for our architecture are found to be 50–70 % smaller than programs for conventional architectures. The importance of the system memory size translates to an emphasis on code size since data is dictated by application. Larger memories mean more power, and optimization power is often critical in embedded applications. In addition, instructions of QC-2 processor specify operands implicitly. This design decision makes instructions independent from the actual number of physical queue words (QREG). Instructions are, then, free from false dependencies. This feature eliminates the need for register renaming unit, which consumes about 4 % of the overall on-chip power in conventional RISC processors (Bisshop et al. 1999). Performance of QC-2 in terms of speed and power consumption is compared with various synthesizable CPU cores as illustrated in Table 6.3. The SH-2 is a popular Hitachi SuperH based instruction set architecture (Arahata et al. 1997). The SH-2 has RISC-type instruction sets and 16 × 32 bit general purpose registers. All instructions have 16-bits fixed length. The SH-2 is based on 5 stages pipelined architecture, so basic instructions are executed in one clock cycle pitch. Similar to our QC-2 core, the SH-2 also has an internal 32-bit architecture for enhanced data processing ability.

**Table 9.5** Speed and power consumption comparisons for various Synthesizable CPU cores over speed (SPD) and area (ARA) optimizations

| Cores | Speed (SPD) | Speed (ARA) | Average Power(mW) |
|---|---|---|---|
| PQP | 22.5 | 21.5 | 120 |
| SH-2 | 15.3 | 14.1 | 187.5 |
| ARM7 | 25.2 | 24.5 | 22 |
| LEON2 | 27.5 | 26.7 | 458 |
| MicroBlaze | 26.7 | 26.7 | 135 |
| QC-2 | 25.5 | 24.2 | 90 |

This evaluation was performed under the following constraints: (1) Family: Stratix; (2) Device: EP1S25F1020; (3) Speed: C6. The speed is given in MHz

LEON2 is a SPARCV8 compliant 32-bit RISC processor. The power consumption values are based on Synopsis software based on reasonable input activities. ARM7 is a simple 32-bit RISC processor and the power consumption values are manufacturer given for hard core. The MicroBlaze core is a 32-bit soft processor. It features a RISC architecture with Harvard-style, separate 32-bit instruction and data buses (Xilinx 2006).

From the result shown in Table 9.5, the QC-2 processor core shows better speed performance for both area and speed optimizations when compared with SH-2, PQP and ARM7 (hard core) processors. The QC-2 has higher speed for both SPD and ARA optimizations when compared with SH-2 processor (about 40 % for speed optimization and 41.73 % for area optimization). QC-2 core also shows 25 % less power consumption when compared with PQP and consumes less power than LEON2 and MicroBlaze processors. However, QC-2 core consumes more power than ARM7 processor, which also has less area than PQP and QC-2 for both speed and optimization (not shown in the table). This difference comes from the small hardware configuration parameters of ARM7 when compared to our QC-2 core parameters.

## 9.6  Conclusion

Soft-core processors are becoming increasingly common in modern multicore SoCs. A soft-core processor is a programmable processor that can be synthesized to a circuit, typically integrated into a larger multicore SoC. This chapter presented architecture and hardware design of a Soft-core Queue processors that can be easily integrated in a multicore SoC system. The core was prototyped on FPGA and fits on a single Stratix device with an internal embedded memory that eliminates the need for external memory module, thereby obviating the need to perform multi-chip partitioning which results in a loss of resource efficiency. Only a few clearly identified components, such as the Barrier and the QREG units, need to be specially optimized at the HDL source level to achieve efficient resources usage.

# Chapter 10
# Dual-Execution Processor Architecture for Embedded Computing

This chapter introduces practical hardware design of a dual-execution processor (DEP) architecture targeted for embedded applications. The architecture is based on a dynamic switching mechanism which allows fast and safe switching between two execution entities at runtime. Several hardware optimization and design techniques are presented in a fair amount of details.

## 10.1 Introduction

Generally, the motivation for the design of a new architecture arises from the technological development, which changed gradually the architecture parameters traditionally used in the computer industry. With these growing changes, the computer architect is faced with answering the question what functionality has to be put on a single chip, giving them an extra performance edge.

The nineties show a tendency towards more complex super-scalar processors. These processors which have the ability to initiate multiple instructions during the same clock cycle, are the latest series of architectural innovations aimed at producing ever-faster microprocessors. Because individual instructions are the entities being executed in parallel, super scalar processors exploit what is referred to as instruction level parallelism by issuing multiple instructions per cycle to each functional unit when dependencies allow. In these processors instructions are not necessarily executed in order; an instruction is executed when processor resources are available and data-dependencies are not violated. To execute instructions Out-of-Order data dependencies among instructions must be disabled by the scheduling system during compilation, run time, or both.

Dynamic scheduling detects dependencies in a set of dynamic instruction stream. The most general form of dynamic scheduling, the issue and execution of multiple OoO (Out-of-Order) instructions, can significantly enhance system performance. Instructions with no dependencies are executed if they meet the

A. Ben Abdallah, *Multicore Systems On-Chip: Practical Software/Hardware Design*,
Atlantis Ambient and Pervasive Intelligence 7, DOI: 10.2991/978-94-91216-92-3_10,
© Atlantis Press and the author 2013

constraints of the issuing algorithm (discussed in later section). There are other issue difficulties: branch predictions, and fast precise interrupt particularly if a fast response time is desired. Interrupts are precise in a processor with Out-of-Order execution, if after the execution of the interrupt routine, the processor state visible to the operating system and application can be reconstructed to the state a processor would have, had all instructions executed in sequence up to the point of an interrupt.

Branch instructions represent about 15–30 % of the executed instructions for many applications, decreases the effectiveness of multiple issues to functional units if instructions following an undecided branch cannot be issued. Performance may be improved by enabling speculative executions as predicted path information. If the gains on correct paths out-balance the losses from nullifying execution effects on incorrect paths, performance improves.

Simply stated, achieving higher performance means processing a given program in a smaller amount of time. Therefore, it is imperative that cycle time and total execution time (TET) for a given application be considered when investigating a new architecture. The Dynamic Fast Issue algorithm (discussed later in Chap. 3) efficiently addresses the aforementioned problems.

From an other hand, as we enter into an era of continued demand for faster and compatible processors as well as different Internet-network appliances using different processor core architectures, it becomes extremely complicated and costly to develop a separate processor for every execution model to satisfies this demand.

Internet applications, which are generally "stack based", have complicated the task of processors designers as well and users, who generally seek high execution speed or high performance as defined by the literature. However, recently the term "high performance" is questioned again by many processor designers and computer users. Some consider that high performance means high execution speed or low execution time of some given applications. Other defines "high performance" differently. They consider that processors, which support several executions model, are the favorite candidates for high performance awards, since switching from processor to processor lead to difficulty and waste of time. This is true especially when users have different applications written for different execution model (Stack and RISC model for example). In this case, users are obliged to run these two applications separately on different machines. In conventional machines, this problem was somehow solved by direct software translation techniques. However, these techniques still suffer from slow translation speed. Sun Microsystems proposed its Stack-based Java processor so that Java code can execute directly.

According to its designers, the JavaChip-I, for example, is a highly efficient Java execution unit design. It delivers up to 20 times the Java performance of x86 and other general-purpose processor architecture, as well as up to five times the performance obtained by just-in-time (JIT) compilers. It is evident that in tern of reduced TET, the solution is better than the indirect way (translation) or the JIT scheme, but in term of compatibility, the processor still suffers from not being able to execute other codes. The dual-execution mode architecture presented in this chapter is addressing this and other problems as a pure-play architectural paradigm, which will integrate Stack and Queue execution model right into the DEP core.

The Queue execution model (QEM) is analogous to the stack execution model (SEM) in that it has operations in its instructions set, which implicitly reference an operand Queue, just as a stack machine has operations, which implicitly reference an operand Queue. Each instruction removes the required number of operands from the front of the Queue operand, performs some computations, and stores the result of computation into the Queue of operands at the specified offsets from the head of the Queue. The Queue of operand occupies continuous storage locations. A special register, called the Queue front pointer (QFP), contains the address of the first operand in the operand Queue. Operands are retrieved from the front of the Queue by reading the location indicated by the QFP register. Immediately after retrieving an operand, the QFP is incremented so that it points at the next operand in the Queue. Results are returned to the rear of the operand Queue indicated by the Queue rear pointer (QRP). It will be shown later in that, the instruction sequence of such execution mode is easily generated from an expression parse trees.

In Stack mode, implicitly referenced operands are retrieved from the head of the operand stack and results are returned back onto the head of the stack. However, in our QEM, operands are retrieved from the front of the Queue of operands and results are returned to the rear of the Queue of operands. For example consider a "sub" instruction. In stack execution model, the sub instruction pops two operands from the top of the stack (TOS), computes the difference and pushes the results back onto the top of the stack. However, in Queue execution mode (QEM), the *sub* instruction removes two operands from the front of the Queue (FOQ), computes their difference, and puts the results at the rear of the Queue (ROQ) indicated by the RQP. In the former case, the result of the operation is available at the TOS. In the later case, the result is behind any other operand in the Queue. This will have an enormous potential to effectively exploit pipelined ALU with a simple hardware, which, due to their hardware structure, normal SEM obviously cannot guaranty. Another advantage of the QEM, discussed later, is the reduced program size compared to conventional RISC processor.

## 10.2  System Architecture

The DEP architecture is a 32-bit processor dual execution mode processor that supports queue (QEM) and stack (SEM) execution modes in a single processor core. The QEM mode uses a first-in-first-out data structure as the underlying control mechanism for the manipulation of operands and results. The QEM is analogous to the stack execution model in that it has operations in its instructions set which implicitly reference an OPQ just as a stack machine has operations that implicitly reference an OPS. Each instruction removes the required number of operands from the front of the OPQ, performs computation, and stores the result of computation into the OPQ at the specified offsets from the tail of the queue. The OPQ occupies continuous storage locations. A special register called queue head (QH) contains the address of the first operand in the OPQ. Operands are retrieved from the front of

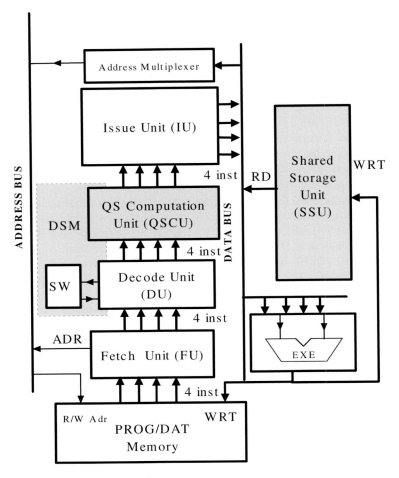

**Fig. 10.1** DEP architecture block diagram

the queue by reading the location indicated by the QH pointer. Immediately after
retrieving an operand, the QH is incremented so that it points to the next operand in
the queue. Result is returned to the rear of the OPQ, which is indicated by the queue
tail (QT). When switched to stack-based mode, the switching circuitry and the
computing unit perform the job of executions-mode-switching and calculates the
sources and destination operands for corresponding instructions.

In the SEM mode, implicitly referenced operands are retrieved from the top of
the OPS and results are returned back into the top of the OPS. For example,
consider a sub instruction. In SEM mode, the sub instruction pops two operands
from the top of the OPS (TOP), computes the difference and pushes the results
back into the top of the stack. However, in QEM mode, the sub instruction
removes two operands from the front of the OPQ, computes their difference, and

puts the results at the rear of the OPQ. In the former case, the result of the operation is available at the TOP. In the later case, the result is behind any other operand in the queue. This will have an enormous impact to effectively exploit pipelined ALU where normal SEM obviously cannot guarantee. The block diagram of the proposed architecture is shown in Fig. 10.1.

### 10.2.1 Pipeline Structure

The execution pipeline operates in five pipeline stages combined with four pipeline buffers to smooth the flow on instructions through the pipeline. The pipeline stages of DEP processor architecture are following:

*Instruction Fetch*: Fetches instructions from the program memory and inserts them into a fetch buffer.

*Instruction Decode*: Decodes instruction's opcodes and operands.

*Queue-Stack Computing*: The processor's computation stage reads information from the DU and uses them to compute each instruction's sources and destination locations in both queue and stack execution models.

*Instructions Issue*: The issue stage issues ready instructions to the execution unit.

*Execution*: Executes issued instructions and sends the results to the Shared Storage Unit or data memory.

### 10.2.2 Fetch Unit

The fetch mechanism is shown in Fig. 10.2. The fetch unit (FU) has a program counter controller (PCCTRL), an increment register (incr), a program counter register (PC), and a fetch buffer (FB). FU fetches instructions from the program memory. In QEM mode, the FU fetches four instructions per cycle. However, for SEM mode it fetches one instruction per cycle. A special fetch mechanism is used to update the fetch counter according to the mode being processed. A special fetch mechanism is used to update the fetch counter according to the mode being processed. FU controls the fetch mechanism by using the PCCTRL which is controlled by *im*, *halt*, *int*, and *return* signals from different units of processor. The *new PC* and *target PC* forces the PCCTRL for fetch from the their new PC value.

### 10.2.3 Decode Unit

The block diagram of decode unit (DU) is shown in Fig. 10.3. The DU decodes instructions opcode and operand. DU has 4 decode circuits (DC), 1 mode selector

**Fig. 10.2** Block diagram of
fetch unit

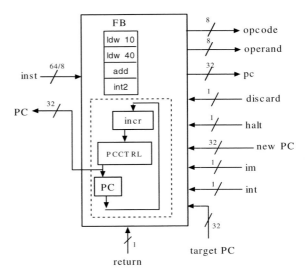

**Fig. 10.3** Block diagram of
decode unit

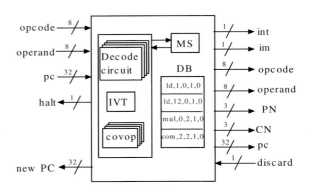

register (MS), 1 interrupt vector table (IVT), and 4 covop registers (covop). In DU, we have implemented the switching mechanism, some part of software interrupt handling mechanism, and the memory address extension mechanism (covop execution). The switching mechanism generates the instruction mode (im) for each instruction. When the DU detects the software interrupt instruction it generates the *new PC* and *int* signals. The DU also generates the number of consumed *CN* and produced *PN* data for each instruction that will be used in the next unit for calculating the sources and destination addresses. The decode buffer (DB) is a buffer where the DU inserts the decoded instructions. When DU gets the *discard* signal, it resets the DB contents. DU detect the halt instruction and generates the *halt* signal for stopping fetch.

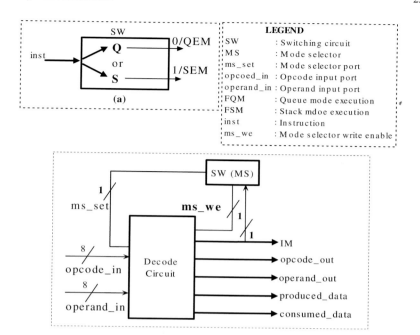

**Fig. 10.4**  Mode-switching mechanism

## 10.2.4 Dynamic Switching Mechanism

DEP uses a simple dynamic hardware mechanism (DSM) to dynamically switch between execution modes. The block diagram of the DSM is shown in Fig. 10.4. The DSM system consists of a switching circuitry (SW) and a dynamic computation unit (QSCU) Akanda (2005). The QSCU unit calculates the sources and destination addresses for instructions in both QEM and SEM modes. The DSM detects the instruction mode by decoding the operand of the "switch" instruction.

After the mode detection, it inserts a mode-bit for all instructions between the current and the next "switch" instruction. Hence, the same operation can be used for both modes. This will increase the resources usability and the overall system performance.

## 10.2.5 Calculation of Produced and Consumed Data

The decode unit calculates the number of PN and CN data by following the Table 10.1. The PN indicates the result of a computation and the CN indicates the operands to be processed. For ALU type instruction, we know that it requires two data for computation and after the computation it makes one result. As a result, the

**Table 10.1** PN and CN calculation with instruction in decode stage. PN means number of produced data and CN means number of consumed data

| Instruction | PN | CN |
|---|---|---|
| ALU | 1 | 2 |
| Shift | 1 | 1 |
| Set register | 0 | 0 |
| Load | 1 | 0 |
| Store | 0 | 1 |
| Control | 0 | 0 |

CN for ALU is 2 and PN for ALU is 1. Figure 10.5 shows the decode mechanism with PN and CN results.

## 10.2.6 Queue-Stack Computation Unit

The Queue-stack computation unit (QSCU) is the back bone of DEP processor architecture. The block diagram of QSCU is shown in Fig. 10.6. The queue and stack instruction have their source and destination information as default and here the question is arise why DEP needs the computation unit. The default information is enough for serial execution model. But, our target is to implement the stack computation model on the parallel queue processor architecture.

For parallel queue computing the computation unit is extremely necessary for knowing each instruction source and destination addresses and default information is not enough for parallel execution models. So, we have designed a shared computation unit for two different kinds of computation models in QSCU. When program mode is in queue the QSCU behaves like queue computation unit and when the program mode is in stack, the QSCU works like stack computation unit. The QSCU can compute the sources and destination addresses for both queue and stack execution model.

We have implemented the *sources-results computing mechanism* in QSCU. The QSCU has two register for calculating the source and destination addresses for parallel queue execution model and these are QH and QT. However, for stack execution model the QT register works like the top of the stack register (TOP). We have designed the *QT/TOP* as shared register for QT and TOP calculation but theoretically it is not shared. The QSCU has a buffer named *queue-stack computation buffer* (QCB). After calculating the source and destination addresses, QSCU sends the instruction (with its source and destination address) to the QCB. When QSCU gets the *discard* signal from execution unit, it resets the QCB contents. The QSCU generates *flag* signal for inform the instruction mode to the next unit (issue).

**Fig. 10.5**  Decode
mechanism: **a** decode for
queue program and **b** decode
for stack program

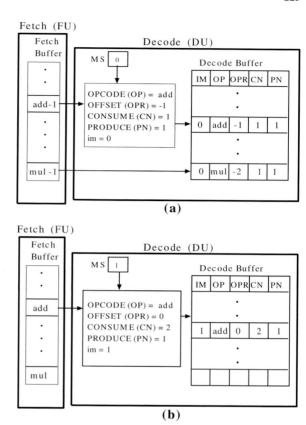

(a)

(b)

**Fig. 10.6**  Block diagram of
queue-stack computation unit

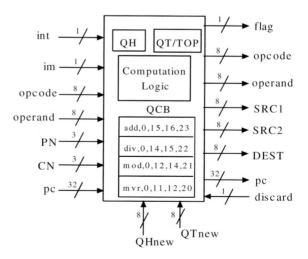

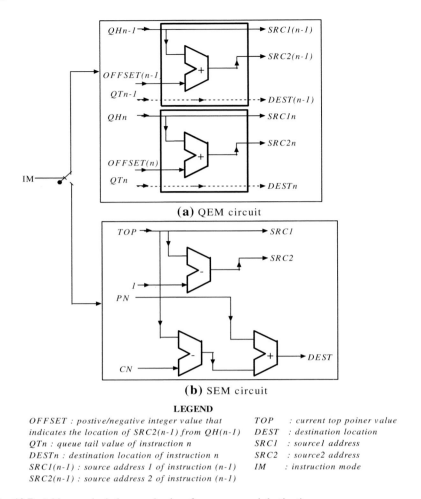

**(a)** QEM circuit

**(b)** SEM circuit

**LEGEND**

*OFFSET : postive/negative integer value that*          *TOP     : current top poiner value*
*indicates the location of SRC2(n-1) from QH(n-1)*      *DEST   : destination location*
*QTn : queue tail value of instruction n*               *SRC1   : source1 address*
*DESTn : destination location of instruction n*         *SRC2   : source2 address*
*SRC1(n-1) : source address 1 of instruction (n-1)*     *IM      : instruction mode*
*SRC2(n-1) : source address 2 of instruction (n-1)*

**Fig. 10.7**  Address calculation mechanism for sources and destination

## 10.2.7 Sources-Results Computing Mechanism

We introduce the sources-results computing mechanism for dual execution mode
processor architecture. This mechanism is controlled by the instruction mode (IM)
which is generated by the DSM. Figures 10.7 and 10.8 show the mechanism of
sources-results computing that is implemented in QSCU. There are two different
circuits (QEM and SEM) controlled by *IM* where the *IM* value is 1 (that means
switch is in *on* mode), the QSCU follows the SEM circuit. Otherwise QSCU
always follows the QEM circuit.

In QEM execution mode, each instruction needs to know its QH and QT values.
The above values are easy to obtain in serial queue execution model, since the QH

**Fig. 10.8** Address
calculation mechanism for
next instruction's source1 and
destination

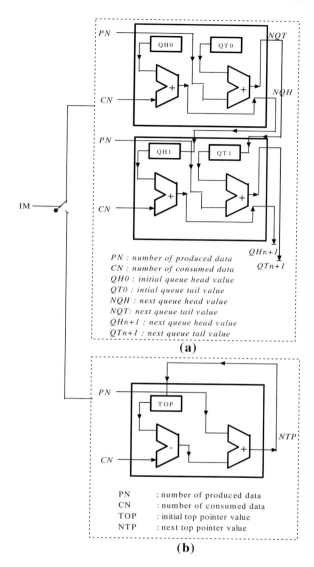

PN : number of produced data
CN : number of consumed data
QH0 : initial queue head value
QT0 : intial queue tail value
NQH : next queue head value
NQT: next queue tail value
QHn+1 : next queue head value
QTn+1 : next queue tail value

**(a)**

PN          : number of produced data
CN          : number of consumed data
TOP         : initial top pointer value
NTP         : next top pointer value

**(b)**

is always used to fetch instructions from the OPQ and the QT is always used to
store the result of the computation into the tail of the OPQ. However, in parallel
execution, which is supported by DEP processor, the values for QH and QT are not
explicitly determined.

Figure 10.7a shows the hardware mechanism used for calculating *source*1 (first
operand), *source*2 (second operand), and destination (result) addresses for current
instruction. The computing unit keeps the current value of the QH and QT
pointers. In QEM, four instructions arrive at this unit in each cycle. The first
instruction uses the current QH ($QH(n - 1)$) in the figure)) and QT ($QT(n - 1)$)

values for *source*1 and destination addresses respectively. As shown in Fig. 10.7a, the *source*2 of a given instruction is the first calculated by adding the *source*1 address to the displacement (OFFSET) $(OFFSET(n-1))$.

Figure 10.8a shows the pointers-update mechanism of current QH and QT values for next instruction. The number of consumed data (CN) field (8-bit) is added to the current QH value (QH0) to find the next QH (NQH) and the number of produced data (PN) field (8-bit ) is added to the current QT value (QT0) to find the next QT (NQT). The other three instructions source and destination addresses are calculated similarly.

In SEM mode, the execution is based on SEM model. The hardware used for calculating *source*1, *source*2, and destination addresses is shown in Fig. 10.7b. It is the same hardware used for calculation of operands in QEM mode. The computing unit keeps the current value of the stack pointer (TOP). One instruction arrives to the QSCU unit each cycle. The *source*1 address is popped from the OPS pointed by the current TOP pointer value (TOP). The *source*2 is calculated by subtracting 1 from current TOP pointer value. The number of consumed data (CN) is subtracted from the current TOP value (TOP) and the number of produced data (PN) is added for finding the result address (DEST). Figure 10.8b shows the hardware mechanism used for calculating the result address for current instruction. The destination address of current instruction points to the next TOP pointer value (NTP), which will be used for next instruction's source1 address.

Figure 10.9a, b show two examples of sources and destination addresses calculations for both QEM and SEM execution models respectively. For simplicity, only two instructions "add −1" and "mul −1" are shown in the fetch buffer (FB). The "MS" is the instruction-mode-selector register and is set to 0 which means that the DEP core is in QEM mode. The DU decodes instructions and calculates several fields for each instruction.

As shown in the Fig. 10.9a, the fields are: IM (instruction mode), OP (opcode), OPR (operand), CN (consumed number), and PN (produced number). The values of IM, OP, OPR, CN, and PN are: 0, add, −1, 1, and 1 for the first instruction "add −1". The same calculation scheme is performed for the following instructions.

Using the mechanism shown in Figs. 10.7a and 10.8a, the source1 (QH1), source2 (QH2), and destination (QT0) addresses for each instruction are calculated in the QSCU stage. Figure 10.9b shows another example illustrating the calculation of TOP, TOP-1, and DEST fields in SEM mode.

## 10.2.8 Issue Unit

The issue unit (IU) has two issue mechanisms and is controlled by the *flag* signal from QSCU. If the program is in queue mode, IU issues four instructions per cycle. In QEM mode, IU checks the memory and register dependencies. IU also checks the availability of the sources and destination addresses. However, in SEM mode the IU issues only one instruction for sequential execution and in this mode IU

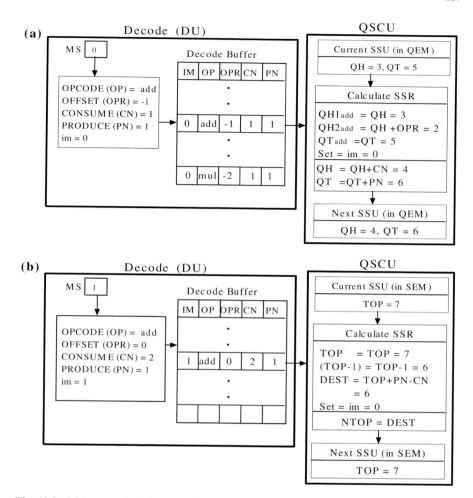

**Fig. 10.9**  Addresses calculation example: **a** QEM mode and **b** SEM mode

does not need to check the dependencies. Figure 10.10 shows the block diagram of the issue unit. The issue mechanism of DEP is quite simple. It is possible for queue programs where always follows the single assignment and there is no false dependency occur in queue and stack storage unit (SSU).

### 10.2.9 Execution Unit

This is the execution and write back unit of DEP architecture. The block diagram of execution unit (EXE) is shown in Fig. 10.11. The ready instructions come from IU with their appropriate source and destination. EXE executes the ready

**Fig. 10.10** Block diagram of the issue unit

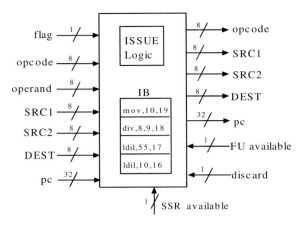

**Fig. 10.11** Block diagram of execution unit

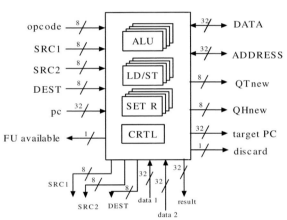

instructions and sends the result to the shared storage unit (SSU) or memory (DM). If the branch is taken then it sends a *discard* signal to previous all units to stop their activities and also sends the *new PC* to the FU and sends the new qh (*QHnew*) and new qt (*QTnew*) or new top (*QTnew*) pointers value to the QSCU. The block diagram of EXE is shown in Fig. 10.11. Four executing four instructions in parallel in QEM, we have implemented 4 ALU units, 4 Ld/St units, 4 set register units, and 1 control unit in EXE. Now, we do not know the behavior of programs and for getting maximum performance in QEM decided to implement 4 units four each ALU, Ld/St units, and set register unit.

### 10.2.10  Shared Storage Mechanism

We have implemented the *shared storage mechanism* in the Shared storage unit (SSU). The SSU is an intermediate storage unit for DEP architecture. The SSU has 32-bit 256 shared registers (SSR) and behaves like a conventional register file (RF). However, in QEM, the system organizes the SSR access as a first-in-first-out (FIFO) latches, thus accesses concentrate around a small window and the addressing of registers is implicit trough the queue head and tail pointers and in QEM, the system organizes the SSR access as a last-in-first-out (LIFO) latches which addressing the register is implicit through the stack pointer. The shared storage mechanism of SSR is controlled by the QSCU. The block diagram of SSU is shown in Fig. 10.12. The SSU has 4 read and 8 write ports for supporting the maximum performance in QEM mode. The 4 ALU type instructions need maximum 4 read and 8 write ports of SSU.

### 10.2.11  Covop Instruction Execution Mechanism

The *covop* instruction execution mechanism is implemented in DU. Figure 10.13 shows the main circuit which implements "covop" instruction for extending memory displacement. The mechanism loads the displacement value in the register covop (11000001 in this example). The value in the covop register is then concatenated with the displacement value of the load instruction (0100) and finally generates, the original displacement value (110000010100) for load instruction (ld).

### 10.2.12  Interrupt Handling Mechanism

We have implemented the software interrupt handling mechanism in the dual-execution mode processor architecture. The Fig. 10.14 shows the different

**Fig. 10.12**  Block diagram of shared storage unit

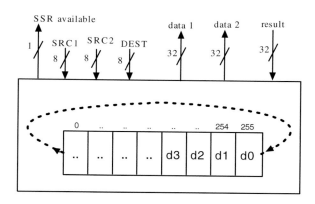

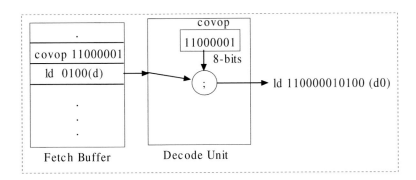

**Fig. 10.13**  Address extension mechanism

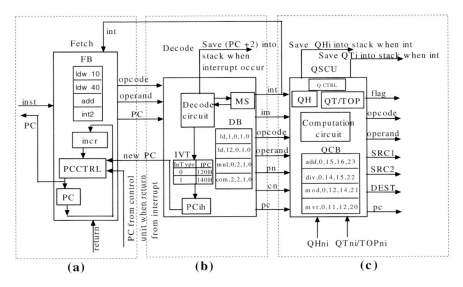

**Fig. 10.14**  Components used for software interrupt handling mechanism in DEP. **a** Fetch Stage with the Program Counter Controller (PCC). **b** Decode stage. **c** Queue-Stack Computation Unit (QSCU)

components used for interrupt handling mechanism. The decode unit (DU) prepares the processor for correct handling of the software interrupt. After an interrupt instruction in the DU is detected, the program counter of the next instruction (PC + 2) is saved into the stack. The DU determines the address of the interrupt handler from the interrupt vector table (IVT) and places the value into the PCih. At the same time the DU sends the *int* signal to the fetch unit (FU) and the interrupt (int) signal to the QSCU.

After receiving the *int* signal and the new value for the PC, the fetch unit stops fetching instructions and resets the fetch buffer. Once finished, the FU resumes the fetching starting from the newest value of PC until the return signal coming from the execution unit is detected.

*Program Counter Controller*: Figure 10.14a describes the Program Counter Controller (PCC) mechanism. There is a controller (PCCTRL) that selects the PC. The *PCCTRL* is controlled by input signals coming from decode and execution units. Normally, *PCCTRL* is selected by normal fetching mode. If there is *int* signal from DU, the PCC is selected by the discard signal and it updates the PC by the new PC. When the PCC gets the return signal with return PC address from the execution unit, it sets the PC as return PC.

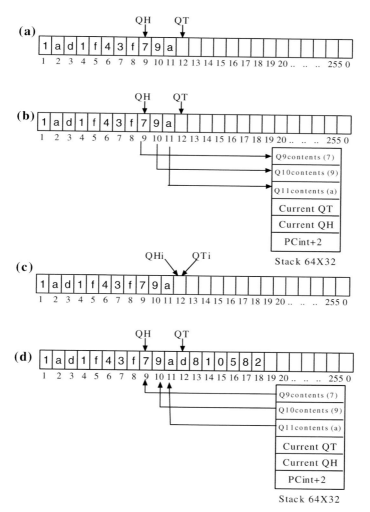

**Fig. 10.15** Queue status when interrupt occur and return from interrupt. **a** Queue status before interrupt, **b** when interrupt occur, **c** Queue: ready for interrupt handler, **d** Queue: when return from interrupt

*Queue-stack status controller*: We have implemented a queue-stack status controller (QCTRL) in QSCU. Figure 10.14 shows the QCTRL mechanism in QEM. Figure 10.14c shows the block diagram of QSCU when the interrupt occur and Fig. 10.15 describes the details of queue status before and after the interrupt. Figure 10.15a shows the present queue contents with present QH and QT pointer addresses. When the QSCU gets the *int* signal from the DU, QSCU saves the current queue status (current QH,QT values, and queue (SSR) contents between QH and QT) into the stack (Fig. 10.15b) and also changes the status of queue. Figure 10.15c shows the new QH (QHi) and QT (QTi) address for the interrupt handler. The QSCU will continue the computation by using the QHi and QTi value until it gets the return signal from Execution unit. When QSCU gets the return signal from EU it will restore the QH address, QT address, and queue contents from the stack recovering the normal queue with correct QH and QT pointer address (Fig. 10.15d).

Figure 10.16 shows the QCTRL mechanism in SEM. In SEM, the QCTRL saves the present TOP value and the stack (SSR) contents into the stack and makes empty the original stack with new TOP pointer(TOPi) (Fig. 10.14b). Then the QSCU will

**Fig. 10.16** Stack status when interrupt occur and return from interrupt. **a** stack status before interrupt, **b** when interrupt occur, **c** stcak: ready for interrupt handler, **d** stcak: when return from interrupt

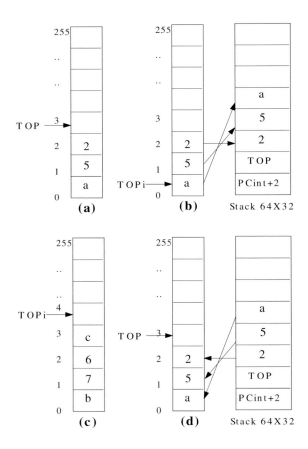

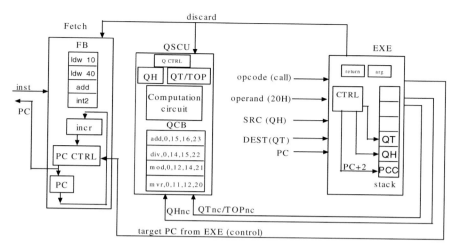

**Fig. 10.17** Components used for subroutine call mechanism in DEP

continue the compuation for stack by using (TOPi) until it gets the return signal from EU (Fig. 10.14c). When QSCU gets the return signal form the EU, it will restore the original stack contents with the original TOP address.

## 10.3 Sub-Routine Call Handling Mechanism

In DEP architecture, we have also implemented the subroutine call handling mechanism. Figure 10.17 shows the different components used for subroutine call handling mechanism. We have designed the call execution mechanism in control unit (CTRL) (Fig. 10.17c). After executing the *call* instruction the CTRL creates a *discard* signal and sends to all previous units (FU, DU, QSCU, and IU) for reset their buffers. At the same time CTRL saves the program counter of the next instruction (pc + 2) into the stack and sends the new target address for call instruction to the FU. After receiving the *discard* signal and the target address (target PC) form the CTRL, the FU stop fetching and reset the FB. After reset the FB, the FU resumes the fetching starting from the new target PC value until the return signal coming from the execution unit is detected. Here, the program counter controller will do the same job what we described for interrupt handling mechanism.

The queue status controller in QSCU resets the QCB and saves the queue status in the stack when it gets the *discard* signal. For saving the return value the CTRL uses a general purpose register (g0) both QEM and SEM mode. In SEM CTRL also uses another general purpose register (g1) for saving the argument. The QCTRL mechanism for subroutine call in QEM is described in Fig. 10.18.

Figure 10.15a shows the present queue contents with present QH and QT pointer addresses. When the CTRL executes the *call* instruction, it saves the

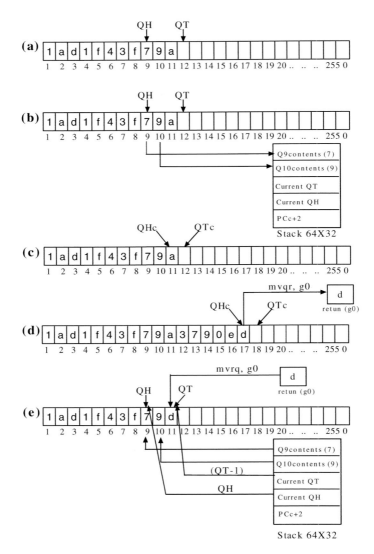

**Fig. 10.18** Queue status when subroutine call and return from call. **a** queue status before call, **b** when execute the call, **c** queue: ready for handle callee program, **d** when execute the return from call (rfc) instruction, and **e** queue: when return from call with return result

current queue status (current QH, QT values, and queue contents between QH and QT) into the stack (Fig. 10.15b) and also changes the status of queue. The original queue has the argument for the callee program at the position of (QT−1) of the original queue and the QCTRL makes a new queue by following the argument of callee program. So, the new head (QHc) will be pointed by the position of (QT−1) and the new QT (QTc) will be pointed by original QT position. Figure 10.15c

**Fig. 10.19** Stack status when subroutine call and return from call. **a** stack status before call, **b** when execute the call, **c** stack: ready for handle callee program, **d** when execute the return from call (rfc) instruction, and **e** stack: when return from call with return result

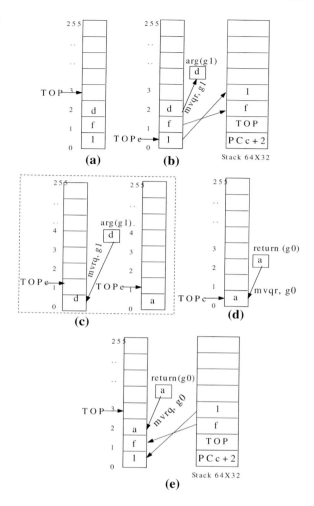

shows QHc and QTc address for the callee program. The QSCU will continue the computation by using the QHc and QTc value until it gets the return signal from execution unit.

When the CTRL executes the return form call (rfc) instruction, it stores the return value into a special return register (g0) is shown in Fig. 10.18d. This moving data from queue to register (mvqr, g0) is generated by programmer for move the QHc contents to the g0 register. Then QTRL sends the return signal to the QSCU and FU. When QSCU gets the return signal from EU it will restore the QH address, QT address (QT−1), and queue contents from the stack recovering the normal queue with correct QH and QT pointer address and the return value from the go register will be move to the QT (Fig. 10.18e). The moving data from register (mvrq, g0) to queue is generated by the programmer for go contents to the QT of the original queue.

Figure 10.19 shows the QCTRL mechanism for subroutine call in SEM. In SEM the QCTRL first saves the argument for callee into a special *arg* register (g1) and then saves the stack (SSR) contents with the present TOP into the stack of CTRL unit and makes a new stack with new TOP (TOPc) (Fig. 10.19b). For moving the TOP contents to the g1 register the programmer will generate the *mvqr,g1* instruction. Then QCTRL moves the g1 register contents (argument of callee) into new stack (Fig. 10.19b). Then the QSCU will continue the computation by using the TOPc pointer until getting the return signal from EU.

When the CTRL executes the return form call (rfc) instruction, it moves the return value into a special return register (g0) is shown in Fig. 10.19d. The programmer will generate the *mvqr, g0* for moving the TOP contents to the g0 register. Then QTRL sends the return signal to the QSCU and FU. When QSCU gets the return signal from EU it will restore the TOP address and stack contents from the stack recovering the normal stack with correct TOP pointer address and the return value from the go register will be move to the TOP (Fig. 10.19e). For moving the g0 contents the programmer generates *mvrq, g0* instruction.

## 10.4  Hardware Design and Evaluation Results

To make the DEP design easy to debug, modify, and adapt, we decided to use a high-level description, which was also used by other system designers, such as works in Maejima (1997), Takahashi (1997). We have developed the DEP core in Verilog HDL. After synthesizing the HDL code, the designed processor gives us then the ability to investigate the actual hardware performance and functional correctness. It also gives us the possibility to study the effect of coding style and instruction set architectures over various optimizations. For the DEP core to be useful for these purposes, we identified the following requirements:

1. High-level description: the format of the DEP description should be easy to understand and modify;
2. Modular: to add or remove new instructions, only the relevant parts should have to be modified. A monolithic design would make experiments difficult; and
3. the processor description should be synthesizable to derive actual implementations.

The DEP has been designed with a distributed controller to facilitate debugging and future adaptation for specific application requirements since we target embedded applications. This distributed controller approach replaces a monolithic controller which would be difficult to adapt. The distributed controller is responsible for pipeline flow management and consists of communicating state machines found in each pipeline.

In this design, we have decided to break up the unstructured control unit to small and manageable units. Each unit is described in a separate HDL module. That is, instead of a centralized control unit, the control unit is integrated with the

**Fig. 10.20** Finite state machine transition for DEP pipeline synchronization

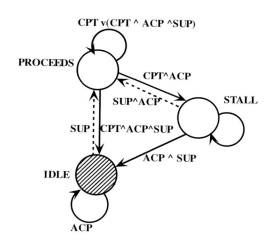

pipeline data path. Thus, each pipeline stage is mainly controlled by its own simple control unit. In this scheme, each distributed state machine corresponds to exactly one pipeline stage and this stage is controlled exclusively by its corresponding state machine. Overall flow control of the DEP processor is implemented by cooperation of the control units in each stage based on communicating state machines. Each pipeline stage is connected to its immediate neighbors and indicates whether it is able to supply or accept new instructions.

In order to estimate the impact of the description style on the target FPGAs efficiency, we have explored logic synthesis for FPGAs. The idea of this experiment was to optimize critical design parts for speed or resource optimizations. In this work, our experiments and the results described are based on the Altera Stratix architecture Lewis (2002). We selected Stratix FPGAs device because it has good trade-offs between routability and logic capacity. In addition it has an internal embedded memory that eliminates the need for external memory module and offers up to 10 Mbits of embedded memory through the TriMatrix TM memory feature. We also used Altera Quartus II professional edition for simulation, placement, and routing. Simulations were also performed with Cadence Verilog-XL tool.

## 10.4.1 DEP System Pipeline Control

In many conventional processors, the control unit is centralized and controls all central processing core functions. This scheme introduces pipeline stalls, bubbles, etc. However, especially for pipelined architecture, this control unit is one of the most complex part of the design, even for processors with fixed functionality Lysecky (2005).

Communication with adjacent pipeline stages is performed using two asynchronous signals, *AVAILABLE*, and *PROCEED*. When a stage has finished processing, it asserts the *AVAILABLE* signal to indicate that data is available to the next pipeline stage. The next stage will indicate whether it can proceed these data by using the *PROCEED* signal. Since all fields, necessary to find what actions are to be taken next, are available in the pipeline stage (for example operation status ready bits and synchronization signals from adjacently stages), computing the next stage is simple. The state transitions of a pipeline stage in the DEP is illustrated in Fig. 10.20. This basic state machine is extended to cover the operational requirements of each stage, by dividing the *PROCEED* state into sub-states as needed. An example is the implementation of the Queue computation stage, where *PROCEED* is divided into sub-states for reading initial addresses values, calculating next addresses values, and addresses fixup (when needed).

## 10.4.2 Hardware Design Result

To simplify the functional verification we developed a front-end tool, which displays the internal state of the processor. The displayed states include: all pipeline stages buffers, SSU and data memory contents. We can easily extend the front-end tool to display several other states at each pipeline stage. For visibility, we only show the state of the SSU and the data memory—the two states are enough for checking the correctness of a simulated benchmark program. This approach allowed us to monitor the program execution as each instruction passes through the pipeline and to identify functional problems by tracing processor state change.

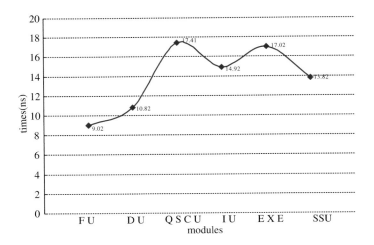

**Fig. 10.21** Critical path for different units

**Table 10.2** DEP Processor hardware configuration parameters

| Items | Configuration | Description |
|-------|---------------|-------------|
| IW | 2 bytes | Instruction width |
| FW | 8 bytes | Fetch width |
| DW | 8 bytes | Decode width |
| SSR | 256 | Shared storage register |
| ALU | 4 | Arithmetic logical unit |
| LD/ST | 4 | Load/Store unit |
| SET | 4 | Set unit |
| BRAN | 1 | Branch unit |
| GPR | 16 | General purpose registers |
| MEM | 2048 word | PROG/DATA memory |

We captured the input and output signals changes for several cases. Table 10.2 shows the hardware configuration parameters of the designed DEP processor.

High-level verification is mainly used to verify functional correctness. Low-level problems such as timing violation cannot be verified directly with high-level verification tools. To ensure correctness of low-level implementation details, interfaces, and timing, we used gate-level simulation to ensure compliance with design specifications. We specified timing and other constraints using a unified user constraints file with the core modules. We also used several test benches to verify the correctness of the architecture for both stack and queue execution models. Table 10.3 shows the design results of the DEP architecture when synthesized for Stratix FPGA device. The synthesis results are measured by Altera Quartus II professional edition and form this tool we have got two kinds of optimization results: speed optimization (SOP) and area optimization (AOP).

The complexities of each module as well as the whole DEP core are given as the number of logic elements (LEs) for both SOP and AOP optimizations. Table 10.3 shows that the EXE uses the 31.89 % of total LEs and the SSU uses 51 % of total LEs. In EXE, we have implemented four ALU, four load/store, and four set register units for executing four instructions in parallel in QEM. For supporting the EXE, we have implemented four write and eight read ports in SSU and SSU has also 32-bit 256 sahred registers. For getting the maximum performance we don't consider about the hardware complexity.

**Table 10.3** Verilog HDL code size for integrated DEP processor

| Description | Modules | Size (Lines) |
|-------------|---------|--------------|
| Fetch unit | fetch.v | 192 |
| Decode unit | decode.v | 1,059 |
| QS computation unit | qscu.v | 327 |
| Issue unit | issue.v | 1,038 |
| Execution unit | exe.v | 2,630 |
| Shared storage unit | ssu.v | 262 |
| Program/data memory | pram.v | 50 |
| Top | cpucore.v | 1,610 |
| Total | | **7,168** |

**Table 10.4** Synthesis results. LEs means Logic Elements. AOP means Area optimization and SOP means speed optimization

| Descriptions | Modules | LE-SOP | LE-AOP |
|---|---|---|---|
| Fetch unit | FU | 345 | 252 |
| Decode unit | DU | 1,395 | 1,269 |
| QS computation unit | QSCU | 489 | 484 |
| Issue unit | IU | 1,794 | 1,588 |
| Execution unit | EXE | 7,543 | 6,213 |
| Shared storage unit | SSU | 12,084 | 8,120 |
| DEP core | DEP | 23,650 | 17,926 |

The design was optimized for balanced optimization guided by a properly implemented constraint table. From the prototyping result, the processor consumes 94.389 % of the total logical elements of the target Stratix EP1S25F1020 FPGA device. As a result, the DEP processor successfully fits on a single FPGA device, thereby eliminating the need to perform multi-chip partitioning which results in a loss of resource efficiency.

Figure 10.21 shows the critical path for each pipeline stage. The evaluation shows that the queue-stack computation stage (QSCU) has the longest delay. This is a largely due to the delays needed for computing the source and destination address for each instruction. The achievable frequency of the DEP core is 64.8 and 62.31 MHz for speed and area optimizations respectively. The performance can be much more improved by using specific layout generation tools and standard libraries. The average power consumption of DEP processor is about 187.5 mW.

Table 10.4 shows the total number LEs for the DEP and the base architecture (PQP). When compared to the PQP core, DEP requires only 2.41 % extra hardware for speed optimization (SOP) and 2.06 % extra hardware for area optimization (AOP). About the speed performance the DEP has loses 12.92 and 11.88 % speed for SOP and AOP optimizations respectively. The required average power consumption is same both for DEP and PQP architectures. The comparison results show that with increasing little extra hardware and lose some speed we have implemented the stack computation model on the base PQP architecture that we are expecting from the beginning of DEP research work.

**Table 10.5** Comparison results between DEP and PQP architecture. Area in LE, Speed in MHz, and Power in mW

| Architectures | LE-SOP | LE-AOP | Speed-SOP (MHz) | Speed-AOP (MHz) | Average Power (mW) |
|---|---|---|---|---|---|
| DEP | 23,650 | 17,926 | 64.8 | 62.31 | 187.5 |
| PQP | 23,065 | 17,556 | 71.5 | 70.1 | 187.5 |

**Table 10.6** DEP speed comparisons

| Cores | Speed-SOP | Speed-AOP |
|---|---|---|
| DEP | 64.8 | 62.31 |
| PQP | 71.5 | 70.1 |
| OpenRisc1200 | 32.64 | 32.1 |
| ARM7 | 25.2 | 24.5 |
| LEON2 | 27.5 | 26.7 |
| MicroBlaze | 26.7 | 26.7 |
| CPU86 | 26.95 | 26.77 |

## 10.4.3  Comparison Results

We have already compared the DEP architecture results with PQP aachitecture and both architecture have been designed by us. So, we have compared our DEP processor performance result with other conventional synthesizable processors. Performance of DEP core in terms of speed and power consumption is compared with various synthesized CPU cores as illustrated in Tables 10.5 and 10.6. The source code for PQP, OpenRisc1200, and CPU86 cores were available. Therefore, we synthesized and evaluated their performance using altera Quartus II professional edition. The other cores data were obtained from corresponding manufacturers performance reports and published work Mattson (2004); EDN (2008).

LEON2 is a SPARCV8 compliant 32-bit RISC processor Gaisler (2004). ARM7 is a simple 32-bit RISC core ARM (1994, 2001). The CPU86 core is fully binary/instruction compatible with an 8086/8088 processor CPU86 (2008). The SH2-DSP (SH7616) and SH3-DSP (SH7710 and SH7720) series processor cores are based on a popular Hitachi SuperH (SH) instruction set architecture Arahata (1997). The SH has RISC-type instruction sets and $16 \times 32$ bit general purpose registers. All instructions have 16-bits fixed length. The SH2-DSP and SH3-DSP are based on 5 stages pipelined architecture, so basic instructions are executed in one clock cycle pitch. Similar to our processor, the SH also has an internal 32-bit architecture for enhanced data processing ability (Table 10.7).

From the results shown in Table 10.5, the DEP core has 49.63 % higher speed than OpenRisc1200 core for both area and speed optimizations. DEP core also has 61.11, 57.56, 58.53 and 58.79 % higher speed than ARM7, LEON2, CPU86, and

**Table 10.7** DEP power consumption comparisons with various synthesizable CPU cores

| Cores | Average power |
|---|---|
| DEP | 187.5 |
| PQP | 187.5 |
| OpenRisc1200 | 1005 |
| SH7616 | 250 |
| SH7710 | 500 |
| SH7720 | 600 |
| ARM7 | 22 |
| LEON2 | 458 |

MicroBlaze cores respectively. When compared with PQP processor, DEP has 12.92 and 11.88 % speed decrease for speed and area optimizations respectively. For power consumption comparison, the DEP core consumes 144.26 and 33.33 % less power than LEON2 and SH7616 cores respectively. It also consumes less power than SH series and OpenRisc1200 cores. However, DEP core consumes more power than the ARM7 core. This difference comes mainly from the small hardware configuration parameters of ARM7 when compared to our DEP core parameters.

## 10.5  Conclusions

This chapter presented architecture and design of a dual-execution mode synthesizable processor. The architecture shares a single instruction set and supports both queue and stack execution modes. This is achieved dynamically by execution mode switching and sources-results computing mechanisms. In overall performance, the DEP architecture is expected to increase the processor resources usability, relative to single core processor.

# Chapter 11
# Case Study: Deign of Embedded Multicore SoC for Biomedical Applications

Electrocardiography (ECG) is an interpretation of the electrical activity of the heart over time captured and externally recorded by electrodes. An effective approach to speed up this and other biomedical operations is to integrate a very high number of processing elements in a single chip so that the massive scale of fine-grain parallelism inherent in several biomedical applications can be exploited efficiently. As a case study, we present in this chapter a real hardware and software design of a multicore SoC architecture, named BANSMOM, targeted for biomedical applications. We start by explaining a novel algorithm that analyses ECG signals in an efficient manner. Then, we explain in details the hardware components of the system as well as the prototyping, and evaluation results.

## 11.1 Introduction

Recent technological advances in wireless networking, embedded microelectronics and the Internet allow computer and biomedical scientists to fundamentally modernize and change the way health care services are deployed. Thus, changes and new services are urgently needed to help cope with the imminent crisis in the health care systems caused by current demographic, social, and economic trends in many countries.

The world population over age 65 is expected to more than double from 357 million in 1990 to 761 million in 2025 (Ben-Abdallah 2009). These statistics clearly underscore the need for more scalable and affordable health care solution. Despite the decreased mortality rate, heart disease and associated complications is one of the main causes of death around the world. Detection of irregularities in the rhythms of the heart is a growing concern in medical research.

Embedded health monitoring systems are approaches to deal with such problems. However, development of such systems faces a number of challenging tasks since they need to often address conflicting requirements for performance, size, and accuracy. In health monitoring applications, a wide range of parameters must be available and processed. Thus, multiple tasks must be performed in order to obtain accurate diagnosis. In most cases, complex computations are required because of the

A. Ben Abdallah, *Multicore Systems On-Chip: Practical Software/Hardware Design*, Atlantis Ambient and Pervasive Intelligence 7, DOI: 10.2991/978-94-91216-92-3_11,
© Atlantis Press and the author 2013

applied detection algorithm. When real time diagnosis are required, a single med-ium-performance processor core might have problems dealing with all tasks.

Electrocardiography is an essential practice in heart medicine. It faces com-putational challenges, especially when 12 or more lead signals are to be analyzed in parallel, in real-time, and under increasing sampling frequencies. Another challenge is the analysis of huge amounts of data that may grow to days of recording.

As we described in Chap. 3, MCSoCs are high performance devices that incor-porate multiple building blocks from multiple sources. An MCSoC may contain general or special purpose fully programmed processors, co-processors, DSPs, dedicated hardware, memory blocks, etc. These systems are becoming a common design alternative in portable devices because it is possible to manufacture a silicon chip including only necessary elements. Certain medical applications require devices capable of providing very accurate information about monitored patients in places where complex clinical systems are not available and parameters such as electrocardiogram characteristics are important to be determined.

In this chapter, we present a case study of a real hardware and software design of a multicore SoC architecture, named BANSMOM, targeted for biomedical applications. The ultimate goal of this multicore system is to monitor elderly people and promote well-being by introducing smart in-body sensors that allow medical professionals to initiate interventions in the home environment. Although the designed system can be slightly modified and used for various biomedical applications, we focus here only on ECG processing and real-time monitoring. The complete system consists of hardware and software components. The hardware part consists of the multicore SoC platform (discussed in Sect. 11.4). While the software part consists of a so called *Period-Peak-Detection (PPD)* algorithm and a real-time interaction interface (discussed in Sects. 11.3 and 11.5).

### *11.1.1   Electrocardiography and Heart Diseases*

Electrocardiography, which is also called ECG/EKG, is generally used to record the electrical impulses which immediately precede the contractions of the heart muscle. This method causes no discomfort to a patient and is often used for diagnosing heart disorders such as coronary heart disease, pericardia or inflam-mation of the membrane around the heart, heart muscle disease, arrhythmia and coronary thrombosis, etc. When using this technique, doctors connect electrodes to the chest, wrist and ankles that are connected to a recording machine. This machine displays, then, the electrical activity in the heart as a trace on a rolling graph or screen. Using the electrocardiography any abnormalities are revealed to the doctor.

This technique can be taken at a doctor's office, hospital or even at home and will provide your doctor with a 24 h record of the patients heart activity from a tape recorder that is worn by the patient. The Doctor or a medical staff can look at the printed graph to see if the heart chambers are contracting with complete regularity which indicates a normal rhythm. If the contractions of the lower heart chambers are extremely irregular this could indicate ventricular fibrillation. When the upper and lower heart chambers are beating independently this could indicate a complete heart blockage. If the upper heart chambers are beating fast and irregular, this can indicate arterial fibrillation.

The electrocardiography is a painless and quick procedure. The electrical impulses in the heart are recorded and amplified on a moving strip of paper. Small metal electrodes are placed on the skin of the patient to measure the flow and direction of the electrical currents in the heart during each heart beat. Each of the electrodes are connected by a wire to a machine that will produce what is called a tracing for each electrode. This tracing represents a particular view or what is called lead of the heart's electrical patterns. In most cases any person who is suspected of having heart disease will have an ECG taken by their doctor. This will aid the doctor in identifying a number of heart problems.

An electrocardiography produces waves that are known as: P, Q, R, S, T and U waves which gives each part of the ECG an alphabetical designation. Figure 11.1 shows an example of a typical ECG wave. As the heart beat begins with an impulse from the senatorial node, the impulse will first activate the upper chambers of the heart or atria and produce the P wave. Then the electrical current will flow down to the lower chambers of the heart or ventricles producing the Q, R and S waves. As the electrical current spreads back over the ventricles in the opposite direction it will produce the T waves. Using this technique doctors can determine where in the heart abnormal rhythms start which allows them to begin to determine the cause.

Many ECG analysis methods use the three peaks Q, R, S and the corresponding intervals between these three peaks. In biomedical terms, this interval from Q to R to S is known as the QRS complex (Desai 2006; Friesen 1990). The well known QRS Pan-Tompkins algorithm locates R-peaks in the ECG signal and calculates the heart period (Tomkins 1985).

A number of other research efforts focus on hardware implementations of health monitoring systems. For example, Christos presented a hardware implementation of the Pan and Tompkins QRS complex (Carey 2008).

**Fig. 11.1** A typical ECG wave

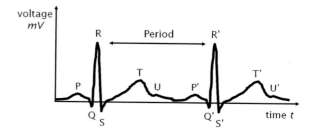

## 11.2  Digital Signal Processing

Before we start describing the PPD algorithm and the system architecture, let us first
review some basic knowledge about digital signal processing (DSP). DSP has been
with us for decades now with some astronomical development in the area over the
years. The world of science and engineering is filled with signals: images from
remote space probes, voltages generated by the heart and brain, radar and sonar
echoes, seismic vibrations, and countless other applications. Digital Signal Processing is the science of using computers to understand these types of data. This
includes a wide variety of goals: filtering, speech recognition, image enhancement,
data compression, neural networks, and much more. DSP is one of the most powerful
technologies that will shape science and engineering in the twenty-first century.

DSP is the processing of signals by digital means. A signal in this context can
mean a number of different things. Historically the origins of signal processing are
in electrical engineering, and a signal here means an electrical signal carried by a
wire or telephone line, or perhaps by a radio wave. More generally, however, a
signal is a stream of information representing anything from stock prices to data
from a remote-sensing satellite. A digital signal consists of a stream of numbers,
usually (but not necessarily) in binary form. The processing of a digital signal is
done by performing numerical calculations.

### 11.2.1  Analog and Digital Signals

In many cases, the signal of interest is initially in the form of an analog electrical
voltage or current, produced for example by a microphone or some other type of
transducer. In some situations, such as the output from the readout system of a
compact disc player, the data is already in digital form. An analog signal must be
converted into digital form before DSP techniques can be applied. An analog
electrical voltage signal, for example, can be digitized using an electronic circuit
called an analog-to-digital converter (ADC). This generates a digital output as a
stream of binary numbers whose values represent the electrical voltage input to the
device at each sampling instant.

### 11.2.2  Signal Processing

Signals commonly need to be processed in a variety of ways. For example, the
output signal from a transducer may well be contaminated with unwanted electrical noise. The electrodes attached to a patient's chest when an ECG is taken
measure tiny electrical voltage changes due to the activity of the heart and other
muscles. The signal is often strongly affected by mains pickup due to electrical

interference from the mains supply. Processing the signal using a filter circuit can remove or at least reduce the unwanted part of the signal. Increasingly nowadays, the filtering of signals to improve signal quality or to extract important information is done by DSP techniques.

### 11.2.3 Analog to Digital Conversion

Signals in the real world are analog: light, sound, heart signal. So, real-world signals must be converted into digital, using a circuit called analog to digital conversion, before they can be manipulated by digital equipment. Scanning a picture for example with a scanner is doing is an analog-to-digital conversion: The scanner is taking the analog information provided by the picture (light) and converting into digital. When voice is recorded or a VoIP solution is used on the computer, an analog-to-digital conversion takes place to convert voice, which is analog, into digital information. Digital information is not only restricted to computers. For talk on the phone, for example, voice is converted into digital since voice is analog and the communication between the phone switches is done digitally. When an audio CD is recorded at a studio, analog-to-digital conversion is taking place, converting sounds into digital numbers that will be stored on the disc.

To get the analog signal back, the opposite conversion digital-to-analog, which is done by a circuit called DAC (Digital-to-Analog Converter) is needed. Playing an audio CD, what the CD player is doing is reading digital information stored on the disc and converting it back to analog so that the music can be heard. There are some basic reasons to use digital signals instead of analog, noise being the number one. Since analog signals can assume any value, noise is interpreted as being part of the original signal. Digital systems, on the other hand, can only understand two numbers, zero and one. Anything different from this is discarded.

Basically Analog-to-digital conversion is an electronic process in which a continuously variable (analog) signal is changed, without altering its essential content, into a multi-level (digital) signal. The input to an analog-to-digital converter (ADC) consists of a voltage that varies among a theoretically infinite number of values. Examples are sine waves, the waveforms representing human speech, heart signals and the signals from a conventional television camera.

The output of the ADC, in contrast, has defined levels or states. The number of states is almost always a power of two—that is, 2, 4, 8, 16, etc. The simplest digital signals have only two states, and are called binary. All whole numbers can be represented in binary form as strings of ones and zeros. Digital signals propagate more efficiently than analog signals, largely because digital impulses, which are well-defined and orderly, are easier for electronic circuits to distinguish from noise, which is chaotic. This is the chief advantage of digital modes in communications. Computers "talk" and "think" in terms of binary digital data; while a microprocessor can analyze analog data, it must be converted into digital form for the computer to make sense of it.

## 11.3 Period-Peak Detection Algorithm

After we reviewed some basics about DSPs, we will now describe in this section a so called Period-Peak Detection Algorithm (PPD) for processing real signal—ECG signals. The PPD algorithm first detects the period and then looks for all peaks. This is the fundamental idea which differ from the known approaches that first find peaks and then period.

The PPD algorithm detects period before finding peaks because there is a high degree of randomness in the ECG signals. The randomness makes finding peaks an erroneous process. What we would get by doing this is the level of correlation these signals have. PPD algorithm computes several parameters: heart period, typical peaks (P, Q, R, S, T, and U), and inter-peak time spans (R-R interval). Peak height and inter-peak time ranging outside normal values, indicating different kinds of diseases, are also detected with the PPD algorithm.

PPD consists of two processing flows (see Fig. 11.2): one that detects period using the autocorrelation function, and another one that detects the number, amplitude and time interval of all peaks.

### 11.3.1 Period Detection

As indicated in Fig. 11.2, the PPD algorithm's *period detection* phase consists of 4 steps: (1) Data reading, (2) Derivation, (3) Autocorrelation, and (4) Finding intervals. The derivation phase finds the discrete derivative of the ECG signal. The derivative function is the best function we can run and which can aid in amplifying signal peaks; therefore, after reading the data of a signal $y$ with samples from memory, a very helpful step is to calculate the derivative of the signal $y(t)$. Equation 11.1 is the derivative function used by the PPD algorithm in the *period detection* phase.

$$\frac{\partial y}{\partial t}(t) \approx \frac{y[n+1] - y[n]}{(n+1) - n} = y[n+1] - y[n] \qquad (11.1)$$

**Fig. 11.2** PPD algorithm processing flow

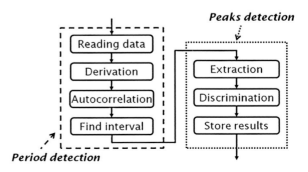

With this derivative, a given peak will be amplified relative to the samples before it, and if the value of $y[n]$ and $y[n+1]$ are near each other (i.e. no peaks) then the difference will look relatively small on the new derivative graph. The advantage of taking the derivative is that the fluctuations taking place in the signal, especially those around the peaks, would be reduced to a near-zero-value. In addition, performance overhead associated with derivative calculation of the ECG signal is negligible compared to the rest of the algorithm.

The *autocorrelation* step finds the period of ECG signals. This step uses autocorrelation function (ACF) defined by Formula 11.2. This ACF is a statistical method used to measure the degree of association between values in a single series separated by some lags. The fixed length ACF is defined by Formula 11.3. By running the ACF on the function $y$ over the recorded data sample, we can easily get the coefficients of the ACF.

$$R_y[k] = \sum_{n=-\infty}^{n=\infty} y[n] \times y[n-k] \qquad (11.2)$$

$$R_y[L] = \sum_{n=0}^{N} y[n] \times y[n-L] \qquad (11.3)$$

where, $R_y$ is the autocorrelation function, $y[n]$ is the filtered ECG signal. $L$ is a positive natural number related to the number of times needed for the calculations to get the period; it is the same as the number of lags of the autocorrelation. Finally, the finding interval step finds interval point in ECG signals based on the results of the autocorrelation step.

The *period detection* detailed computation steps are shown in Fig. 11.3. As it is shown in the above flow-chart, the actual *period detection* phase consists of seven steps (Fig. 11.4). Figures 11.5, 11.6, 11.7 and 11.8 describe the detailed computations of the main steps.

## 11.3.2 Peaks Detection

As shown in Fig. 11.2, the second phase of the PPD algorithm is the *peaks detection* phase and consists of 3 main steps: Extraction, Discrimination, and Store results. The *extraction* step discriminates significant peaks from calculated interval information in *period detection* phase. The *discrimination* step finds 6 peak-points (P, Q, R, S, T and U) from the extracted peaks (Ben-Abdallah 2010, 2009). Finally, the *store* step stores interval and peak information in the buffer. The *peaks detection* detailed computation is shown in Fig. 11.4.

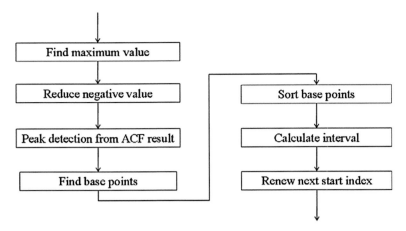

**Fig. 11.3** Period detection computation details

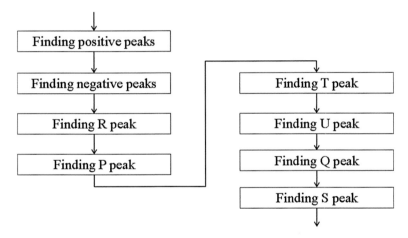

**Fig. 11.4** Peaks detection computation details

## 11.4 Multicore SoC Architecture and Hardware Design

Figure 11.9 shows the block diagram of the multicare SoC system architecture that was designed in hardware. As shown in this figure, the processing of a given ECG signal from one lead is performed in four major phases: (1) signal reading, (2) filtering, (3) analysis, and (4) display. In the remaining of this section, we will explain these processing stages in detail.

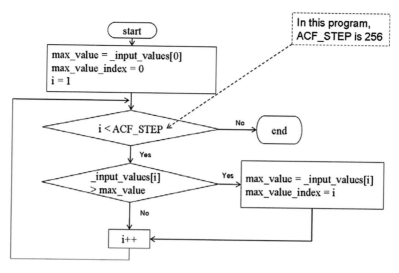

**Fig. 11.5** Period detection: finding maximum value algorithm. The autocorrelation step (*ACF_STEP*) is set 256

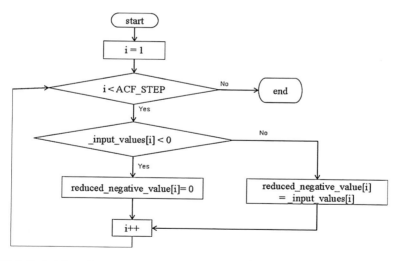

**Fig. 11.6** Period detection: reduce negative value algorithm

### 11.4.1 Signal Reading

First of all we have to note that the number of data inputs from the external sensors (leads) is extensible to 15 leads or more (see Fig. 11.9). The size of data is included in data read from the sensors. Analog Digital Converter (ADC) converts

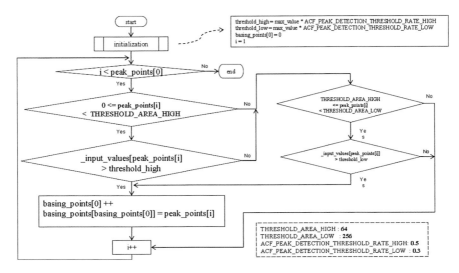

**Fig. 11.7**  Period detection: find base points

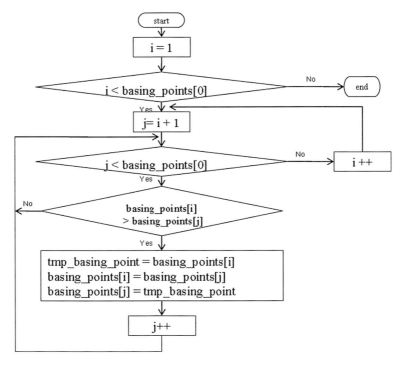

**Fig. 11.8**  Period detection: sort base points

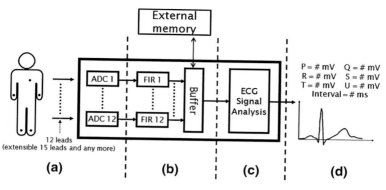

**Fig. 11.9** High-level view of the BANSMOM system architecture. **a** Signal reading, **b** filtering, **c** analysis, **d** display

analog data into digital data so a contiguous ECG signal is converted into a discrete ECG signal. As a result, filter processing and analysis processing can be easily done.

## 11.4.2 Filtering

The band-pass filter reduces the influence of muscle noise, 60 Hz interference, baseline wander, and T-wave interference. This filter cascaded the low-pass and high-pass filters described below to achieve a 3 dB passband from about 5–11 Hz (Figs. 11.9 and 11.10).

A low pass filter only allows low frequency signals from 0 Hz to its cut-off frequency, *fc* point to pass while blocking those any higher. The difference equation of the filter is shown in Formula 11.4. Where $T$ is the sampling period, the cutoff frequency is about 11 Hz.

$$y(nT) = 2y(nT - T) - y(nT - 2T) + x(nT)$$
$$- 2x(nT - 6T) + x(nT - 12T) \qquad (11.4)$$

The other type of filtering is called high-pass filter. Its design is based on subtracting the output of a first-order low-pass filter from an all-pass filter (i.e., the samples in the original signal). The difference equation of the filter is shown in the Formula 11.5. Where the cutoff frequency is about 5 Hz.

$$y(nT) = 32x(nT - 16T) - [y(nT - T)$$
$$+ x(nT) - x(nT - 32T)] \qquad (11.5)$$

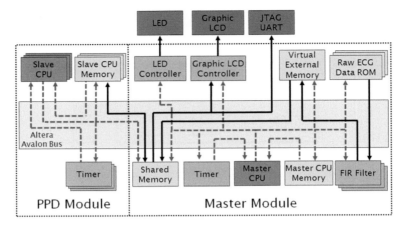

**Fig. 11.10**  Prototyped multicore SoC block diagram

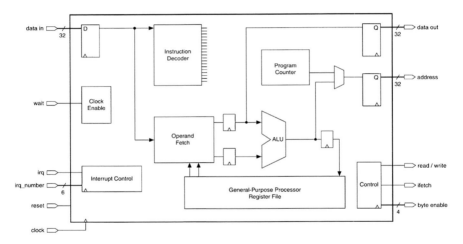

**Fig. 11.11**  Nios II core architecture block diagram

### 11.4.2.1  Noise Filtering

Noise filtering uses a bandpass filter that is based on the Finite Impulse Response (FIR) filter. The bandpass filter reduces the influence of muscle noise, 50 Hz interference, baseline wander, and T-wave interference. Digital filters process digitized or sampled signals. A digital filter computes a quantized time-domain representation of the convolution of the sampled input time function and a representation of the weighting function of the filter. They are realized by an extended sequence of multiplications and additions carried out at a uniformly spaced sample interval. The digitized input signal is mathematically influenced by the DSP program. These signals are passed through structures that shift the clocked data into summers (adders), delay blocks and multipliers. These structures change the mathematical values in a predetermined way: the resulting data represents the filtered or transformed signal.

Digital filters are a very important part of DSP. Filters have two uses: signal separation and signal restoration. Signal separation is needed when a signal has been contaminated with interference, noise, or other signals. For example, imagine a device for measuring the electrical activity of a baby's heart (EKG) while still in the womb. The raw signal will likely be corrupted by the breathing and heartbeat of the mother. A filter might be used to separate these signals so that they can be individually analyzed. Signal restoration is used when a signal has been distorted in some way. For example, an audio recording made with poor equipment may be filtered to better represent the sound as it actually occurred.

Finite Impulse Response (FIR) filter is a basic type of digital filter. FIR filters have no non-zero feedback coefficient in the general form of the digital filter difference equation. That is, the filter has only zeros, and once it has been excited with an impulse, the output is present for only a finite N number of computational cycles. The FIR filter uses noise rejection and waveform extraction for ECG algorithm. The data from analog/digital converter is finite and is a discrete digital signal; therefore, BANSMOM system uses FIR filter. This filter is popular among liner digital filters and the most safety in another filter within finite data. The FIR filter is composed of three parts: delay element, multiplier, and adder. Formula 11.7 is the difference equation for FIR filter that is defined by the relationship between input signal and output signal.

$$y[n] = a_0 x_n + a_1 x_{n-1} + \cdots + a_N x_{n-N} \tag{11.6}$$

$$= \sum_{i=0}^{N} a_i x_{n-i} \tag{11.7}$$

$N$ is filter order that corresponds to the number of taps. $xn$ are current or previous filter inputs. $y[n]$ is the current filter output. $ai$ are the filters coefficients that correspond to impulse response. A FIR filter works by multiplying an array of the most recent n data samples by an array of constants, and summing the elements of the resulting array. The filter then inputs another sample of data and repeats the process.

## 11.4.3  Data Processing

Correlation is calculated between the acquired segment and a pattern which has been previously obtained. For each analyzed patient, the pattern segment is

```
************************************************************
*            The University of Aizu                  *
*        Embedded Multicore System Research           *
*            -- AIZUDAI BANSHOM Project --            *
*                        Author:Yasuyoshi Haga *
*                    Last Update Date:Jan 22, 2010.   *
******* Period-Peaks Detection Processing Report *******
Sample Data:MIT-BIH Normal Sinus Rhythm Database No.16483 from PhysioBank
Filter lag:0.195s

*** Start of Processing

Range of processing: 0.000s - 2.000s
  Interval:0.625s [0.000s - 0.625s]
  PPP=0.047s, PPV=0.008mV
  QPP=0.086s, QPV=-0.292mV
  RPP=0.125s, RPV=0.492mV
  SPP=0.164s, SPV=-0.309mV
  TPP=0.344s, TPV=0.176mV
  UPP=0.602s, UPV=0.080mV
  R-R Interval:0.125s [0.000s - 0.125s]

  Interval:0.617s [0.625s - 1.242s]
  PPP=0.672s, PPV=0.003mV
  QPP=0.711s, QPV=-0.280mV
  RPP=0.750s, RPV=0.455mV
  SPP=0.797s, SPV=-0.291mV
  TPP=0.969s, TPV=0.175mV
  UPP=1.227s, UPV=0.085mV
  R-R Interval:0.625s [0.125s - 0.750s]
```

**Fig. 11.12**  Software simulation output

assumed to contain regular ECG signals where a signal's QRS complex is contained so that any further ECG pulses can be correlated with it. High correlation values correspond to pulse detection. Pattern extraction is performed by the main processor. Once obtained, it is transferred and stored to the off-chip memory. The off-chip memory starts to receive data samples directly from the ADC. Data samples are stored in a Queue (FIFO). Correlation pattern is calculated, and pulse alignment is evaluated. When the input signals in the Queue are aligned with the pattern, a high correlation value will be obtained, and a signal indicating the presence of a new pulse is generated. External monitor outputs the analyzed results. The output data is peaks of each typical wave (P, Q, R, S and T), heart rate and entire waveform (see Figs. 11.12 and 11.15).

## 11.4.4 Processor Core

For Master and Slave cores, we adopted the Nios II soft-core which is a 32-bit embedded-processor architecture designed. Nios II incorporates many enhancements over the original Nios architecture, making it more suitable for a wider range of embedded computing applications, from DSP to system-control. The Nios II architecture is a RISC style architecture. The soft-core nature of the Nios II processor lets the system designer specify and generate a custom Nios II core, tailored for his or her specific application requirements. Of course, system designers can extend the Nios II's basic functionality by adding a predefined memory management unit, or defining custom instructions and custom peripherals.

Nios II processor is designed for 5-stage pipelines, with separate data and instruction Harvard structure. Nios II has its own dedicated architecture and instruction set to support 32 bits hardware multiplication and division instructions. It has 32 general purpose registers. Users can also customize up to 256 instructions according to their needs. Figure 11.11 shows a simple block diagram of the Nios II core. Reader can reefer to on-line literature (Nios II 2012) for more details.

## 11.5  Real-Time Interaction Interface Development

The monitoring part is crucial for the real time diagnosis with BANSNOM system. The existing methods of ECG monitoring are characterized by a manually-intensive work flow for data acquisition, formatting and visualization. Besides, they are most often relying on multiple serial processes and several software packages (Fig. 11.13).

The developed Real-Time Interaction (RTI) interface is a robust web based application. This feature allows the user to deal with the high requirements of biomedical data monitoring, such as the real time constraint in addition to the interaction and the synchronization issues between the medical staff side and the patient side.

The RTI tool uses PHP (2012) as a server side and Mysql (2012) as a data base management system. The ECG waveform is displayed with a library based on Java-script. Moreover, the dynamic update is ensured by Ajax technology to allow the user to interact directly with the data coming from the local storage without needing to refresh the page. The incoming data is stored in a dedicated table in Mysql database. Each node has its own table that contains all data classified by recording date. This classification allows the medical staff to visualize any specific data at any desired date and time. In addition, by building the RTI tool as a web application, one can improve the mobility of the monitoring task without distributing it or installing any specific software. Thus, the medical staff can consult the ECG data at real-time from anywhere through an Internet browser. In other words, the user/doctor can easily interact with patients at any time as long as the Internet connection is established.

### 11.5.1  Data Capturing

The output of the processing part is the coordinates of each peak for each corresponding node. To continue on the same way of mobility, the processed data coming from BANSMOM node(s) are transmitted to the database through the

**(a)**

```
$.ajax({
        //Call the script to get new peak
        url: 'live-server-data.php',
        success: function(point) {
        var series = chart.series[0],

    // add the peak
        chart.series[0].addPoint(point, true, shift);

        // call it again after one second
         setTimeout(requestData, 1000);
                },
                cache: false
        });
```

**(b)**

```
<?php include 'get_data.php'; ?>

    var dataFromPHP = [ <?php echo join($data, ',') ?> ] ;

/* preprocess data */
var newData = [];function pointExists(array, key) {
    for (var i = 0; i < array.length; i++) {
        if (array[i][0] == key) {
            return true
        };
    }
    return false;
}


/* 1) create only one point */
for (var i = 0; i < dataFromPHP.length; i++) {
    if (!pointExists(newData, dataFromPHP[i][0])) {
        newData.push(dataFromPHP[i]);
    }
}
```

**Fig. 11.13  a** Get live-data, **b** Get previous-data

Internet and the corresponding table in MySQL is updated automatically. Figures 11.14 and 11.15 show BANSMOM system running snapshot and the external monitoring interface respectively.

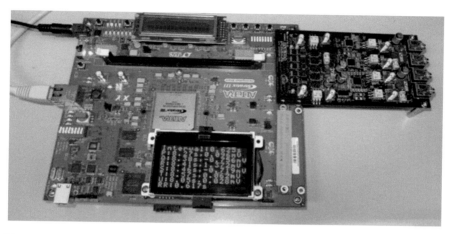

**Fig. 11.14** Multicore SoC system running snapshot

## 11.5.2 Data Display and Analysis

The coordinates of the ECG graph from each node are first transmitted through the Internet and sent to the database. This process is done as long as there are new incoming data. The continuity of the update process gives us a wide range of ECG data classified by capture date. The real time charting library implemented in the web visualization tool will manipulate this huge amount of data. So, the medical staff can consult the latest incoming data at real time (a marker is implemented to show that there are new incoming data) or it can re-consult previous data.

As it is shown in Fig. 11.15, the tool contains four main modules. The most important one is the ECG viewer itself with the capability to display the data from three leads at the same time. The second module (window) displays the nodes which already sent data to the database. The remaining utilities are dedicated for the information related to the node (patient).

Figure 11.13b illustrates the PHP script for consulting previous ECG data. In the case of visualizing live incoming data, an Ajax call is executed; this execution returns the last peaks that have been added to the database as shown in Fig. 11.13a.

## 11.6  Design Results

### 11.6.1 Hardware Complexity

The system was designed in Verilog HDL. Figure 11.10 shows the block diagram of the prototyped system. The master module consists of the Altera Nios II core (NiosII 2012), four on-chip memories (used for raw ECG data storage,

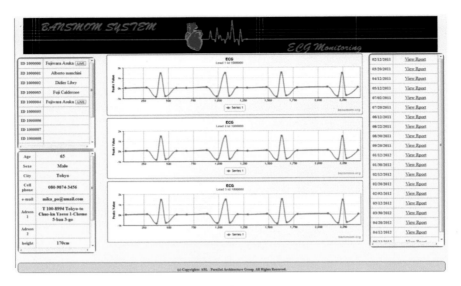

**Fig. 11.15** Interactive RTI tool displaying ECG waves

**Table 11.1** Hardware complexity

| System model | Logic utilization | | | | MEM bits | Speed | Power |
|---|---|---|---|---|---|---|---|
| | ALUTs | ALUTs | REG | Total (%) | | (MHz) | (mW) |
| 1-lead | 9,769 | 16 | 11,669 | 14 | 1,207,312 (21 %) | 97.89 | 677.00 |
| 2-lead | 17,169 | 32 | 21,297 | 26 | 1,810,384 (32 %) | 95.82 | 716.31 |
| 3-lead | 24,592 | 48 | 30,947 | 38 | 2,413,840 (43 %) | 92.52 | 754.84 |
| 4-lead | 32,047 | 64 | 40,566 | 50 | 3,016,976 (54 %) | 92.25 | 784.31 |

processor memory, shared memory and virtual external memory), an interrupt timer, a graphics LCD controller, a LED controller and a JTAG UART (used for connection with host PC). One PPD node (slave) consists of Nios II core, on-chip memory, and an interrupt timer.

The FIR filter module is generated by Altera MegaCore Function. The specification of this filter is as follows: filter step is 51, sample rate is 128, and cutoff frequency is from 5 to 15 Hz. Table 11.1 shows logic synthesis result. For example, one configured with 1-lead (only one PPD module), the logic utilization is about 14 %, the total block memory bits is about 21 %, and The total power dissipation is about 677 mW.

## 11.6.2 Performance Evaluation

We used real sample data from PhysioBank data base (PhysioBank 2011) for testing the correctness and the accuracy of BANSMOM system. Table 11.2 shows

**Table 11.2** Performance evaluation

| Recode (No.) | Detected RR interval (# of interval) | Failed detection (# of interval) | Execution time (s) |
|---|---|---|---|
| 16265 | 14 | 7 (50 %) | 6.787 |
| 16273 | 13 | 3 (23 %) | 6.959 |
| 16420 | 14 | 5 (36 %) | 6.791 |
| 16773 | 10 | 1 (10 %) | 6.511 |
| 16786 | 10 | 3 (30 %) | 6.524 |
| 17052 | 9 | 2 (22 %) | 6.182 |
| 18177 | 15 | 5 (33 %) | 8.316 |
| 18184 | 8 | 3 (38 %) | 4.860 |

the test results over various configurations. Figure 11.12 shows the simulation screen capture of the processing report. PPP, QPP, RPP, SPP, TPP and UPP mean P, Q, R, S, T and U Peaks. On average, the PPD algorithm achieves fair accuracy of about 69 %.

## 11.7  Conclusion

Recent technological advances in wireless networking, microelectronics and the Internet allow computer and biomedical scientists to fundamentally modernize and change the way health care services are deployed.

Electrocardiography is a commonly used, non-invasive procedure for recording electrical changes in the heart. The record, which is called an electrocardiogram (ECG or EKG), shows the series of waves that relate to the electrical impulses which occur during each beat of the heart. The results are printed on paper or displayed on a monitor. The waves in a normal record are named P, Q, R, S, T, U and follow in alphabetical order.

MCSoCs are high performance devices that incorporate multiple building blocks from multiple sources. An embedded multicore SoC may contain general or special purpose fully programmed processors, co-processors, DSPs, dedicated hardware, memory blocks, etc. These MCSoC systems are becoming a common design alternative in portable devices because it is possible to manufacture a silicon chip including only necessary elements.

This chapter exploits the technology of parallel processing to process the electrocardiography computational kernels in parallel. The idea is to implement the traditional multi-lead bulky electrocardiogram on a programmable embedded multicore SoC which is small and more efficient. The presented solution paves the way for real-time processing diagnosis of heart-related diseases. Prototyping of Multicore SoC on FPGA involves building a functional system model that lets the designer evaluate various aspects of a design, and provide a realistic projection about the final product implementation. Having a prototype available provides more accurate power-performance evaluations. For example, prototypes make accurate area estimations feasible, as well as hardware complexity overhead and energy consumption measurements.

# References

2006 Edn DSP directory, http://www.edn.com/dspdirectory

A. Abnous, J. Rabaey, Ultra-low-power domain-specific multimedia processors, in *Proceedings of the IEEE VLSI Signal Processing Workshop* (IEEE Press, Piscataway, 1996), pp. 459–464

Advanced RISC Machines Ltd, ARM Architecture Reference Manual, 02 Sept 2001

Advanced RISC Machines Ltd, ARM7DMI Data Sheet, (1994)

Advancel Logic Corporation, Tiny2J Microprocessor Core for Javacard Applications, http://www.advancel.com

A.V. Aho, R. Sethi, J.D. Ullman, *Compilers Principles, Techniques, and Tools* (Addison Wesley, New York, 1986)

M. Akanda, A. Ben-Abdallah, S. Kawata, M. Sowa, An efficient dynamic switching mechanism (DSM) for hybrid processor architecture, in *Proceedings of Springer's Lecture Note in Computer Science, LNCS-3824*, 6–9 Dec 2005, pp. 77–86

M. Akanda, A. Ben-Abdallah, M. Sowa, On the design of a dual-execution mode processor: architecture and preliminary evaluation, in *Proceedings Springer's Lecture Note in Computer Science*, LNCS-4331, 1–4 Dec 2006, pp. 37–46

F. Akyildiz, S. Weilian, S. Yogesh, E. Cayirci, A survey on sensor networks. IEEE Commun. Mag. **40**(8), 102–114 (2002)

R. Allen, K. Kennedy, *Optimizing Compilers for Modern Architectures* (Morgan Kaufman, San Francisco, 2002)

D. Alpert, D. Avnon, Architecture of the pentium microprocessor. IEEE Micro **13**(3), 11–21 (1993)

A. Alsolaim, J. Becker, M. Glesner, J. Starzyk, Architecture and application of a dynamically reconfigurable hardware array for future mobile communication systems, in *IEEE International Conference on Field-Programmable Custom Computing Machines*, 2000, pp. 205–214

Altera Design Software, http://www.altera.com/

Altera, http://www.altera.com/devices/fpga/stratix-fpgas/stratix-ii/stratix-ii/features/architecture/st2-lut.html. Accessed 29 Jan 2012

F. Arahata, O. Nishii, K. Uchiyama, N. Nakagawa, Functional verification of the superscalar SH-4 microprocessor, in *Compcon97, the Proceedings of the International conference Compcon97*, Feb 1997, pp. 115–120

ARM: Advanced microprocessor bus architecture (AMBA) specification, v.2.0 (1999), http://www.arm.com/

ARM: Amba overview (2007), http://www.arm.com

H. Balakrishnan, V. Enkata, N. Padmanabhan, A comparison of mechanisms for improving TCP performance over wireless links. IEEE/ACM Trans. Netw. **5**(6), 756–769 (1997)

S. Bell, B. Edwards, J. Amann, Tile64-processor: a 64-core SoC with mesh interconnect, in *Solid-State Circuits Conference*, 2008

A. Ben Abdallah, *Multicore Systems On-Chip: Practical Software/Hardware Design*,
Atlantis Ambient and Pervasive Intelligence 7, DOI: 10.2991/978-94-91216-92-3,
© Atlantis Press and the author 2013

263

A. Ben Abdallah, Y. Haga, K. Kuroda, An efficient algorithm and embedded multicore implementation for ECG analysis in multi-lead electrocardiogram records, in *IEEE Proceedings of the 39th he International Conference on Parallel Processing Workshop*, San Diego, 13–16 Sept 2010, pp. 99–103

A. Ben Abdallah, M. Sowa, Basic network-on-chip interconnection for future gigascale MCSoCs applications: communication and computation orthogonalization, in *Proceedings of Tunisia-Japan Symposium on Society, Science and Technology (TJASSST)*, 4–9 Dec 2006

A. Ben Ahmed, A. Ben Abdallah, ONoC-SPL customized network-on-chip (NoC) architecture and prototyping for data-intensive computation applications, in *IEEE Proceedings of The 4th International Conference on Awareness, Science and Technology*, 2012, pp. 257–262

A. Ben Ahmed, A. Ben Abdallah, K. Kuroda, Architecture and design of efficient 3D network-on-chip (3D NoC) for custom multicore SoC, in *IEEE Proceedings of BWCCA-2010*, Nov 2010

A. Ben-Abdallah, Dynamic instructions issue algorithm and a queue execution model toward the design of hybrid processor architecture, Ph.D. thesis, Graduate School of Information Systems, the University of Electro-Communications, Mar 2002

A. Ben-Abdallah, M. Arsenji, S. Shigeta, T. Yoshinaga, M. Sowa, Queue processor for novel queue computing paradigm based on produced order scheme, in *Proceedings of HPC, IEEE CS*, Jul 2004

A. Ben-Abdallah, S. Kawata, T. Yoshinaga, M. Sowa, Modular design structure and high-level prototyping for novel embedded processor core, in *Proceedings of the 2005 IFIP International Conference on Embedded and Ubiquitous Computing (EUC'2005)*, Nagasaki, 6–9 Dec 2005, pp. 340–349

A. Ben-Abdallah, S. Kawata, T. Yoshinaga, M. Sowa, Modular design structure and high-level prototyping for novel embedded processor core, in *Proceedings of the 2005 IFIP International Conference on Embedded And Ubiquitous Computing (EUC'2005)*, Nagasaki, Japan, 6–9 Dec 2005, pp. 340–349

A. Ben-Abdallah, M. Sarem, M. Sowa, DRA: Dynamic register allocator mechanism for FARM microprocessor, in APPT99, 1999

A. Ben-Abdallah, S. Kawata, M. Sowa, Design and architecture for an embedded 32-bit QueueCore. J. Embed. Comput. **2**(2), 191–205 (2006)

A. Ben-Abdallah, T. Yoshinaga, M. Sowa, High-level modeling and FPGA prototyping of produced order parallel queue processor core. J. Supercomput. **38**(1), 3–15 (2006)

A. Ben-Abdallah, T. Yoshinaga, M. Sowa, High-level modeling and FPGA prototyping of produced order parallel queue processor core. Int. J Supercomput. **38**(1), 3–15 (2006)

L. Benini, G. de Micheli, System-level power optimization: techniques and tools, in *Proceeding International Symposium Low-Power Electronics Design*, San Diego, CA, 1999, pp. 288–293

L. Benini, G. de Micheli, E. Macii, Designing low-power circuits: practical recipes. IEEE Circ. Syst. Mag. **1**, 6–25 (2001)

B. Bisshop, T. Killiher, M. Irwin, The design of register renaming unit, in *Proceedings of Great Lakes Symposium on VLSI*, 1999

E. Bolotin, I. Cidon, R. Ginosaur, A. Kolodny, QNoC: QoS architecture and design process for network-on-chip. J. Syst. Arch. **50**, 105–128 (2004)

L. Bononi, N. Concer, Simulation and analysis of network on chip architectures: Ring, spidergon and 2D mesh. DATE 2006, pp. 154–159

A.D. Booth, A signed binary multiplication technique. Quart. J. Mech. Appl. Math. **4**, 23–40 (1951)

S. Borkar, Design challenges of technology scaling. IEEE Micro. **19**(4), 23–29 (1999)

B. Brey, *The Intel Microprocessors*, 6th edn. (Prentice Hall, Upper Saddle River, 2003)

C-5 Network Processor Architecture Guide, C-Port Corp., North Andover, MA, 31 May 2001

Cadence Design Systems, http://www.cadence.com/

A. Canedo, Code generation algorithms for consumed and produced order queue machines, Master's thesis, University of Electro-Communications, Tokyo, Japan, Sept 2006

A. Canedo, A. Ben-Abdallah, M. Sowa, A GCC-based compiler for the queue register processor, in *Proceedings of International Workshop on Modern Science and Technology*, May 2006, pp. 250–255

A. Canedo, A. Ben-Abdallah, M. Sowa, A new code generation algorithm for 2-offset producer order queue computation model, in the Journal of Computer Languages, Systems and Structures, to appear 2007

A. Canedo, A. Ben-Abdallah, M. Sowa, Code generation algorithms for consumed and produced order queue machines, Master Thesis, Graduate School of Information Systems, University of Electro-Communications, Sept 2006

M.G. Carey, Electrocardiographic predictors of sudden cardiac death. J Cardiovas Nurs **23**(2), 175–182 (2008)

L.P. Carloni, P. Pande, Y. Xie, Networks-on-chip in emerging interconnect paradigms: advantages and challenges, in *Proceedings of the 3rd ACM/IEEE International Symposium on Networks-on-Chip (NOCS09)*, San Diego, CA, May 2009

V. Catania, R. Holsmark, S. Kumar, M. Palesi, A methodology for design of application specific deadlock-free routing algorithms for NoC systems, in *Proceedings of International Conference on Hardware-Software Codesign and System Synthesis*, Oct 2006

L.M. Censier, P. Feautrier, A new solution to coherence problems in multicache systems. IEEE Trans. Comput. **c-20**(12), 1112–1118 (1978)

D. Chaiken, C. Fields, K. Kurihara, A. Agarwal, Directory-based cache coherence in large-scale multiprocessors. Computer **23**(6), 49–58 (1990)

C.H. Chao, K.Y. Jheng, H.Y. Wang, J.C. Wu, A.-Y. Wu, Traffic–and thermal-aware run-time thermal management scheme for 3D NoC systems, in *Proceedings of ACM/IEEE International Symposium Networks-on-Chip (NoCS)*, Grenoble, France, May 2010, pp. 223–230

A.A. Chien, J.H. Kim, Planar-adaptive routing: low-cost adaptive networks for multiprocessors. J. ACM **42**(1), 91–123 (1995)

CPU86 8088/8086 FPGA IP Core, http://www.ht-lab.com/

M. Creeger, Multicore CPUs for the Masses, QUEUE, Sept 2005

W.J. Dally et al., Route packets, not wires: on-chip interconnection networks, in *Proceedings of DAC*, 2001, pp. 684–689

W.J. Dally, Express cubes: improving the performance of kary-n-cube interconnection networks. IEEE Trans. Comput. **40**(9), 1016–1023 (1991)

S. Das et al., Technology, performance, and computer aided design of three-dimensional integrated circuits, in *Proceedings of International Symposium on Physical Design*, 2004

B. Dave, G. Lakshminarayama, N. Jha, COSFA: Hardware-software co-synthesis of heterogeneous distributed embedded system architectures for low overhead fault tolerance, in *Proceedings of IEEE Fault-Tolerant Computing Symposium*, 1997, pp. 339–348

A.V. de Mello, L.C.O.F.G. Morales, N.L.V. Calazans, Evaluation of routing algorithms on mesh based NoCsm, Technical report, FACULDADE DE INFORMATICA—PUCRS, Brazil, 2004

G. De Micheli, R. Ernst, W. Wolf, Readings in hardware/software co-design (Morka Kaufmann Publishers, San Francisco). ISBN:1-55860-702-1

G. De Micheli, R. Ernst, W. Wolf, *Readings in Hardware/Software co-design* (Morka Kaufmann Publishers, San Francisco, 2001). ISBN:1-55860-702-1

A.D. Desai, T.S. Yaw, T. Yamazaki, A. Kaykha, S. Chun, V.F. Froelicher, Prognostic significance of quantitative qrs duration. Am J Med **119**(7), 600–606 (2006)

K. Dev, *Multi-Objective Optimization Using Evolutionary Algorithms* (John Wiley and Sons Ltd, New York, 2002) pp. 245–253

K. Diefendorff, K. Dubey, How multimedia workloads will change processor design. IEEE Comput. **30**(9), 43–45 (1997)

F. Doughs, P. Krishnan, B. Marsh, Thwarting the power hungry disk, in *Proceedings of the 1991 Winter USENIX Conference*, 1994

F. Douglis, F. Kaashoek, B. March, R. Caceres, K. Li, J. Tauber, Storage alternative for mobile computers, in *Proceedings of the First USENIX Symposimum on Operating Systems Design and Implemnetation*, 1994

J. Dowdeck, Inside Intel Core Microarchitecture and Smart Memory Access, Intel, 2006

P. Erik, P. Harris, W. Steven, E.W. Pence, S. Kirkpatrick, Technology directions for portable computers. Proc. IEEE. *83b*(4), 63–57 (1995)

R. Ernst, J. Henkel, T. Benner, Hardware-software co synthesis for microcontrollers, IEEE Design and Test, Dec 1993, pp. 64–75

B. Feero, P.P. Pande, Performance evaluation for three-dimensional networks-on-chip, in *Proceedings of IEEE Computer Society Annual Symposium on VLSI (ISVLSI)*, 9–11th May 2007, pp. 305–310

M. Fernandes, J. Llosa, N. Topham, Using queues for register file organization in VLIW. Technical Report, ECS-CSG-29-97, University of Edinburgh, Department of Computer Science, 1997

B. Flachs, S. Asano, S.H. Dhong, H.P. Hofstee, G. Gervais, R. Kim, T. Le, P. Liu, J. Leenstra, J. Liberty, B. Michael, H.-J. Oh, S. M. Mueller, O. Takahashi, A. Hatakeyama, Y. Watanabe, N. Yano, The microarchitecture of the streaming processor for a CELL processor, in *Proceedings of the IEEE International Solid-State Circuits Symposium*, Feb 2005, pp. 184–185

M. Franklin, Notes from ENEE759M: Microarchitecture, Spring 2008

G.M. Friesen, T.C. Jannett, M.A. Jadallah, S.L. Yates, S.R. Quintand, H.T. Nagle, A comparison of the noise sensitivity. IEEE Trans. Biomed. Eng. *37*(1), 85–89 (1990)

Z. Fu, X. Ling, The design and implementation of arbiters for network-on-chips, in *IEEE, Industrial and Information Systems (IIS), 2010 2nd International Conference*, vol. 1 (2010), pp. 292–295

Gaisler Research Laboratory, *LEON2 XST User's Manual*, 1.0.22 edition, May 2004

D. Geer, For Programmers, Multicore Chips Mean Multiple Challenges, Computer, Sept 2007

N. Genko, G. De Micheli, D. Atienza, J. Mendias, R. Hermida, F. Catthoor, A complete network-on-chip emulation framework, in *Proceedings of Design, Automation and Testing in Europe Conference*, Mar 2005, pp. 246–251

C.J. Glass, L.M. Ni, The turn model for adaptive routing, in *Proceedings of 19th Annual International Symposium Computer Architecture*, May 1992, pp. 278–287

D. Gohringer, M. Hubner, V. Schatz, J. Becker, Runtime adaptive multi-processor system-on-chip: RAMPSoC, in *International Symposium on Parallel and Distributed Processing*, Apr 2008, pp. 1–7

B.T. Gold, Balancing performance, area, and power in an on-chip network, Master's thesis, Department of Electrical and Computer Engineering, Virginia Tech, Aug 2004

GOMP: An OpenMP implementation for GCC, http://gcc.gnu.org/projects/gomp

K. Goossens, J. Dielissen, A. Radulescu, The Athereal network on chip: concepts, architectures, and implementations. IEEE Design and Test of Computers, 2005

L. Goudge, S. Segars, Thumb: reducing the cost of 32-bit RISC performance in portable and consumer applications, in *Proceedings of COMPCON '96*, 1996, pp. 176–181

K. Govil, E. Chan, H. Wasserman, Comparing algorithms for dynamic speed-setting of a low-power cpu, in *First ACM International Conference on Mobile Computing and Networking (MOBICOM)*, 1995

M. Gowan, L. Biro, D. Jackson, Power considerations in the design of the alpha 21264 Microprocessor, in *CAD1998, The 35th Design Automation Conference*, Jun 1998, pp. 726–731

A. Habibi, M. Arjomand, H. Sarbazi-Azad, Multicast-aware mapping algorithm for on-chip networks, in *19th International Euromicro Conference on Parallel, Distributed and Network-Based Processing*, Feb 2011, pp. 455–462

M.M. Hafizur Rahman, S. Horiguchi, High performance hierarchical torus network under matrix transpose traffic patterns, in *Proceedings of 7th International Symposium on Parallel Architectures, Algorithms and Netowrks (ISPAN04)*, Hong Kong, China, May 2004

Y. Haga, A. Ben Abdallah, A.B. d Kuroda, Embedded MCSoC architecture and period-peak detection (PPD) algorithm for ECG/EKG processing, in *The 19th Intelligent System Symposium (FAN 2009)*, 2009, pp. 298–303

P.J.M. Havinga, G.J.M. Smit, Energy-efficient wireless networking for multimedia applications, in *Wireless Communications and Mobile Computing*, vol. 1 (Wiley, New York, 2001), pp. 165–184

P.J. Havinga, G. Smit, M. Bos, Energy-efficient wireless ATM design, in *Proceedings wmATM'99*, 2–4 June 1999

L.S. Heath, S.V. Pemmaraju, A.N. Trenk, Stack and queue layouts of directed Acyclic graphs: Part I. SIAM J Comput. **23**(4), 1510–1539 (1996)

L.S. Heath, S.V. Pemmaraju, Stack and queue layouts of directed acyclic graphs: Part I. SIAM J. Comput. **28**(4), 1510–1539 (1999)

J. Hennessy, D. Patterson, *Computer Architecture: A Quantitative Approach* (Morgan Kaufman, San Diego, 1990)

J.L. Hennessy, D.A. Patterson, *Computer Architecture A Quantitative Approach* (Morgan Kaufmann Publishers Inc., San Francisco, 1996)

R. Holsmark, A. Johansson, S. Kumar, On connecting cores to packet switched on-chip networks: A case study with MicroBlaze processor cores, in *7th IEEE, Workshop DDECS 04*, Apr 2004

T. Holwerda, Intel: Software Needs to Heed Moore's Law

http://ultratechnology.com/

http://www.arm.com/products/CPUs/ARM926EJ-S.html

J. Hu, R. Marculescu, Exploiting the routing flexibility for energy/performance aware mapping of regular NoC architectures, in *Proceedings of DATE'03*, 2003, pp. 688–693

X. Huang, S. Carr, P. Sweany, Loop transformations for architectures with partitioned register banks, in *Proceedings of the ACM SIGPLAN workshop on Languages,Ccompilers and Tools for Embedded Systems*, 2001, pp. 48–55

IEEE Standard for Binary Floating-point Arithmetic, ANSI/IEEE Standard 754, 1985

IEEE task P754, A proposed standard fr binary floating-ponit arithmetic. IEEE Comput. **14**(12), 51–62 (1981)

Intel Corporation, Mobile intel pentium III processor in BGA2 and micro-PGA2 packages, revision 7.0, 2001

Intel Corporation, mobile power guidelines 2000, ftp://download.intel.com/design/mobile/intelpower/mpg99r1.pdf, Dec 1998

International Technology Roadmap for Semiconductors, 2003 Edition, System Drivers

International Technology Roadmap for Semiconductors, 2005 Edition

ITRS, http://public.itrs.net/

A. Jalabert, S. Murali, L. Benini, G. Michelli, Xpipes compiler: a tool for instantiating application specific networks-on-chip, in *Proceedings of Design, Automation and Testing in Europe Conference*. IEEE, 2004, pp. 884–889

S. Jang, S. Carr, P. Sweany, D. Kuras, A code generation framework for VLIW architectures with partitioned register banks, in *Proceedings of the 3rd International Conference on Massively Parallel, Computing Systems*, 1998

J. Janssen, H. Corporaal, Partitioned register file for TTAs, in *Proceedings of the 28th Annual International Symposium on Microarchitecture*, 1995, pp. 303–312

JazelleTM-ARM Architecture Extensions for Java Applications, White Paper, http://www.arm.com

A. Jerraya, *Multiprocessor System-on-Chip* (Morgan Kaufman Publishers, San Francisco, 2005). ISBN:0-12385-251-X

J. Joyner, P. Zarkesh-Ha, J. Meindl, A stochastic global net-length distribution for a three-dimensional system-on-chip(3D-SoC), in *Proceedings of 14th Annual IEEE International ASIC/SOC Conference*, Sept 2001

G. Kane, J. Heinrich, *MIPS RISC Architecture* (Prentice Hall, Upper Saddle River, 1992)

R. Kessler, The alpha 21264 microprocessor. IEEE Micro **19**(2), 24–36 (1999)

J. Kim, J. Balfour, W.J. Dally, Flatterned butterfly topology for on-chip networks, in *Proceedings of the 40th International Symposium on Microarchitecture*, 2007, pp. 172–182

K. Kim, H.Y. Kim, T.G. Kim, Top-down retargetable framework with token-level design for accelerating simulation time of processor architecture, in *IEICE Transaction Fundamentals of Electronics, Communications and Computer Sciences*, vol. E86-A, No. 12, Dec 2003, pp. 3089–3098

J. Kim, C. Nicopoulos, D. Park, V. Narayanan, M.S. Yousif, C.R. Das, A gracefully degrading and energy-efficient modular router architecture for on-chip networks, in *Proceedings of the 33rd International Symposium on Computer Architecture*, 2006, pp. 138–149

K. Kissel, MIPS16: High-density MIPS for the embedded market, Technical report, Silicon Graphics MIPS Group, 1997

J. Kistler, Disconnected operation in a distributed file system, Ph.D. thesis, Carnegie Mellon University, School of Computer Science, 1993

W. Knight, Two heads are better than one. IEEE Review, Sept 2005

J. Knobloch, E. Micca, M. Moturi, C.J. Nicol, J.H. O'Neill, J. Othmer, E. Sackinger, K.J. Singh, J. Sweet, C.J. Terman, J. Williams, A single-chip, 1.6-billion, 16-b MAC/s multiprocessor DSP. IEEE J. Solid-State Circuits **35**(3), 412–424 (2000)

B.U. Kohler, C. Hennig, R. Orglmeister, The principles of software QRS detection. Engineering in Medicine and Biology Magazine, IEEE. **21**(1), 42–57, Jan/Feb2002

J.P. Koopman, *Stack Computer* (Ellis Horwood Limited, Chichester)

D. Koufaty, D.T. Marr, Hyperthreading technology in the netburst microarchitecture. IEEE Micro **23**(2), 56–65 (2003)

R. Kravets, P. Krishnan, Application driven power management for mobile communication springer science. Wirel. Netw **6**(4), 263–277 (2000)

G. Kucuk, O. Ergin, D. Ponomarev, K. Ghose, Energy efficient register renaming. Lecture Notes in Computer Science, vol. 2799/2003 (2003), pp. 219–228

D. Kulkarani, W.A. Najjar, R. Rinker, F.J. Kurdahi, Fast area estimation to support compiler optimization in FPGA-based reconfigurable systems, in *IEEE Symposium on Field-Programmable Custom Computing Machines*, Napa, California, Apr 2002, pp. 239–247

S. Kumar, A. Jantsch, J.-P. Soininen, M. Forsell, et al., A network on chip architecture and design methodology, VLSI, 2002, in *Proceedings of IEEE Computer Society Annual Symposium*, 25–26 Apr 2002, pp. 105–112

A. Kumar, L.-S. Peh, P. Kundu, N.K. Jha, Express virtual channels: towards the ideal interconnection fabric, in *Proceedings of the 34th International Symposium on Computer Architecture*, 2007, pp. 150–161

R. Kumar, V. Zyuban, D.M. Tullsen, Interconnections in multicore architectures: understanding mechanisms, overheads and scaling, in *Proceedings of 32nd International Symposium on Computer Architecture*, Madison, USA, 2005, pp. 408–419

K. Lahiri, A. Raghunathan, S. Dey, Efficient exploration of the SoC communication architecture design space, in *Proceedings of IEEE/ACM ICCAD'00*, 2000, pp. 424–430

M. Lam, Software pipelining: an effective scheduling technique for VLIW machines, in *Proceedings of the ACM SIGPLAN 1988 conference on Programming Language design and Implementation*, 1988, pp. 318–328

G. Leary, K.S. Chatha, Design of NoC for SoC with multiple use cases requiring guaranteed performance, in *23rd International Conference on VLSI Design*, Jan 2010, pp. 200–205

H.G. Lee, N. Chang, U.Y. Ogras, R. Marculescu, On-chip communication architecture exploration: a quantitative evaluation of point-to-point, bus, and network-on-chip approaches. ACM Trans. Design Autom. Electron. Syst. **12** (2007)

C. Lee, M. Potkonjak, W.H. Mangione-Smith, MediaBench: a tool for evaluating and synthesizing multimedia and communications systems, in *30th Annual International Symposium on Microarchitecture (Micro '97)*, 1997, p. 330

C.K. Lennard, P. Schaumont, G. de Jong, A. Haverinen, P. Hardee, Standards for system-level design: practical reality or solution in search of a question?, in *Proceedings of Design Automation and Test in Europe*, Mar 2000, pp. 576–585

D. Lewis et al., The stratix logic and routing architecture, in *FPGA-02, International Conference on FPGA*, 2002, pp 12–20

X. Li, O. Hammami, Network-on-chip performance evaluation by on-chip hardware monitoring network: OCP-IP Benchmarks on 48-core, in *DAC 2011 Workshop on Diagnostic Services in Network-on-Chips*, 5 Jun 2011

K. Li, R. Kumpf, P. Horton, T. Anderson, A quantitative analysis of disk drive power management in portable computers, in *Proceedings of the 1994 Winter*, USENIX, 1994

F. Li, C. Nicopoulos, T.D. Richardson, Y. Xie, N. Vijaykrishnan, M.T. Kandemir, Design and management of 3D chip multiprocessors using network-in-memory, in *ISCA*, 2006, pp. 130–141

M. Li, Q.A. Zeng, W.-B. Jone, DyXY–a proximity congestion-aware deadlock-free dynamic routing method for network on chip, in *Proceedings of Design Automation Conference*, 2006, pp. 849–852

F. Li, C. Nicopoulos, T. Richardson, Y. Xie, V. Narayanan, M. Kandemir, Design and management of 3D chip multiprocessors using network-in-memory. ACM SIGARCH Comput. Archit. News **34**(2), 130–141 (2006)

J. Liang et al., An architecture and compiler for scalable on-chip communication. IEEE Trans. VLSI Syst. **12**(7), 711–726 (2004)

Y. Liu, S. Chakraborty, W.T. Ooi, A. Gupta, S. Mohan, Workload characterization and cost-quality tradeoffs in MPEG-4 decoding on resource-constrained devices, in *Workshop on Embedded Systems for Real-Time Multimedia*, Sept 2005, pp. 129–134

M. Loghi, F. Angiolini, D. Bertozzi, L. Benini, R. Zafalon, Analyzing on-chip communication in a MPSoC environment, in *Proceedings of the Conference on Design Design Automation and test in Europe*, vol. 2 (Feb 2004), pp. 16–20

J. Lorch, A complete picture of the energy consumption of a portable computer, Master's thesis, Department of Computer Science, University of California, Berkeley, 1995

J. Lorch, Modeling the effect of different processor cycling techniques on power consumption, Performance Evaluation Group Technical Note 179, ATG Integrated Sys, Apple Computer, 1995

J.R. Lorch, A.J. Smith, Reducing processor power consumption by improving processor time management in a single user operating system, in *Second ACM International Conference on Mobile Computing and Networking (MOBICOM)*, 1996

J.R. Lorch, A.J. Smith, Software strategies for portable computer energy management. IEEE Pers. Commun. **5**(3), 60–63 (1998)

J. Losa, E. Ayguade, M. Valero, Quantitative evaluation of register pressure on software pipelined loops. Int. J. Parallel Prog. **26**(2), 121–142 (April 1998)

R. Lysecky, F. Vahid, A study of the speedups and competitiveness of FPGA soft processor cores using dynamic hardware/software partitioning, in *Proceedings of Design Automation and Test in Europe (DATE'05)*, Munich, Germany, vol. 1, Mar 2005, pp. 18–23

H. Maejima, M. Kinaga, K. Uchiyama, Design and architecture for low power/high speed RISC microprocesor:SuperH. In IEICE Trans. Electron. **E80**(12), 1539–1549 (1997)

S.A. Mahlke, W.Y. Chen, P.P. Chang, W. Mei, W. Hwu, Scalar program performance on muliple-instruction-issue processors with a limited number of registers, in *Proceedings of the 25th Annual Hawaii Int'l Conference on System Sciences*, 1992, pp. 34–44

S. Mandal, N. Gupta, A. Mandal, J. Malave, J. Lee, R. Mahapatra, NoCBench: a benchmarking platform for network on chip, in *Workshop on Unique Chips and Systems (UCAS)*, 2009

T. Martin, Balancing batteries, power and performance: System issues in CPU speed-setting for mobile computing, Ph.D, Dissertation, Carnegie Mellon University, Department of Electrical and Computer Engineering, 1999

R. Matthew, J. Rey Ringenberg, D. Ernst, T.M. Austin, T. Mudge, R.B. Brown, MiBench: a free, commercially representative embedded benchmark suite, in *IEEE 4th Annual Workshop on Workload Characterization*, 2001, pp. 3–14

D. Mattson, M. Christensson, Evaluation of synthesizable CPU cores, Master's Thesis, Department of Computer Engineering, Chalmers University of Technology, 2004

H. McGhan, M. O'Connor, PicoJava: a direct execution engine for Java bytecode. Comput. Trans. **31**(10), 22–30 (1998)

H. Mehta, R. M. Owens, M. J. Irwin, R. Chen, D. Ghosh, Techniques for low energy software, in *Internatzonal Symposzum of Low Power Electronics and Design*, IEEE/ACM, 1997, pp. 72–75

J. Merrill, GENERIC and GIMPLE: A new tree representation for entire functions, in *Proceedings of GCC Developers Summit*, 2003, pp. 171–180

R. Merritt, CPU designers debate multi-core future, EETimes Online, Feb 2008

R. Merritt, X86 Cuts to the Cores, EETimes Online, Sept 2007, http://www.eetimes.com/showArticle.jtml?articleID=202100022

J.M. Montana, M. Koibuchi, H. Matsutani, H. Amano, Balanced Dimension-Order Routing for k-ary n-cubes. Keio University, Yokohama. International Conference on Parallel rocessing Workshops, Department of Information and Computer Science, 2009, pp. 499–506

G. Moore, Cramming more components onto integrated circuits, Electronics Magazine. Accessed 2006-11-11, p. 4

F.G. Morales et al., HERMES: an infrastructure for low area overhead packet-switching networks on chip, integration. VLSI J. **38–1**, 69–93 (2004)

K. Mori, A. Ben Abdallah, K. Kuroda, Design and evaluation of a complexity effective network-on-chip architecture on FPGA, in *The 19th Intelligent System Symposium (FAN 2009)*, Sep 2009, pp. 318–321

K. Mori, A. Esch, A. Ben Abdallah, K. Kuroda, Advanced design issue for OASIS network-on-Chip architecture, in *IEEE International Conference on BWCCA*, 2010, pp. 74–79

P. Morrow, M. Kobrinsky, S. Ramanathan, C.-M. Park, M. Harmes, V. Ramachandrarao et al., Wafer-level 3D interconnects via Cu bonding, in *Proceedings of the 21st Advanced Metallization Conference*, Oct 2004

S.S. Muchnick, *Advanced Compiler Design and Implementation* (Morgan Kaufman, San Francisco, 1997)

R. Mullins, A. West, S. Moore, Low-latency virtual-channel routers for on-chip networks, in *Proceedings of the 31st International Symposium on Computer Architecture*, 2004, pp. 188–197

*Multiprocessor System-on-Chip* (Morgan Kaufman Publishers, San Francisco, 2005). ISBN:0-12385-251-X

S. Murali, G. De Micheli, SUNMAP: a tool for automatic topology selection and generation for NoCs, in *Proceedings of Design Automation Conference*, 2004

Mysql, http://www.mysql.com/

F.N. Najm, A survey of power estimation techniques in VLSI circuits. IEEE Trans. VLSI Syst. **2**(4), 44–55 (1994)

Nios II Processor, http://www.altera.com/literature/lit-nio2.jsp

D. Novillo, Design and implementation of tree SSA, in *Proceedings of GCC Developers Summit*, 2004, pp. 119–130

K. Obrien, Z. Sura, T. Chen, T. Zhang, Supporting OpenMP on cell. J. Parallel Prog. **36**(3), 289–311 (2008)

S. Okamoto, Design of a superscalar processor based on queue machine computation model, in *IEEE Pacific Rim Conference on Communications, Computers and, Signal Processing*, 1999, pp. 151–154

R.G. Olsen, *OCP Based Adapter for Network-on-Chip Master Degree* (Technical University of Denmark, Kongens Lyngby, 2005)

OpenCores, http://opencores.org/. Accessed Jan 2012

OpenMP: API specification for parallel programming, http://openmp.org

U.Y. Orgas, R. Marculescu, It's a small world after all: NoC performance optimization via long-range link insertion. IEEE Trans. VLSI Syst. **14**(7), 693–706 (2006)

P6 Power Data Slides provided by Intel Corp. to Universities

J. Pan, W.J. Tompkins, A real-time QRS detection algorithm. IEEE Trans. Biomed. Eng. **32**, 230–236 (1985)

P.P. Pande, C. Grecu, M. Jones, A. Ivanov, R. Saleh, Performance evaluation and design trade-offs for network-on-chip interconnect architectures. IEEE Trans. Comput. **54**(8), 1025–1040 (2005)

M.S. Papamarcos, J.H. Patel, A low-overhead coherence solution for multiprocessors with private cache memories, in *ISCA '84 Proceedings of the 11th, Annual International Symposium on Computer Architecture*, 1984, pp. 348–354

S. Pasricha, N. Dutt, M. Ben-Romdhane, Constraint-driven bus matrix synthesis for MPSoC, in *Asia and South Pacific Design Automation Conference (ASPDAC 2006)*, Yokohama, Japan, Jan 2006, pp. 30–35

V.A. Patankar, A. Jain, R.E. Bryant, Formal verification of an ARM processor, in *Twelfth International Conference on, VLSI Design*, 1999, pp. 282–287

V.F. Pavlidis, E.G. Friedman, 3-D topologies for networks-on-chip. IEEE Trans. VLSI Syst. **15**,1081–1090 (2007)

M. Pedram, Power minimization in IC design: principles and applications. ACM Trans. Des. Automat. Electron. Syst. **1**(1), 3–6 (1996)

G. Philip, B. Christopher, P. Ramm, *Handbook of 3D integration: Technology and Applications of 3D Integrated Circuits*, Wiley-VCH, Weinheim, 2008

PHP Hypertext Preprocessor, http://www.php.net/

PhysioBank, http://www.physionet.org/physiobank/

S. Pinter, Register allocation with instruction scheduling, in *Proceedings of the ACM SIGPLAN 1993 Conference on Programming Language Design and Implementation*, 1993, pp. 248–257

M. Postiff, D. Greene, T. Mudge, The need for large register file in integer codes, Technical Report, CSE-TR-434-00, University of Michigan, 2000

S. Prakash, A. Parker, SoS: synthesis of application-specific heterogeneous multiprocessor systems. J. Parallel Distrib. Comput. **16**, 338–351 (1992)

B.R. Preiss, V.C. Hamacher, Data flow on queue machine, in *ISCA 1985, 12th International Symposium on Computer Architecture*, Boston, Aug 1985, pp. 342–351

B. Preiss, C. Hamacher, Data flow on queue machines, in *12th International IEEE Symposium on Computer Architecture*, 1985, pp. 342–351

Pthread Standard, http://standards.ieee.org/findstds/

A. Pullini, F. Angiolini, D. Bertozzi, L. Benini, Fault tolerance overhead in network-on-chip flow control schemes, in *Proceedings of Symposium Integrated Circuits System Design*, Sept 2005

Quartus II Handbook Version 11.0 Vol 3: Verification, Chapter 10: PowerPlay Power Analysis (Altera Corporation, San Jose, 2010)

Quartus II Handbook Version 11.0 Vol. 3: Verification, Chapter 6: The Quartus II TimeQuest Timing Analyzer (Altera Corporation, San Jose, 2011)

J. Rabaey, L. Guerra, R. Mehra, Design guidance in the power dimension, in *Proceedings of the ICASSP*, 1995

R.S. Ramanujam, B. Lin, Near-optimal oblivious routing on three dimensional mesh networks, in *Proceedings of IEEE International Conference on Computer Design*, Lake Tahoe, CA, 2008

M.S. Rasmussen, Network-on-chip in digital hearing aids, in *Informatics and Mathematical Modeling*, Technical University of Denmark, DTU, Richard Petersens Plads, Building 321, DK-2800 Kgs. Lyngby, IMM-Thesis-2006-76, 2006

R. Rau, Iterative modulo scheduling: an algorithm for software pipelining loops, in *Proceedings of the 27th annual international symposium on Microarchitecture*, 1994, pp. 63–74

R. Ravindran, R. Senger, E. Marsman, G. Dasika, M. Guthaus, S. Mahlke, R. Brown, Partitioning variables across register windows to reduce spill code in a low-power processor. IEEE Trans. Comput. **54**(8), 998–1012 (2005)

J. Rosethal, in *JPEG Image Compression Using an FPGA*, Master of Science in Electrical and Computer Engineering, University of California Santa Barbara, Dec 2006

J.M. Rulnick, N. Bambos, Mobile power management for maximum battery life in wireless communication networks, in *Proceedings of IEEE INFOCOM 2006*, 1996

F.A. Samman, T. Hollstein, M. Glesner, Multicast parallel pipeline router architecture for network-on-chip, in *Proceedings of the Conference on Design, Automation and Test in Europe (DATE 08)*, Munich, Germany, Mar 2008, pp. 1396–1401

H. Schmit, B. Levine, B. Ylvisaker, Queue machines: hardware compilation in hardware, in *FCCM'02, 10th Annual IEEE Symposium on Field-Programmable Custom Computing Machines*, 2002, pp. 152–161

T. Schonwald, J. Zimmermann, O. Bringmann, W. Rosenstiel, Fully adaptive fault-tolerant routing algorithm for network-on-chip architectures, in *Proceedings of 10th Euromicro Conference on Digital System Design Architectures, Methods and Tools*, 2007, pp. 527–534

Semiconductor Industry Association, The National Technology Roadmap for Semiconductors: Technology Needs, Sematche Inc., Austin, 1997, http://www.sematech.org

R.A. Shafik, P. Rosinger, B.M. Al-Hashimi, MPEG-based performance comparison between network-on-chip and AMBA MPSoC, 2008 in *IEEE Design and Diagnostics of Electronic Circuits and Systems*, Bratislava, Slovakia, Apr 2008, pp. 16–18

M. Sheliga, E.H. Sha, Hardware/software co-design with the HMS framework. J VLSI Sig Process Syst **13**(1), 37–56 (1996)

M. Sheliga, E.H. Sha, Hardware/software co-design with the HMS framework. J. VLSI Signal Process. Syst. **13**(1), 37–56 (1996)

K.M. Sivalingam, J.C. Chen, P. Agrawal, M. Srivastava, Design and analysis of low-power access protocols for wireless and mobile ATM networks. Wirel. Netw. **6**(1), 73–77 (2000)

J.E. Smith, G. Sohi, The microarchitecture of superscalar processors. Proc. IEEE **83**(12), 1609–1624 (1995)

Sowa Laboratory, www.sowa.is.uec.ac.jp

M. Sowa, Fundamental of queue machine, Technical Reports, SLL97302, the University of Electro-Communications, Sowa Laboratory, 2000

M. Sowa, PQP: parallel queue processor with high parallelism, simple hardware and low power consumption, Technical Report, SLL030331, the University of Electro-Communications, Sowa Laboratory, Jun 2003

M. Sowa, Queue processor instruction set design, Technical Report, SLL 00303, the University of Electro-Communications, Sowa Laboratory, 2000

M. Sowa, A. Ben Abdallah, T. Yoshinaga, Parallel queue processor architecture based on produced order computation model. J. Supercomput. **32**(3), 217–229 (2005)

M. Sowa, A. Ben-Abdallah, T. Yoshinaga, Parallel queue processor architecture based on produced order computation model. Int. J. Supercomput. HPC **32**(3), 217–229 (2005)

Sparc-International, The SPARC Architecture Manual, Version 8 (Prentice Hall, Upper Saddle River, 1992)

K. Srinivasan et al., Linear programming based techniques for synthesis of network-on-chip architectures, in *Proceedings of ICCD*, 2004

STMicroelectronics, http://www.st.com/internet/com/home/home.jsp

O. Strgm, E.J. Aas, An implementation of an embedded microprocessor core with support for executing byte compiled java code, in *Proceedings of the Euromicro Symposium on Digital Systems Design*, 2001, pp. 396–399

C.L. Su, A.M. Despain, Cache designs for energy efficiency, in *Proceeding of the 28th Hawaii International Conference on System Science*, 1995

SuperH RISC engine SH-1/Sh-2/Sh-DSP Programming Manual, http://www.renesas.com

H. Suzuki, O. Shusuke, A. Maeda, M. Sowa, Implementation and evaluation of a superscalar processor based on queue machine computation model. IPSJ SIG **99**(21), 91–96 (1999)

H. Takahashi, S. Abiko, S. Mizushima, A 100 MIPS high speed and low power digital signal processor, IEICE Trans. Electron. **E80**(12), 1546–1552 (1997)

The Message Passing Interface (MPI) standard, http://www.mcs.anl.gov/research/projects/mpi/

Tilera, Tile 64 Product Brief, Tilera, 2008

Tilera: TILE64 processor family, http://www.tilera.com/products/processors.php

V. Tiwari et al., Reducing power in high-performance microprocessors, in *CAD 1998, 35th Design Automation Conference*, San Francisco, Jun 1998, pp. 732–737

V. Tiwari, S. Malik, P. Ashar, Guarded evaluation: pushing power management to logic synthesis/design. IEEE Trans. Comput. Aided Des. Integr. Circ. Syst. **17**(10), 1051–1060 (1998)

V. Tiwari, S. Malik, A. Wolfe, Power analysis of embedded software: a first step towards software power minimization. IEEE Trans. Very Large Scale Integr. **2**(4), 437–445 (1994)

A.W. Topol, J.D.C. La Tulipe, L. Shi, D.J. Frank, K. Bernstein, S.E. Steen, A. Kumar, G.U. Singco, A.M. Young, K.W. Guarini, M. Ieong, Three-dimensional integrated circuits. IBM J. Res. Dev. **50**(4/5), 491–506 (2006)

S. Tyagi, Extended Balanced Dimension Ordered Routing Algorithm for 3d-Networks. Centre for Development of Advance Computing, Noida. India International Conference on Parallel Processing Workshops, 2009, pp 499–506. http://www.iacqer.com/Proceedings

G. Tyson, M. Smelyanskiy, E. Davidson, Evaluating the use of register queues in software pipelined loops. IEEE Trans. Comput. **50**(8), 769–783 (2001)

T. Uesaka, Architecture and design of OASIS NoC with short-path link (SPL), graduation thesis, University of Aizu, Fukushima, School of Computer Science and Engineering, 2011

T. Uesaka, OASIS NoC topology optimization with short-path link, Technical Report, ASL Systems Architecture Group, School of Computer Science and Engineering, University of Aizu, Fukushima, 2011

N. VijayKrishnan, Issues in the design of JAVA processor architecture, Ph.D. thesis, University of South Florida, Tampa, FL-33620, Dec 1998

D. Wall, Limits of instruction-level parallelism. ACM SIGARCH Comput. Archit. News **19**(2), 176–188 (1991)

M. Weiser, B. Welch, A. Demers, S. Shenker, Schedlibng for reduced cpu energy, in *Proceedings of the First Symposium on Operating System Design and Implementation (OSDI)1994*, 1994

G.F. Welch, A survey of power management techniques in mobile computing operating systems. ACM SIGOPS Operating Syst. Rev. **29**(4), 47 (1995)

D. Wentzlaff et al., On-chip interconnection architecture of the tile processor. IEEE Micro **27**, 15–31 (2007)

F. Wolf, *Behavioral Intervals in Embedded Software: Timing and Power Analysis of Embedded Real-Time Software Process* (Kluwer Academic Publishers, Boston, 2002)

M. Wolfe, *High Performance Compilers for Parallel Computing* (Addison-Wesley, New York, 1996)

Xilinx MicroBlaze, http://www.xilinx.com/xlnx/

Xilinx, Virtex-5 Family Overview, Feb 2009

L. Xin, C.s. Choy, ? Low-latency NoC router with lookahead bypass, in *IEEE International Symposium on Circuits and Systems (ISCAS)*, 2010, pp. 3981–3984

S. Yan, B. Lin, Design of application-specific 3D networks-on-chip architectures, in *Proceedings of International Conference of Computer Design*, Oct 2008, pp. 142–149

H. Yasuyoshi, A. Ben Addallah, Architecture and design of application specific multicore SoC, Graduation Thesis, The University of Aizu, Feb 2010

Y. Ye, S. Borkar, V. De, A new technique for standby leakage reduction in high-performance circuits, *Symposium on VLSI Circuits*, Honolulu, Hawaii, 1998, pp 40–41

J. Zalamea, J. Llosa, E. Ayguade, M. Valero, Software and hardware techniques to optimize register file utilization in VLIW architectures. Int. J. Parallel Prog. **32**(6), 447–474 (December 2004)

Printed in the United States
By Bookmasters